Superwomen
and the
Double Burden

Milica Antic lives in Škofja Loka, Slovenia and teaches sociology at a secondary school. She is a member of the group Women for Politics. Her current research centres on women's experience in the field of politics.

Mita Castle-Kanerova, exiled from Czechoslovakia in 1968, now lectures at the Polytechnic of North London. Her areas of interest include comparative social policy, women, history and politics in east/central Europe. She spent one semester lecturing at the Charles University in Prague in spring 1991 where she was awarded an honorary professorship. She now visits Czechoslovakia regularly after 21 years of enforced break.

Chris Corrin lives and works in Glasgow teaching politics at Glasgow University. She has worked with academics and activists in Hungary and neighbouring countries since 1984. Her present work involves expanding women's access and information on health care and reproductive rights throughout central and eastern Europe and investigating women's opportunities for achieving changes. She is currently co-secretary of the European Forum of Socialist Feminists and co-convenor of the Women's Commission of the Helsinki Citizens Assembly. She has published a number of articles on women and socialism and women's situation within Hungarian society. Her book *Magyar Women's Lives 1940s–1990s* is forthcoming with Macmillan,1992.

Barbara Einhorn is based at the University of Sussex in Brighton. She has been researching literature and women in the former GDR for many years. Her book on the relationship of the individual to society as reflected in GDR novels between 1949 and 1969 was published in West Germany in 1976. Her current comparative research is on the situation of women and women's movements in the former GDR, Poland, Hungary and Czechoslovakia.

Hilary Pilkington lives and works in Birmingham teaching Soviet Politics and Society at the Centre for Russian and East European Studies at Birmingham University. She became interested in women's experience in the Soviet Union while living in various cities there over several years. Her other research is concerned with youth culture.

Jolanta Plakwicz lives and works in Warsaw. An English translator by profession, she specializes in women's literature. She was a member of an informal feminist group in the 1980s and a co-founder of the Polish Feminist Association in 1989.

Edited by Chris Corrin

Superwomen and the Double Burden

Women's experience of change in central and eastern Europe and the former Soviet Union

SECOND STORY Press

FEMINIST PUBLISHERS

CANADIAN CATALOGUING IN PUBLICATION DATA

Superwomen and the double burden

ISBN 0-929005-34-1

1. Women–Central Europe.   2. Women–Eastern Europe, Eastern.
3. Women – Soviet Union.   I. Corrin, Chris

HQ1587.886 1992   305.4'0943   092-093716-0

Published in Great Britain by Scarlet Press 1992

Published in North America by
SECOND STORY PRESS
760 Bathurst St.
Toronto, Canada M5S 2R6

Contents

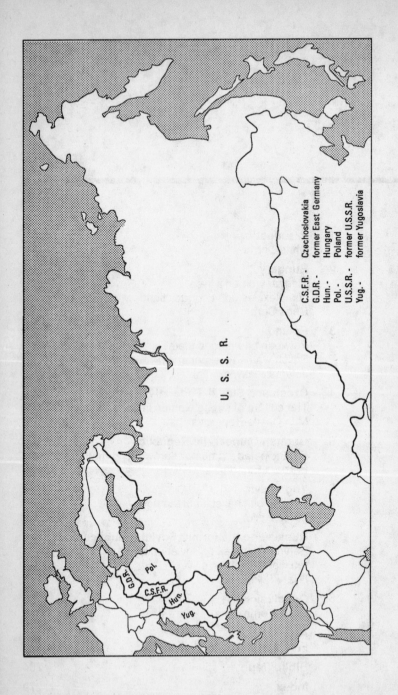

C.S.F.R. - Czechoslovakia
G.D.R. - former East Germany
Hun. - Hungary
Pol. - Poland
U.S.S.R. - former U.S.S.R.
Yug. - former Yugoslavia

U. S. S. R.

Pol.

G.D.R.

C.S.F.R.

Hun.

Yug.

1 Introduction

Chris Corrin

This book has been written for those wanting to learn more about the situation of women in central and eastern Europe and the former Soviet Union.[1] It is intended as an introduction to the theoretical, official and *actual* situations of women in these formerly 'Soviet-type' countries. To understand the revolutionary upheavals that swept across Europe in 1989 and their implications for women, some basis of knowledge of the social, political and economic conditions of these societies *before* the later 1980s – how they developed and differed from each other – is required. This book seeks to lay such a foundation.

At the outset it must be stated that the choice of countries included has been based on access to analyses on the questions under consideration. Had it been possible to include studies on Romania, Bulgaria and Albania this would have been welcomed, but no such studies were available to us when compiling the present work. It is known that women in Romania faced massive obstacles in their everyday lives not least of which was the Ceausescu regime's policy of women having to have five children. In Bulgaria and Albania change has been slower than elsewhere, and women have fewer opportunities within these countries to change their situations. Yet change has affected all three countries, with safe abortions now available in Romania and possibilities for more initiatives by women in Bulgaria and Albania who are now able to travel to overseas conferences and to establish better links within central and eastern Europe and elsewhere. Studies are currently being compiled on certain aspects of women's situations in Albania, Bulgaria and Romania which will add depth to comparative work in this field.

Our stress is on political change only in so far as the political systems of these countries helped to create centralized, statist environments in which politics, in its very narrowest sense, dominated most other spheres of life. Within such a context the outcomes of policy, intended and unintended, had different consequences among various groups and were accepted, or not, according to a multiplicity of factors. Cultural traditions and histories of the countries concerned and women's experience within these environments are of pivotal importance when considering how changes were mediated and experienced.

There are several reasons why such a book is timely, not least because all of these countries have undergone enormous changes since World War Two, and particularly in the last few years. In addition, while much has been written on women's experience in some countries – USSR, Germany, Czechoslovakia[2] – there is less material available on others – Poland, Yugoslavia and Hungary.

The countries making up what has long been referred to as 'the Soviet Union and eastern Europe' have never formed a monolithic bloc. Certainly 'eastern Europe' could not be viewed merely as an evenly coloured region on the world map. Cultural, historical and traditional differences are enormous, as the basic figures on ethnic groups and languages spoken show. The massive divergences between peoples living in the former Soviet Union have become more apparent as conflicts have emerged, and one of the aims of the book is therefore to correct the erroneous assumption of 'sameness'.

The study of women

Do women make up a collective entity that we can study? I have argued this point elsewhere[3] and would only reiterate here that essentially there can be no general grouping of women worldwide, or within countries or cultures. Women have never been, and indeed cannot become, one 'category'. There are fundamental differences between women, in terms of economic activity, household pattern and lifestyle, yet the party/state systems in these various countries systematically produced policies based on a specific collective identity – 'women'.

Women suffer inequalities on the basis of their ability to give birth to children and are thereby often assigned gender qualities that are socially, and often officially, constructed. Many of the expectations imposed on women result in their direct and indirect oppression *as women* in terms of childbearing, caring and as women workers.

In this book we have used both qualitative and quantitative methods – interviews, small surveys and statistical data – to chart the course of Soviet-styled societies, including the use of certain statistics about which a cautionary note is required. Given that in some contexts these are the *only* nationwide figures available to give background information we have made use of them. It is important to note that the reliability of some figures is tainted by the fact that statistical information in these countries became a crucially important aspect of policy making. It can be seen from the different contributions that the availability of *reliable* information varies widely between countries and where accurate information on, for example, women's health care or frequency of divorce was not available, these factors could not be assesssed.

Almost all research and centrally gathered information in these societies was controlled – knowledge is power, and certain types of knowledge underpin certain directions of policy. For sociologists wishing to look at social problems such as poverty or the situation of vulnerable groups in society, there were officially erected barriers that discouraged work of a politically sensitive nature. Thus, information on the proportions of women working in certain fields, claiming benefits, and so on, must be seen as providing only basic background for consideration of the complexities of women's lives. It is to be hoped that more qualitative studies will become available in the future.

Throughout the book it becomes clear that there are obvious differences between the former Soviet societies and those of neighbouring countries, not least because the Soviet revolutionary history goes back to 1917 and because the Soviet Union has been the dominant power in this region for the past 50 years. The focus of the present work is primarily on the Russian Republic. Given the break-up of the former Soviet Union it is expected that more detailed studies will be carried out by women in the various new republics, and indeed some such studies have begun (see bibliography). A principal difference between the former Soviet Union and the countries in central and eastern Europe concerns the type of party/state system in place in each.

Soviet revolutionary history goes back to 1917 with a rich theoretical tradition, including work on women's liberation and mobilization. As is clear from Chapter 7, there has been much theorizing within the former USSR about certain aspects of the so-called 'woman question', so that there is a body of sociological theory that contains at least a minimal history of experimentation with new social relations, including those between men and women. When considering countries other than the Soviet Union the extent of the imposition of rigid Stalinism from roughly 1947–48 cannot be overemphasized. Stalin had regained his authoritarian grip over political affairs in the Soviet Union following the defeat of the Nazis and the systems created in the central and eastern European countries that came under the Soviet sphere of influence were rigid and highly centralized. They could be seen as 'anti-women' in that women's liberation was viewed purely in terms of labour-force participation, with none of the revolutionary notions concerning communal living, sexual liberation or the socialization of housework. The difference between having a system implanted by an outside power and having one to which people could claim inheritance is also a major psychological factor to be taken into account. The periodic uprisings in this region, including those in Germany in 1953, Poland and Hungary in 1956, Czechoslovakia in 1968, and Poland in 1976 and 1980–81 all bear witness to two sets of forces at work. These two forces, the national traditions arising from each society and the centralizing overseeing forces of the Soviet authorities, tended periodically to clash with each other.

Change over time?

In each of these countries centralized, highly bureaucratic administrative systems have been maintained to a greater or lesser degree. Yet as the case studies show, developments within Poland from 1981 meant that a new political formation was being placed on the agenda. In Hungary from the late 1960s experiments with economic reforms were raising numerous questions concerning social-market economies and the necessity or otherwise for democratization to accompany economic reform. In 1985 the advent of Gorbachev in the Soviet Union seemed to open a window on previously closed viewpoints. The massive upheavals in 1989 opened the gates to changes in this part of the world.

Just as the orientations of these countries differed in the past, so too will their paths diverge in the future. Despite the differences between women in terms of age, occupation, family commitment, certain 'blanket' changes will affect many women as workers (unemployment) and mothers (closing of child-care facilities).

In terms of the book's methodology and the reliability of statistical data it was decided to use the

authors' concrete knowledge of long acquaintance
with the situations to gather together hitherto
neglected aspects of how women have experienced
change. In order to give depth to our consideration
in terms of data a variety of works are cited, from
small-scale interviews to the aggregated statistical data
for which the state-controlled statistical offices in
these countries were infamous. We recognize that
some of these relatively unreliable statistics can be
used as no more than a guide, but because currently
they are the only national source available we offer
them as background information. The statistical
bureaux throughout the Soviet Union and central
and eastern Europe were supported by the
communist authorities in each of these countries and
are undergoing vast changes in the current period. It
is doubtful whether the emerging statistical
organizations will be able to redress this balance
retrospectively for some time. Other, smaller
ethnographic sources are noted for reference, in the
native language where considered appropriate.
Ethnographic research is generally carried out as
small-scale qualitative research projects based on in-
depth interviews and discussions. While the study of
the general discipline of 'sociology', albeit within a
somewhat limited framework, was to a certain extent
'allowed' to develop in these societies, political
analysis was not actively encouraged. It will become
apparent that the social sciences were controlled in
many different ways in these societies in order to
serve the official viewpoint. These were large-scale
funded projects such as those on demographic
questions but the small-scale, generally privately
funded studies were semi-illegal. For instance poverty
did not legally exist, having been overcome within
the socialist transitions. While all social scientists
could testify that in practice this was not the case,
there was no research funding available to investigate
instances. No large-scale studies of poverty could be
carried out, yet very useful ethnographic work was
done in several areas.

This lack of political analysis is of particular concern in terms of issues affecting women, such as certain pro-natalist and equal opportunities policies and such debates as 'services versus benefits'; for example state child-care in crèches and kindergartens versus maternity/child-care benefits for mothers (later made available to fathers in some cases) to care for children in the home.

Communist revolution

When historians and social and political analysts speak or write of revolutionary situations they often use the Bolshevik revolutionary situation from 1917 onwards as an example of a situation in which there was intense societal upheaval for several years. The experience and influence of the Soviet Union was pivotal to post-war reconstruction for the nations within Europe. It is important to remember the relatively low level of economic development at the time of the socialist transformations. This was certainly the case with the Soviet Union, Bulgaria and Romania. Yet there were obvious divisions between the so-called 'developed' countries such as Czechoslovakia, Germany and, to some extent, Hungary and Poland and the less developed countries that were more dependent on agricultural production and that had less diverse industrial bases.

Some history books retell the 'communization' of central and eastern Europe as a liberating epoch in which these societies began the path of development towards communism, on the road to socialism. Certainly in the late 1940s and early 1950s various groups of people within these societies did have some faith in a 'new' future, a belief that perhaps their society was being shaped for a more egalitarian, more dynamic socialist future. The reality for many though was such that they believed the 'Stalinization' of their nations was leading backwards and downwards rather than on to a brighter new future.

For women great changes were taking place. Other writings show the unfortunate reduction of Marxist theory that led some politicians to believe that *the* major step on the way to women gaining liberation was to encourage them to join the work-force in great numbers. In this way Marxist ideology was actually modified or reduced, in that the early revolutionary thinkers did recognize the need radically to alter familial relations and women's domestic responsibilities, but these aspects were later downplayed or ignored. In the Soviet context of the 1920s there is evidence of real social and political questioning of the ways in which women were working and of the ways in which domestic work could become socialized. By the time the Soviet Union was encouraging/imposing the implementation of this system within central and eastern Europe genuine experimentation with the socialization of domestic work and child-care was not on the agenda. As we know there were steps taken to lift some of the burdens from the family units – that is, women's extra work – but these did not actually come into force until the 1960s, when women had experienced the true horrors of the *Stakhanovite* and bleakly Stalinist 1950s. The Stakhanov movement encouraged workers to compete to achieve higher and higher results, often totally unrealistically.

It was not immediately apparent that working eight hours each day for less money than men and generally in unskilled or semi-skilled work still meant that women would come home to more work. The hoped-for socialization of household tasks and child-care did not actually happen. Crèches and nurseries were built in these countries, but not until well into the 1960s and even then there were differing levels of benefits and services. Generally many women were still expected to look to their older female relatives for suitable child-care. If they had no women relatives then women neighbours or their older children had to fill the gaps.

Of course, in the immediate years after the war many households had no men in them. In such situations the women were more or less forced to become 'superwomen', heading the household as the main provider as well as the main carer and domestic worker. Some women remember these formative years in central and eastern Europe as an exciting time, one that heralded promise. But any such excitement was short-lived; for many it lasted only for the brief period between 1947 and 1950. After this time the structural oppression of the centralized communist system started to impact on all areas of social, economic and political life. This is when we begin to see the uprisings against the imposed system – in East Germany in 1953 and in Poland and Hungary in 1956. Important areas of criticism and comparison were opened up by Stalin's death and by Khrushchev's secret speech – the speech given to the twentieth Party congress of the Communist Party of the Soviet Union which 'admitted' some of the errors of Stalinism and opened the way for debate over the legitimacy of certain aspects of centralized, communist rule in central and eastern Europe.

It was the way in which these uprisings were suppressed that led each nation into different survival strategies. In Poland and Hungary these strategies were to lead to longer term resistance. In Poland resistance culminated in the events leading up to the establishment of Solidarity for independent worker representation in negotiations with the communist state bureaucracy. In Hungary it often took the form of intellectual oppositional groupings – the secret publication of banned material (termed *samizdat* material) created a climate in which the Kádárist compromise, the 'social contract' by which the Kádár regime managed to placate Hungarian society after the revolution in 1956, could be pressured into more compromise, especially with regard to the liberalization of the economy and the recognition of the second economy. Rather than confronting the state forces directly in the form of strike activity, Hungarian workers appeared to work 'around' the state forces to some extent, within the semi-legalized alternative economy, often working in two or three jobs.

The late de-Stalinization in Czechoslovakia and the depth of the thaw during the Prague Spring meant that the Soviet repression from 1968 onwards bit very deeply into the social, political and intellectual fabric of Czech and Slovak societies. The Charter 77 movement began with a charter being signed by 242 signatories. Initially it was a largely intellectual opposition movement but it steadily gained workers' support and played a vital role of issuing 'documents' and making publicity concerning the repression of political activists in Czechoslovakia. The developments within Charter 77 were closely watched and tentatively supported within both western and eastern Europe.

In Yugoslavia on the other hand, the break with Stalin in 1948 and the experimentation with workers' councils appeared on the surface to offer possibilities for a more 'successful' experiment in 'socialist' planning. After Tito's death political life seemed to be 'suspended' between immobility and crisis. Events during the 1980s showed just how deeply entwined the ethnic tensions and political power struggles have now become.

In the Soviet Union, Khrushchev's hasty removal and the long period of stagnation under Brezhnev seemed to smooth over any cracks in the unity of the peoples of the various republics.

Women's liberation within socialist theory

There are various ways of assessing the situation of women in any society. Often the present is compared with the past, and practice with claims. In this context it is important for us to remember that in order to understand the history of claims concerning women's liberation in the former Soviet Union and central and eastern Europe we need some knowledge of the prevailing strategy for achieving social change within the communist model. Here the theoretical bases of 'women's liberation through socialism' are important. What were the official expectations of, and for, women's involvement in the development of these so-called socialist societies? What roles were viewed as 'women's roles' within these societies and what was the role of social policy towards achieving women's 'liberation'? How did state and societal forces intervene and shape the processes in which women were able to construct their identities and carry on their lives?

It is apparent that these so-called 'socialist' societies could not, in reality, be compared with a Marxist model. Yet the basic essence of socialist theory is *equality*, an egalitarianism based on the eradication of oppression in terms of class, race, gender or any other societal inequity. These societies publicly stressed an emphasis on policies directed towards women's equality.

The Marxist materialist conception of history explains the way in which humans can act on their environment in a politically conscious movement to create a more egalitarian situation in which human potential can be developed. These Soviet-type societies emphasized at least a *formal* commitment toward societal change in terms of creating more egalitarian social relations. Since at least the mid-nineteenth century socialist political movements explicitly stated that women's liberation was an *integral* part of the *communal* revolutionary project. The socialization of domestic work was envisaged by early Marxists as another stage in the equalizing of relations between men and women in society. Yet the contradictions of the double burden from which women suffered in all 'socialist' societies – as good public workers/mothers/wives/domestic workers were to become all too apparent.

Although Engels had something to say about household work becoming privatized under capitalism, and about women's alienated position as 'slaves of the workers', his work here was partial and was reduced by later Bolshevik thinkers. Engels viewed the family solely in the context of the social division of labour, and assessed women's oppression mainly with reference to different forms of ownership. He concentrated more on prehistory than on the family in capitalist society, and on the family generally, rather than on women's oppression in particular. It is clear that neither Marx, Engels nor later Marxist theorists attempted a systematic study of the specific oppression of women. Put crudely, liberation was to be gained by workers' efforts to control the external world of work.

Engels outlined two essential preconditions for women's emancipation – women's participation in the work-force and the socialization of domestic work – which could not happen together under capitalism, but would have to take place in a system in which industry was socialized or communally owned, and in a society in which the nuclear family model did not underpin private property and profits.

Lenin was more concerned with *practical* goals and favoured the politicization of women, which he believed would lead both to women's liberation and to successful revolution. In his work both the duality of women's oppression and the double-edged nature of women's revolutionary participation are apparent. The Bolsheviks needed women's support and participation to overthrow the old order, and the primary concern was to reduce working women's oppression so that they might realize their interests. Lenin speaks of the double oppression of women in terms of the old bourgeois laws that kept women in inequality and domestic drudgery. Such laws as divorce laws and illegitimacy would be replaced by new legislation guaranteeing women's rights. The second element – women's oppression by 'household bondage', this 'petty domestic economy' – would be harder to abolish and replace.

And what of attempts by women to problematize the sexual division of labour? Even in the works of writers such as Alexandra Kollantai, Inessa Armand and others in the 1920s there is both self-censorship and external constraint. Inessa Armand and Alexandra Kollontai, the first two directors of the *Zhenotdel* (an organization set up to encourage women into active politics), writing against the backdrop of revolution in the Soviet Union, shared with Bebel, Engels and Marx the belief that women's liberation was only possible under socialism. Like Lenin they realized there would be nothing 'automatic' in this. Change could not come merely from new economic structures or legislation but had to take place in the family, in domestic labour, maternity, child-rearing and sexual relations. Both women viewed reorganization of domestic labour and child-rearing as being fundamental to the transformation of the family. Unfortunately, they too underestimated the enormity of social change this would require. When they broadened their analyses to the dynamics of sexuality, Lenin and other revolutionaries disapproved of this 'bourgeois self-indulgence'. Much has been written on the divide between so-called 'bourgeois' and 'socialist' feminists.[4]

The importance of this Marxist theoretical work on women's liberation lies in the fact that in their analyses of the socialization of housework and child-care tasks, the economic benefits of women's participation in the public sphere were overestimated, or rather the high costs (economic and psychological) of making available public utilities for meals, laundry and child-care were radically underestimated. As Heitlinger (1979) points out, Lenin thought only of the savings in labour time when housework would be socialized, but another outcome would be that previously unpaid domestic work would become waged work, requiring equivalent payment.[5]

The psychological costs for women were not considered and, as will be seen, this public/private, valued/undervalued dichotomy in work was to prove a heavy burden for women. In an optimistic vein Kollantai states that:

Instead of working woman cleaning her flat, the communist society can arrange for men and women whose job it is to go round in the morning cleaning rooms.
(Buckley, 1989, p.45)

Not only would such cleaners need to be paid for their work but men would have to be prepared and able to carry out such jobs.

Socialism and 'bourgeois feminism'

For Kollantai and other revolutionaries of this time the aims of the so-called 'bourgeois feminists' were insufficient because they left capitalism intact. The basic issue in question was that if women's gains depended on the wider gains of the proletarian cause there was no universal 'women's cause' and there could be little unity between bourgeois women and revolutionary women. It was around this time that the value of separate women's organizations was questioned and found to be counter-productive. The question of separate women's organization has remained a central point of contention in socialist and feminist politics throughout the world. For women who want to work autonomously in republics of the former Soviet Union and central and eastern Europe today, the legacy of decades of propaganda concerning the divisiveness of 'women-only' working and the dangers of problematizing home life is very apparent. The fact that gender roles and socialization were not tackled in the revolutionary writings allowed the ill-founded belief that women would be released from their domestic burden without men assuming any new domestic roles. The implications of male–female relations and the means by which women were subordinated to men were nowhere thoroughly analysed. Notions of sisterhood were viewed as out of step with the class-based analysis of Marxists.

Such notions of sisterhood today have to grapple with many questions, not least those raised by black women countering many 'white feminist' assumptions. In terms of socialist–feminist conceptions of equality, questions have now arisen concerning the applicability of certain 'socialist' ideas for central European women's politics, given that many elements of 'socialist' thinking have become discredited. This is something to be borne in mind when considering not only possibilities for change but also the ways in which change may be brought about.

It is well to reiterate the deep reluctance of many socialists to countenance any autonomous women's movements or indeed to see that women's oppression raises particular questions for women as social beings. The old class dualisms as well as the divisions between socialism and bourgeois feminism remain, often implicit, within the arguments around political change to end women's inequality. Sometimes there are new twists in such discussions. Certainly 'socialist–feminist' activists in the western world are now assimilating discussions and decisions that central and eastern European women have undertaken in the rejection of so-called 'socialist' values. In turn, women from the so-called 'socialist' countries in Europe are questioning what their old regimes were actually about. In addition the debates concerning civil society in the liberalizing atmosphere of central and eastern European countries have a new urgency, as do notions of the 'dictatorship of the market'.[6]

Women's liberation

Women's liberation is concerned with the abolition of oppression from which half of the adult population suffer because of their gender – because they are women. The term 'gender' is used here instead of 'sex' because the former takes into account all of the social phenomena that overlie the basic biological differences between men and women. Child-care is generally viewed as 'women's work'. While it remains the case that only women can give birth to and suckle children, all other child-care duties can be undertaken by either men or women. Such a division of labour by gender has not occurred 'naturally' but has been socially constructed and can therefore be changed by people's actions.

It is useful here to remember the distinction between liberal rights and socialist duties to productive labour. Much of the current debate in central and eastern European countries is concerned with the concepts of *choice*. The fact that women and men will now have some choice over employment (less so over unemployment perhaps) is a situation that will be new to many, and future decisions will be viewed within this context.

The spurious equality that women are often officially cited as having gained in the work-place has been used to mask a broader form of inequality in terms of the 'feminization' of certain occupations, for example certain types of doctor, with less pay, longer hours and worse working conditions than in several of the male professional preserves. There is no checking and little documentation in some cases. As our work shows, men generally do not take child-care leave even where parental leave is a legal opportunity. Attitudes are such that employers might view men who take leave as less serious about their careers. Such attitudes are not surprising in a climate where domestic work and child-care is looked down on as a secondary occupation, or not 'real' work. There are few countries in the world where women's domestic work and care of children is actually valued and recognized as being worthwhile.

Divisions of labour

As noted the sexual division of labour has little to do with biology but a great deal to do with what societies have come to expect of women. It is evident that throughout the world caring for children is mainly carried out by women and is seen a 'woman's role'. The majority of domestic work such as cooking, cleaning, shopping and general caring duties is carried out by women. Yet in most 'socialist' states women were accorded an equal role in production – that is, they were expected to engage in paid, public work. Indeed it was the very encouragement of women to become part of the public work-force that Engels viewed as one step on the way to liberating women from domestic slavery.

On the one hand the patterns of economic growth in the Soviet Union and central and eastern Europe, based as they had been on a quantitative expansion of the labour-force, depended heavily on the involvement of women in the labour-force. On the other hand, the strong emphasis that was placed on increasing stocks of capital goods led to wage disparities between 'preferred' industrial occupations, largely dominated by men, and the 'non-preferred' occupations in the basically feminized sectors. This emphasis, combined with other socio-political factors concerning expectations of 'women's roles', meant that low priority was accorded to recognition of women's heavy domestic responsibilities and to the equalizing of opportunities and responsibilities among all adults. The false division between the 'first' external, important world of men and the 'second' domestic, unimportant world of women and children accounts for a good deal of misunderstanding, frustration and basic power imbalance between men and women. The high abortion rates in many countries testify to the uneven power relationship between the sexes in that women have been unable to represent their own basic interests in avoiding unwanted pregnancies or not having pregnancies carried to term. Yet this fundamental power imbalance in which women were in a weakened position to represent their primary interests was seldom, if ever, recognized and seriously considered in these centralized regimes.

Attitudes have a big role to play in changing certain conditions for women, and while legislation is important, laws alone cannot guarantee change: if particular laws are not seriously implemented and maintained with the will to follow through, to check on equal pay and opportunities, then women will continue to be oppressed; received wisdoms on femininity and masculinity – notions of 'women's roles' and 'men's roles', what is 'natural' behaviour and where women's 'best interests' lie – must be challenged and opened up, to viewpoints not previously entertained under the former regimes. Such a rethinking could have important repercussions in many western countries, where insights into such matters are often lacking.

Work and family

The productivity and fertility of women, and the conflict between work and family have important consequences for state structures and planning in the countries under consideration. In social terms, the consequences include the dampening of women's creative input by illness and tiredness precluding involvement in community or national affairs. Adults in multiple working situations tend to have less energy for children, family members and each other.

Industrial development has had contradictory implications for sex equality, as can be noted in each of the case studies. While there are variations between the countries considered, there are apparent similarities in terms of the rhetoric of women's equality not matching up to the reality of women's lives.

There are several specific reasons put forward as to why women in these societies remained second-class citizens.

1   The countries that became known as eastern Europe were actually taken over at height of Stalinism and so suffered many of the effects of war-time rhetoric: the concept of 'motherland', and the esteemed values of 'family' after war, when more babies were wanted yet there were fewer men, so that women workers had to become 'superwomen'. Both Hungary and the GDR also experienced the 'motherland' syndrome fighting alongside the Nazis. As ex-enemy countries of the USSR they additionally suffered by having to pay reparations and financial penalties. All of the countries under Soviet control were influenced by the very undemocratic, centralized and top-down political style then apparent within the Soviet Union.

2   The Stalinist policies of rapid industrialization which gave marked priority to the expansion of capital-intensive sectors, and consequent low priority to recognizing and easing women's burden in the home and with child-care.

3   The minimal restructuring of family units and the backward-looking attitude towards women's unpaid work underpinning 'socialist' development in much the same way as it did within capitalist development. Although in the years immediately after the Bolshevik revolution some genuinely revolutionary attempts were made to free women from the oppression of male dominance in sexual affairs and family life, this was not on the agenda when the

central and eastern European countries came under Soviet influence. There were few sustained attempts at communal living and those that were tried were so underfunded that conditions were appalling.

4   The survival and reinforcement of traditional values and attitudes of male supremacy. The domestic division of labour was not problematized, and state forces became paternal 'protectors' of women, 'allowing' them certain rights. Irene Dölling a well-known German writer, notes that a form of state socialist patriarchy retained control over women's lives by 'caring for' them in a paternal way which excluded any autonomous women's activities and any belief that women were capable of making gains for themselves.

5   The lack of educational campaigns aimed at breaking down conservative images of 'sex roles' and positive encouragement for women to organize for themselves. The institutionalization of 'women's councils' of various sorts within each of these countries showed the Communist Party's desire – need – to control every area of social and political life. Any women's groupings other than the official ones then became *de facto* unnecessary and generally illegal.

6   The nature of state socialist power structures, where no groups were tolerated outside party structures. No movements of any kind could realistically develop within this kind of totalizing control. Peace movements, environmental groups and economic criticisms of state control were all severely repressed within these countries. It is hardly surprising that women's groups did not form or survive during this bleak period.

Quality of life   If the leaderships in these countries had been less preoccupied with rapid economic growth and more with human welfare, attention could have been channelled into some of the areas that affect the quality of people's lives – basics such as having space in which to live, with children sleeping apart from parents, and younger families not having to live with grandparents and other relatives. Adequate child-care facilities could have been developed; cafeterias within work-places could have been improved; and some reliable household durables may have been developed and made available.

The blatant and widespread destruction of the environment in many parts of the former Soviet Union and central and eastern Europe has also led to a rapid deterioration in the quality of people's lives. Not only have industrially related deaths increased in certain occupations such as chemical industries, quarrying and foundry work, but whole areas of common land, lakes and rivers have been devastated and laid waste for years to come. The air in certain areas of cities such as Budapest is literally unsafe for young children to breathe at particular times of day. The heritage of the former regimes in these countries is a heavy one indeed.

Structure of the case studies

The case studies cover three main areas:

1. women as producers and reproducers – workers and mothers

2. women as decision makers – participation and representation

3. women's personal autonomy

Within these categories there are obvious variations in terms of priorities and evaluations, and some fairly apparent similarities.

Issues concerning women and work highlight the relatively undeveloped notions of valued/under-valued work, paid/unpaid work in terms of women's relationships to work and their perceptions of what work involves. Here the context of 'love labour' could prove to be very important in future research.[7] Tensions between public, paid work and domestic work, including housework, child-care, buying food and responsibility for creating domestic environments are apparent in this context, and here the 'superwoman' complex arises. At this time of transition unemployment is an important factor.

Situations differ quite radically between countries, but many of the issues involve similar problems. Horizontal and vertical gender structuring of the labour-market are apparent in terms of the areas in which women work and their pay differentials, including labour legislation and protective legislation. Included in this is the lack of opportunities for women to gain new skills, and adequate training in all chosen fields.

Issues concerning the double burden form the bridge in this section between production and reproduction. The two are very much linked, as our title *Superwomen and the Double Burden* suggests, and it is apparent that women's 'duties' as workers/mothers are prioritized in many countries over their 'rights' to contraception and abortion.

In the arena of reproduction we see the fusion of rights and duties, with the state guarding women's 'duties' as mothers. The whole range of 'benefits' available to women, such as child-care, days off with sick children, protection from certain sorts of work (yet women still do very dirty and dangerous work in other fields), are geared towards 'encouraging' women to be good workers and good mothers. The psychological effects of this worker–mother duality and the confusion women suffer as producers–reproducers are considered.

Figures were often quoted in the Soviet Union on the so-called 'demographic crisis' that structured the debate on women's childbearing and fertility. The needs of the state are often cited in this context as if it is a 'natural' expectation that women should control their fertility only in certain ways and for particular reasons. In Hungary and Poland arguments concerning the 'dying out' of the nation have resulted in women's needs or desires being given very low priority. Family ideology has regarded the family as the basic social unit and a key source of social and economic stability. A nuclear family model of a particular type underpinned the economic systems of state socialism so that women's 'double burden' was very necessary to the smooth functioning of these systems.

The section on women as decision makers includes women's input into policy making and political activity, as well as every-day decision making in terms of deciding the family budget. The areas considered include women's involvement in social change and politics in its broadest sense, be this party politics, organizational or trade union activity, or decentralized small grass-roots groupings.

Ways in which women resist change are considered in terms of 'passive' and 'active' participation/activity. Choosing not to vote, or not to marry, can be examples of such activity. Choosing to live alone or as lesbians are other examples. In this context the old official women's organizations were important. Women often viewed such institutionalized representation as being carried out within 'paper' organizations, and as such wanted nothing to do with them. The legacy of such organizations differs across the countries considered. There is discussion of the variety of women's groupings now developing, and the wide range of the different groups from 'feminist' to anti-feminist, including women in favour of women's rights to control their fertility and women who are anti-abortion. In the former Yugoslavia a Party of Women was formed, and ideas on the development of women's parties were, and still are, being discussed elsewhere. The question of whether or not women are taken seriously as a political force is an important one.

In our final section on women's personal autonomy we are concerned with how women see themselves, and with their aspirations. Societal images of women often veer between images of devoted mothers and images of prostitutes. What sorts of women are acceptable? What sorts of women are tolerated? How can women achieve a balance in their lives within these conflicting demands? How are issues such as prostitution, rape, violence, discussed by the authorities, the press, among women? Has there been much opening up on topics of sexuality? Differences are apparent concerning the degree to which such topics have been discussed, and in some of the central and eastern European countries there is still almost total taboo on such thinking.

With the new governments in place there has been an assumption that there is more room for discussion of issues and initiatives within an activated 'civil society'. Sometimes it is implicitly supposed that in this situation there will automatically be more 'space' for women to be heard, to become active and to participate in broader, differentiated ways. As is apparent in the feminist groupings, which are very much struggling against entrenched beliefs, this is not necessarily true.

For some women though, the 'value vacuum' has been heightened since the demise of statist socialism, and this has often meant that women wish to turn – return – to Christian values and to spiritual aspects of life. As can be seen, religious factors have a variety of parts to play in the lives of women in the countries considered. The coalition of Church/state forces is generally one that seeks to constrain women's choices, certainly in terms of reproductive rights. The responsibility often felt by women to instill into their children moral guidance as 'good people' often includes some measure of religious feeling. How does this combine with the role of the Church in terms of images of women? Despite the opening up since 1989 it is apparent that women's options often remain very limited and that certain religious attitudes can lead to further limitation of women's choices.

Trends in transition

Some argue that the paternal state oppression of women is being replaced by oppression by the market. Certainly, increased availability of pornography and sexual advertising are obviously harmful to women's interests and are at odds with the authorities' stated desires to encourage 'good mother' qualities. Are 'good' and 'bad' women's images being strongly reinforced by this so that women who are raped will always be viewed as 'bad' women and thereby deserving to be raped? Will such women also be refused abortions? The case studies attempt to cover these broad topics within a contextualized background.

The studies are loosely grouped into three main areas, with the countries of Hungary, Czechoslovakia and Poland forming the first group. These countries are now often grouped together as being the three most 'western-looking' states in terms of their outlook towards economic integration with western Europe and their perceived stress on consolidating democratic political structures and pluralistic societies. In the study on Hungary I have brought out apparent similarities between the situation for Hungarian women and those in other countries while highlighting those circumstances that are unique to Hungary. Features such as the early introduction of paid child-care leave with job guarantees, from 1967, and the existence of the semi-legal second economy from the early 1970s made the situation for women in Hungary markedly different from women in neighbouring countries.

For women in Poland, Jolanta Plakwicz highlights the unusual combination of Church and state forces in attempts to criminalize abortion rights. Written from her perspective as a feminist activist, Jolanta is clear that women's rights are currently being restricted in Poland and that the political changes since the late 1980s have actually decreased women's opportunities within Polish society in a variety of ways.

In her work on Czechoslovakia, Mita Castle-Kanerova points to the changing situation for women in terms of the general social regeneration of Czech and Slovak societies. There are many groups now forming in which women can participate and attempt to shape certain aspects of the changes within their society.

In the second grouping are the studies of those countries that have somewhat different histories: the former GDR as part of Germany; the former

Yugoslavia comprising several national groupings moulded together and having broken from Soviet influence as early as 1948; and the former Soviet Union itself, the dominant power in the region.

Barbara Einhorn points to the situation for women in the GDR as having been perhaps 'better' than that of women in other central and eastern European countries. She notes that women's access to child-care facilities was very good within the GDR as the state had managed to turn rhetoric into reality in this area. The GDR was also relatively more prosperous than the Soviet Union and most of the other countries under consideration.

In her work on the former Yugoslavia, Milica Antic explains the complications that arise for women from the manipulation of ethnic tensions and power struggles by state officials. She explores the ways in which women suffer from the expectations of bearing children 'for the nation' or having their children deemed undesirable, as the case may be. Women's groups that have been formed in recent years have attempted to be anti-nationalist in their aspirations, despite the practical difficulties involved.

In the Soviet context Hilary Pilkington points to the wealth of written material and shows that, despite the quantity, much of this material has remained unproblematized in key areas. Certainly the every-day situation for women in the former USSR did not neatly fit within the rhetoric of the party. Women are facing new challenges during this period of immense societal upheaval and are facing them in a variety of ways. The current 'resexualization' of this society is challenging the ways in which women's sexuality is socially constructed, while the atmosphere of glasnost has placed women's questions back on the agenda.

In each study attempts are made to posit some of the future trends in the transitionary period these countries are experiencing.

Notes

1   The term 'central and eastern Europe' is used to highlight the understanding that 'eastern Europe' was a term taken largely from a military context of cold war. No such region was actually recognized by the inhabitants of the countries under consideration. The use of 'central and eastern Europe' also has a more regional connotation which can include countries such as Austria, and which for our purposes also includes more southern countries such as Yugoslavia.

2   The material noted in the bibliography is much more extensive on these countries. One particularly useful comparative early work is that of Alena Heitlinger, 1979.

3   See Corrin, 1990.

4   See initially Buckley, 1989 and Lapidus, 1978.

5   For a more detailed analysis of this point see Heitlinger, 1979.

6   There has been some discussion, particularly in Hungary, concerning the harmful consequences of certain market-oriented drives, including certain aspects of privatization. Whether this critical discussion will be broadened to include social welfare considerations remains to be seen.

7   The term 'love labour' was the subject of a recent paper by Kathleen Lynch of the Department of Education, University College Dublin, given at The Galway Labour Group Conference 'Socialism at the Crossroads' in November 1991.

2

Hungary
Magyar women's lives:
complexities and contradictions

Chris Corrin

Area	93 030 km^2.
Population	10 375 000 including 5 388 000 women.
Capital	Budapest.
Languages	Hungarian (Magyar) official, Romani, German, Slavic.
Races and ethnic groups	Magyar 96 per cent of which up to 1 million are of Romani (gypsy) origin and are counted as Hungarian. German 1.9 per cent, Slovak 1.00 per cent, Croatian 0.8 per cent, Romanian 0.3 per cent, Serbs and Slovenes both 0.05 per cent. Many more Romanians have settled in Hungary since the purges in 1989.
Religions	Roman Catholicism approximately 60 per cent, Protestant (Calvinist), Jewish.
Education	Free and compulsory from six to 16 years. At 14 choices are made between gymnaziums and technical and vocational schools. Girls make up about two-thirds of students in gymnaziums, which provide education in many fields including preparation for university entry. Only a minority of female graduates continue their studies at university or other higher educational institutions. Because girls prefer to study in these secondary grammar schools, which provide a general education only, they are not guaranteed strong chances for work. Boys and men tend to attend mainly vocational schools and obtain up-to-date skills.
Birth rate	In 1990 11.7 per 1000 population.
Death rate	In 1990 13.8 per 1000 population.
Infant mortality	In 1989 15.8 per 1000 live births.
Life expectancy	Female 73.8; male 65.4 (1989).
Currency	Forint (July 1991, exchange £1=128 forints). Now almost convertible; no major difference in legal/illegal exchanges.
Women's wages as a percentage of men's	Women still earn 70–80 per cent of men's wages, but this varies across sectors. Most women remain in the lower levels of the income brackets. While the earnings of 75 per cent of women were below the national average in the 1980s, this was the case with only 33 per cent of men.

Equal pay policy	Guaranteed in law in Article 70B of the Hungarian constitution (amended 1972).
Agreed minimum wage	On 1 April 1991 official minimum monthly wage in Hungary was set at 7000 forints (US $100). Average personal income in 1990 was 13 205 forints (gross), 9960 forints (net).
Production	Agricultural: corn, wheat, sunflower oil, potatoes, sugar beets, vegetables, wine grapes, fruit, dairy produce.
	Industrial: transport equipment (mainly buses), textiles, pharmaceuticals, measuring equipment.
Women as a percentage of the labour-force	Total active earners 4 467 000, of which women make up 1 992 500 (1990). Included in this figure are over 200 000 women on child-care leave.
Employed women's occupational indicators	In the 1980s the majority of women still entered the job market without professional skills, despite rising educational levels.
	The sectoral distribution of women wage earners in 1988 was 29.4 per cent in services (non-material sector), 29.1 per cent in industry, 16.4 per cent in agriculture and forestry, 15.3 per cent in commerce, 5.1 per cent in transport, post and telecommunications, 3.0 per cent in construction and industry, 0.9 per cent in water works and supply, and 0.8 per cent in 'others'.
Unemployment	Little reliable gender-specific data available. Of those receiving unemployment benefit in 1990 it appears that women were less affected by unemployment than men.
	In January 1989 the unemployment benefit scheme was launched.
	In 1990 of those unemployed for less than 180 days there were 34 377 women (51 131 men), with average unemployment benefits of 4959 fts (6542 fts for men); of those unemployed for 180–360 days there were 1524 women (2245 men), with average unemployment benefits of 3845 fts (4367 fts for men). Estimates on future trends range widely from 5 to 20 per cent of the work-force in the next two years.

This study considers the situation of women in Hungarian society from the late 1940s to the early 1990s. The main concentration is on the later period, with a focus on the ways in which the transitional changes now taking place are affecting women, and how women in turn are bringing about changes. As with other countries in this study, women in Hungary share certain experiences common to the 'soviet-type' systems: worker–mother dualities; rigid politics, with economic considerations dictating social questions; bureaucratic and unnecessarily rigid approaches in education and social services generally; and, of course, the 'double burden' that women face.

Given the enormous upheavals that have taken place during the last few years in Hungary, and the need for new agendas in most fields, opinions on support for women's rights and attitudes towards feminist initiatives are divided, with the majority of men, and women, feeling that such matters are not of great importance. Even within the political parties and trade unions, women's issues are viewed as being relatively unimportant. It is becoming an 'in' joke in Hungary among those thinking about women's politics and feminism, that Hungarian society is anti-feminist despite the fact that there are very few feminists in Hungary. This is something to be seriously considered. There is a certain ridiculing of anything that is seen to bear a feminist hallmark; it is seen as either irrelevant to women's needs, or a sign of women's failure to be *real* mothers and women. It has been suggested (see, for example, Tóth and Gabor, 1989) that this is to do with the more rural, traditionalist nature of Hungarian society that has not historically been as western looking as, say, German society.

Language also plays a part, in that the classics of feminism, from Simone de Beauvoir to Germaine Greer and beyond, were not translated into Hungarian, unlike the central works of other 'isms'. Indeed, very few, if any, of the major feminist works have yet been translated. Despite this there are active groups of women in Hungary, including the Feminist Network, groups against pornography, women involved in environmental campaigns and professional women. All are organizing to improve women's opportunities within Hungarian society and to protect some of their rights, such as abortion rights which have now come under threat of limitation.

Political changes

A centre-right coalition came to power in Hungary in April 1990, made up of the Hungarian Democratic Forum (the largest party, with 164 seats), the Smallholders (44 seats) and the Christian Democratic People's Party (21 seats). The nature of this coalition is predominantly conservative/moderate and somewhat nostalgic, looking back to a romanticized Hungarian past where there were 'solid' values of Christianity, family and a sense of nation. Such nostalgia is distinctly double-edged where women are concerned. If notions of 'ideal families' are again to be supported, women's unpaid, undervalued work within the home will be neither recognized nor problematized. Limitations on women's rights – to employment or to control their bodies, sexually and in childbearing – fall within these nostalgic reminiscences.

Unfortunately, of the three major parties in opposition, none has specifically highlighted women's issues in any way. The largest party, the Free Democrats (SzDSz, 92 seats), did have a small women's group for some time but it was not well accepted within the male hierarchy. One woman member of the party, Ottilia Solt, is sympathetic to women's needs, alongside those of other oppressed groups such as Jews and gypsies. The Young Democrats (FIDESZ) have several active young women members and have invited feminists and members of the National Gay Council to air their views in the party publication, *Hungarian Orange (Magyar Narancs)*. A section of the old Communist Party, now involved in the Hungarian Socialist Party, still maintains women's rights to employment, but given that this was really the only 'right' women were 'allowed' by the communists it remains somewhat transparent.

Background developments

As in most other central and eastern European countries the influence of Soviet economic development became decisive in Hungary after 1948. For these societies this meant a concentration on heavy industrial development at the expense of diversification and consumer goods production. These developments took place alongside a 'top-down' approach in which goals were dictated by the five-year plans within which economic solutions to social questions were sought. Yet in the late 1940s there were many who worked hard in Hungary and elsewhere for a 'socialist' future, believing that a more just world could be developed.

The key to understanding this period lies within the realm of Stalinist politics. It is vital to recognize that the types of development that were being encouraged or pressed on these societies were modelled on those of the rigid, hierarchical and basically despotic regime existing at the time within the Soviet Union. This type of development had no connection with Marxism or with the creation of egalitarian living conditions, but a great deal to do with power and influence. The dominant influence in the region, the Soviet Union, pressed its demands hard, especially in 'ex-enemy' countries such as Hungary. Enterprises formerly controlled by the Germans were put under Soviet control and reparations were demanded. It is clear that from 1948 the state apparatus in Hungary was in a strong position vis-a-vis Hungarian society. Unfortunately in the Stalinist state-socialist context this meant that the state was exercising power via coercion. Such coercion varied over time with different circumstances, and volumes have been written on the direct confrontation between major elements of Hungarian society and the oppressive state in 1956.

This was certainly a turning point in state/society relations in Hungary and many thousands died in the violent confrontation. The consequence included primarily a realization for critically active Hungarian people that power politics in terms of Soviet influence in central and eastern Europe was a major factor. The Soviet Union had 'control' over Hungary within its sphere of influence, and neither the USA nor other countries were likely to intervene in any attempts by Hungarians to liberate themselves from this situation. János Kádár took over the leadership of the Hungarian Communist Party (HSWP) after the 1956 revolution and remained one of the more popular 'eastern European' leaders until May 1988 when he was 'retired' and replaced by Károly Grósz. The fundamental recognition of the status quo by Hungarians was certainly a helpful starting point for Kádár's 'normalization' policies. With this came a consequential recognition on the part of active oppositionists of the necessity for different strategies of resistance. Women were active in various ways in this resistance, as will be considered below.

The Stalinist government placed contradictory expectations and obligations on women in Hungary, centering on the rhetoric of 'socialist emancipation' or 'liberation'. Women were entering the work-force in large numbers and in previously 'male' preserves, yet there were few changes in the domestic scene either qualitatively or quantitatively. In time, during the 1960s, crèches and kindergartens were built to ease child-care arrangements but the quality of working mothers' lives remained devastatingly low.

Essentially the dual role of worker-mother has never been fully problematized in Hungary. The unrealistic expectations placed upon 'successful' women to emulate 'superwomen' generally leads to great strains, affecting both physical and psychological health. That the domestic sphere remains women's primary responsibility has meant that the full weight of the 'double burden' has rested on women's shoulders.

In turn, this historical situation will impact on the decisions women now face in Hungary, in terms of *choices* about work. Many women appear very willing to give up low-paid, low-skilled work in favour of a 'family wage' for their spouses. Whether such 'family wages' will become a reality remains to be seen.

As will be considered, Hungary was undergoing radical economic experimentation from the late 1960s, which in stops and starts dramatically changed the organization of the Hungarian economy into the 1980s. The economic changes had obvious social effects, not least on the number of jobs that some people could undertake (mainly men) and on the price rises that accompanied the lifting of subsidies. Both of these factors had important consequences for women's lives during the 1970s and 1980s and in many ways made aspects of their situation very different from their counterparts' in other 'ex-socialist' countries.

Women as producers and reproducers – workers and mothers

Unlike the situation in some other European states, Hungarian industry did not begin with an emphasis on textiles (industries which have generally been considered prime female employers), and the significant involvement of women in industrial occupations did not begin until light consumer industries developed around the early 1900s. It was during World War Two that women began to be employed in large numbers. With men away working as soldiers, their places in the factories were taken by women in ever-increasing numbers. The aftermath of this war was devastating in Hungary, especially for women. Almost 200 000 men died, disappeared or were captured, and women were left to support millions of families. The increased demands for labour, and the consequent increase in economic activity rates for women, meant that between 1949 and 1960 almost 75 per cent of the increase in the numbers of economically active people arose from the fact that many women had joined the labour-force. From 1960 into the late 1980s, as Table 2.1 shows, women's labour-force participation continued to increase. It is important to bear in mind the fact that during the 'socialist' period (certainly until the changes with the New Economic Mechanism from 1968) Hungarian people had to work, and the state remained the sole employer. The changes with the NEM meant that more private businesses were set up and more people worked for themselves. Hungarian people remained legally bound to work right up until 1989 but obviously with the dangers of unemployment, rules on vagrancy or lack of work-place credentials were not strictly applied.

A significant percentage of Hungary's industry is centralized in Budapest – with the increase in private enterprises, there are even more workers in Budapest than the legal number of persons employed. The situation for rural women differs greatly from that of urban working women. There are fewer good job opportunities in rural areas, and women tended to commute from villages to towns in larger numbers in the 1980s. Some young women leave rural areas to work in towns, living in hostels. Despite the fact that women have consistently stated their desire for part-time work, this was considered expensive and difficult to implement under the old authorities. Approximately 3 per cent of women worked part-time in 1989. This percentage is expected to increase as a result of the changes that have taken place since that date.

Table 2.1   **Labour-market participation rates by sex (%)**

	Men	Women
1960	92.2	49.9
1970	87.3	63.7
1980	97.4	70.7
1985	82.5	74.1
1989	80.5	73.9

(Source: *Statisztikai Évkönyv*, 1989)

As Table 2.1 shows, the policy of full employment meant that by 1985 women's participation rates were almost as high as those of men.

In 1976 women workers made up 44.8 per cent of the work-force, but only 20.4 per cent of skilled workers;

in 1984 women workers made up 45.5 per cent of employed people, yet they made up only 21.9 per cent of skilled workers (*Statisztikai Évkönyv*, 1984). In this context then, it is apparent that although women made up almost half of the work-force employed in industry they constituted less than a quarter of skilled workers. The fact that women have consistently been denied opportunities for training is a recurrent theme in literature assessing women's work. Although this is the case in both the east and the west it is particularly so in central and eastern Europe. Here again we find the notion of women's work as being secondary to men's work, with echoes of women's 'real duties' being within the home.

Women in agriculture

Employment and training opportunities for women working in agriculture have decreased in the last 20 years. Hungary is now self-sufficient in major agricultural products, and has some capacity to export, although it has lost its Soviet market, at least temporarily. At the same time there has been a massive decline in agricultural employment as a result of the increased investments in large production units and the import of western harvesting and processing technology.

In this transitional period, from the late 1980s, more fundamental changes have been taking place within agricultural organization. At present women are to be found, above all, in horticulture and gardening, fruit growing and poultry breeding. These areas are particularly labour intensive with little or no mechanization. The vast majority of private plot farming, carried out by traditional primitive means, falls to women. Although women members of agricultural co-operatives can theoretically attain the same jobs, and wages, as men, in practice the annual income of women reaches only about 86 per cent of the income of male members.

One factor here is the deep-seated male prejudice against women working in the same jobs, yet even if this were not the case, the lack of training for women would still be a major problem. Few women employed in agriculture have the necessary school qualifications – an eighth grade primary school education – to enable them to receive certain types of training. New employment opportunities are harder to find in rural areas and this results in many women remaining in their original agricultural occupations. It is in the more industrialized areas such as plant production that male labour-power is absorbed by the demand for skills. As in other areas of work, there are opportunities for men to find professional, non-agricultural work that does not separate them from their usual environment. However, since the 1960s there has been a massive increase in the number of workers commuting to work. In 1980 roughly 25 per cent of men and over 15 per cent of women commuted to their work. Those who commute weekly or monthly live in lodgings at their place of work. Many commuters are caught in a situation that points up the differences between their two ways of life – rural home situation versus urban, industrial working environment. There is evidence to suggest that many commuters would prefer to retain their rural home life.

Women in hostels

There is a group of women who actually leave their rural environment and make their homes in the many industrial hostels in the towns and in Budapest. These women generally move away from their villages when they are quite young, from the age of 16.

In the feminized industries such as textiles some hostels have as many as 1000 members. Often the rooms are filled to capacity, with as many as 10 beds in a single room. Detailed studies written in Hungary on the kind of life that young women in such hostels lead (Mátyus, 1980) show that it is often a very bleak and disappointing experience. Although the girls are promised an education, and most factories do provide lessons, the environment in which lessons take place is not conducive to learning, and to live in a hostel is generally to take on a very low status.

Given this situation, marriage is viewed as the primary escape route. Yet as all the romantic and

sexual life of these young women has to take place
either in bars or on the street, the outcome of many
romances is abortion and shame for the women
involved. Often the women cannot return to their
villages as to do so would mean breaking the contract
that they or their parents have signed. Such contracts
take several forms, the main feature being that the
young women agree to work for a particular
enterprise for a specified time. In return, the
employers offer 'training and education'. Penalties are
enforced if the contract is broken – money they can't
afford to pay. The result is that they are forced to
make the best of a very bad situation.

**Women in
leading positions**

Improvement in the number of women achieving
leading positions in Hungary has been slow and
discrimination has decreased only slightly. In 1978 it
was noted that although 82 per cent of workers in the
health service were women, only 15 per cent were
leaders (Koves, 1978, p. 10). This situation has been
similar among teachers and in other institutional
centres. Women's representation has been, and
remains, poor in public life and executive structures.
The input of women at high level within
governmental structures was practically nil, as can be
seen in terms of decision making, yet in the years
1960–80 the numbers of women in leading positions
did increase as Table 2.2 shows.

Table 2.2   **Proportion of women in leading positions**

	1960	1970	1980
Managers of enterprises/ directors of institutions	7.4	6.4	12.1
Directors of co-operatives	2.4	2.9	5.6
Leaders in public admin	8.1	11.8	19.6
Leaders in municipal admin	12.5	15.3	29.1
Technical managers/chief engineers/works managers	1.7	4.2	3.1
Financial managers/ business executives	21.0	33.8	40.9

(Source: Kulcsár, 1981, p. 6)

As far back as 1977 it was clearly recognized that discrimination against women in this area existed. In an article entitled 'Women in Leading Positions', published in a leading Hungarian newspaper *Népszabadság* in December 1977, István Koncz claimed that there was a general belief that women could not do such work, as leading positions demand total attention, a permanent readiness and often unlimited working hours. It was seen that able women between the ages of 30 and 40 in Hungarian society generally had to make a choice between leadership and family duties, and that they tended to choose the latter. Yet this is at best a very limited 'choice'. The fact that women may be considered too old for training at the age of 40, when they are generally relieved of child-care, yet men are considered to be at the peak of their intellectual and creative force at 40 or 45, tells us a good deal about the not-so-subtle discrimination that works against women. Koncz argued that the objective conditions that limit women from attaining leading positions *can* be changed, and that those who view such conditions as fixed do women a double disservice of perpetuating false 'beliefs' which in turn have practical consequences (Koncz, 1977). Women are expected to achieve much higher standards than their male counterparts simply in order to show that they are capable. The comment 'I have to prove myself better than the men to show them I can do it' is not an uncommon one.

Nevertheless, the numbers of women in leading posts did increase between 1980 and 1989, except in the political arena. While there are no precise figures available on women in leading posts since the political changes in 1989, it is undoubtedly the case that women are seen to be taking a leading role in certain high-level jobs in banking, commerce and private industry. This will certainly be one key feature of change for women in the 1990s.

Job segregation

It is apparent that women remained caught in the trap of job segregation according to gender. While it is true that from the late 1940s women took up more

challenging jobs that had not previously been carried
out by women, early conditions were grim – there
are tales of women having to drown foetuses at the
building sites on which they worked. Infrastructural
and financial support for working mothers lagged far
behind their labour-force participation rates.
Conditions improved somewhat into the 1960s and
beyond, but no concrete, systematic attempts were
made to overcome some of the contradictions
between parenting and work outside the home.
There also remained obvious differences in the types
of work undertaken by women and men.

Table 2.3   **Distribution of active wage earners by staff groups in
the socialist sector – state companies and
collectives (%)**

	1 January 1985		1 January 1988	
	Men	Women	Men	Women
Manual workers:	78.5	59.5	78.2	58.3
skilled	45.4	12.1	46.0	14.4
semi-skilled	23.4	30.0	23.1	29.8
unskilled	9.7	15.9	9.1	14.1
Non-manual workers:	21.5	40.5	21.8	41.7
engineering	9.7	3.5	9.7	3.5
administrative office work	7.0	10.5	7.0	11.4
health/culture	3.5	12.4	3.5	11.8
book keeping/ accountancy	1.3	14.1	1.6	15.0

(Source: Ladó, 1991, p. 30)

It is evident from the figures in Table 2.3 that
women predominate in semi-skilled work in the
socialist sector and make up the majority of those
working in offices, health and cultural activities, and

in bookkeeping and accountancy work. Women are much less well represented in skilled work and in engineering. Other statistics for women's work show that the industries employing more than 50 per cent women are: telecommunications and vacuum engineering; printing; textiles and leather; the fur and shoe industry; and handicrafts and homecrafts. Those branches in which skilled women actually predominate – the textile and clothing industry, and handicrafts and homecrafts – can be seen as 'feminized' in that women form the majority of the workers and the wages and conditions are poor. Some argue that this work neatly parallels women's work within the home, yet it needs to be borne in mind that such work can be among the 'heaviest' in terms of the work-load and physical stamina required.

The deskilling of women's work is a common feature of industry in Hungary, as elsewhere. Instances of this, and discussion of working conditions generally, were reported in various newspapers and radio discussions during the 1980s. Often women's places of work are crowded and very noisy, the light is dim and the ventilation systems inefficient. In certain places employing mainly women workers the air is filled with gas, smoke and dust. Such conditions have increased the likelihood of early retirement for women. Unfortunately, because women's earnings are generally less, on average, than those of men, and women still sometimes receive less for doing the same job, women choose to 'make up' their money by working night shifts and holidays. Enterprise managers often take advantage of this fact by employing women to do extra overtime.

Education and training

Education in Hungary is compulsory for eight years and is free. There is no gender-biased choice of subjects – such as girls taking home economics and boys taking metalwork. Indeed, given the rigid centralization of the system, there is very little curriculum choice at all in the first eight years of schooling. Children attend primary and secondary school from the age of six and have to make a decision at 14 about whether or not to study further.

One major criticism of the Hungarian system is that such an important once-and-for-all decision takes place at such an early age. Some pupils enter 'gymnaziums' in order to prepare for college or university; others go to technical schools. Whereas girls tend to form up to two-thirds of gymnazium pupils, only a minority continue their studies at universities or other higher educational institutions. A variety of vocational schools and centres offer teaching in specific skills.

Table 2.4   **Choice of further education at the age of 14 (%)**

	1980		1987	
	Male	Female	Male	Female
Skill/training school	57.8	36.1	57.2	36.7
Technical college	24.3	26.7	25.9	27.7
Gymnasium	13.8	27.7	14.1	28.1
Total	**95.9**	**90.5**	**97.2**	**92.2**

(Source: Eberhardt, 1991, p. 12)

As full-employment was an essential political goal (until 1988) attainment of education and training became important in the context of 'who does what'. In 1987, of those girls in vocational training (34 per cent of the total of all in training), the majority were involved in 'feminized' training – around 98 per cent of the total training in garment and textiles, and making up 80 per cent of those training in the leather industry. Yet girl apprentices also constituted 85 per cent of chemical trainees, 70 per cent in construction materials and 57 per cent in printing (Eberhardt, 1991, p. 13). As in many other countries women are predominant in the teaching professions in Hungary, making up 100 per cent of kindergarten teachers and almost 90 per cent of primary school teachers, yet they make up only 45 per cent of science teachers.

Equality at work

As in other countries under consideration, the legal status of women in Hungary in terms of equality of earnings has long been recorded – since 1949. This is repeated in the 1972 constitution, where paragraph 2 of article 70/B states that 'for equal work everyone, without difference, has the right to equal pay'. However the reality of the extent to which equal pay principles have been implemented is not so positive. Although pay differs according to qualifications, experience, length of service and actual position within a firm, women consistently earn less than men. Equal pay for work of equal value is not something that regularly arises in Hungarian trade union disputes. While in the 1970s the Women's Council, supported by the Communist Party, argued for, and in some cases gained, equal pay for women entering the labour-market, women cleaners still generally earned less than male 'industrial' cleaners, the only difference in their work being its designation.

In terms of the equal treatment of women in work it is apparent that in Hungary, as elsewhere, the 'protective' legislation works against women being able to enter certain jobs. Work such as mining, flying aeroplanes, driving trains, lorries, tractors and other agricultural machinery were all closed to women. Since 1990 some work, for example on certain agricultural machinery, is now open to women. Frictional, that is temporary sectoral, unemployment may well have created job shortages, as indeed it did in bus driving where women are now 'allowed' to participate, and do so in large numbers. It seems that a basic attitudinal stance has to change whereby women are valued for their skills and abilities rather than categorized in terms of their usefulness within the home and viewed as a 'flexible' work-force.

Domestic work

Efforts to socialize housework in Hungary have fallen far short of what was required for working mothers not to suffer the full burden of their double shifts.

From the late 1950s attempts were made to provide subsidized eating places. Although eating places such as factory dining-rooms and cheap restaurants were relatively inexpensive to provide and maintain, they were often of very poor quality and the choice available to diners was extremely limited. While most new factories did have dining provision it was neither on the scale nor of the quality originally envisaged by planners in the early 1960s. Similarly such provision of laundries as still exists is seen to be expensive to maintain, and as such this provision has not, nor is it likely to become, easily available in many localities.

Certain aspects of household work in Hungary need to be outlined. Labour-saving equipment is still not readily available to the 'average' Hungarian. Necessities – certainly for households with young children – such as modern, *reliable* washing machines are expensive and difficult to obtain. Washing machines do exist in many households, but it is commonplace for a great deal of time to be spent in trying to fix them or attempting to obtain spare parts for them. Tumble dryers are rare.

Unlike in many western countries where 'household shops' can be done each week or month, with such items as milk, eggs and even yoghurt, potatoes and fruit juices being delivered, in Hungary much shopping still needs to be done daily. This means queuing to pay, as shops are fairly crowded, and even in the larger supermarkets it is not always possible to get everything that is required. Carrying bags on crowded trams, especially with young children, can be difficult as the packaging of foodstuffs in Hungary is remarkably poor. The milk, which is sold in very flimsy polythene bags, can leak on to the rest of the shopping. These seemingly small incidents become a surprisingly major irritant on top of a busy day at the factory/office/school.

Cleaning in Hungary is not made easier by handy squeezy mops or spray cleaners. Most floor cleaning is done with a form of headless brush around which a cloth is draped, and most of the cleaning products are of below-average quality in terms of speed cleaning. The problems apparent with washing machines also apply to vacuum cleaners. Of the two main types available, the Czechoslovakian ones are difficult to obtain spare parts for and the Russian makes, while less reliable, are easier to repair. In households without a reliable handyperson the cost of repairs is often prohibitive.

Added to this, the educational system is such that children generally need some parental guidance with homework, and giving this help often falls to women.

In terms of 'help' for women within the home, in Hungary children tend to carry out even less housework then men. Some women, remembering their own shortened childhoods in which they were carrying out responsible jobs, would like more help from their children; others, realizing that their children are tired after school and often have a good deal of homework to complete, believe it is easier to carry out the jobs themselves.

Child-care provision

It is important to set the services/benefits debate for child-care within the economic climate of the time. The general economic situation in the mid 1960s was one in which the previous rapid annual growth had slowed somewhat, and signs of lower growth were apparent. Economists tended to view these changes as marking the end of a period of extensive growth and they proposed structural change in the economy. Some structural change was realized within the New Economic Mechanism (NEM) (see page 34), and it was at this time that the fear of unemployment began to be felt. Certain economists believed that full implementation of the NEM would result in unemployment, and as full employment was a principal socialist value several safeguards were established to avoid unemployment. The child-care grant/benefit can be viewed as part of this process.

The fact that later economic studies have shown an apparent labour shortage in Hungary in the 1970s is irrelevant in this context, since the indicators pointing towards a situation of surplus labour were what formed the basis on which the child-care grant was created. Not only was home-care by mothers much cheaper than institutional provision, but it had the added bonus of flexibility – the removal of a section of women from the work-force for periods of time.

Since the introduction of the child-care grant (GYES) in 1967 and the child-care fee (GYED) from 1985, more and more Hungarian women have chosen to stay at home to care for their young children. The child-care grant was a flat-rate benefit, roughly equivalent to 40 per cent of salary and available for two years. It has been replaced by the child-care fee which is a higher benefit tied to a percentage of previous earnings (75 per cent) and is available for three years. Many women stay at home for at least 18 months and sometimes for the full three years after their 24 weeks' maternity leave. Since 1982 this has been a parental allowance, so that either parent may stay at home once the child has reached the age of one.

The network of child-care services includes crèches, kindergartens and after-school care, however the success of both provision and utilization of services has been mixed in Hungary. In the late 1980s there was room in crèches for only about 15 per cent of children under three years. A major obstacle to furthering this network is the high cost of investment and maintenance. The introduction of the child-care grant and benefit have been very important here, as paying women to stay at home to care for their children is obviously much cheaper than maintaining crèches.

In the three to five age group the provision is better, with up to 70 per cent of children being placed. However, parents pay 20–40 per cent of real costs and often the food is poor and resources cannot stretch to new educational toys. With the move towards a more market-oriented approach it is probable that many kindergartens will become privatized, as they have elsewhere in the region, so that only those who can afford to pay for care will be able to guarantee it. Several firms have closed their child-care facilities recently as a means of saving money.

For the six to 13 age group education is both compulsory and free and works on the basis of morning or afternoon attendance. When both parents work their children attend the so-called 'daytime schools' which are very ill-provided. Children are given lunch and remain under supervision until their parents collect them. Yet generally teachers have little time to do more than sit with children, and when there are not enough teachers very large groups of children of differing age groups simply gather with nothing to do for the rest of the day, knowing that they have to remain there until their parents can collect them. It is easy to see how mothers could have 'guilt feelings' about having to leave their children in such unsuitable circumstances, yet there is little choice.

By early 1991 it was realized that several firms were choosing to close work-place nurseries that were considered too costly, and some enterprises stated that in the current economic climate, women on child-care leave could not be guaranteed posts at the expiry of their leave.

Working mothers   Hungarian commentators often refer to the increased expectations and pressures placed on 'modern' Hungarian women regarding their performances as working mothers. Most women in Hungary have been expected to contribute substantially by paid employment to the household budget as well as to carry out the majority of household work and child-care. If children are in kindergartens it is often the mother who takes them and collects them each day. Studies have shown that the average length of time women enjoy as leisure time is substantially lower than that of men, and working mothers have the least 'free' time. Mária Márkus points out that:

All this leads to a situation where there no longer exists any 'natural' behaviour for women and everything has to be 'explained'. (Márkus, 1975, p. 35)

Women at home feel the need to explain why they are not out working, and women in employment without family feel they must 'explain' this. Women trying to fulfil both aspects often have bad consciences in terms of not being 'good workers' if at home with sick children, or not being 'good mothers' when they are at work. Tensions between home life and 'productive' life have also become apparent in terms of the shortage of houses in Hungary. Due to the lack of apartments, those who can afford to often attempt to build their own homes and this is actively encouraged by the state. As the work generally falls to men, this has meant that women are often further pushed into domestic work and child-care. This tension between economic production and social reproduction has certainly caused great strains for women themselves, and within relationships on both the individual and social levels.

'Socialist families' in theory and practice

In Hungary, as in other countries of this region, during the socialist period ideals of the 'socialist family' were officially upheld. Generally the 'socialist family' was considered to be more democratic and collectivist, and was regarded as more of a genuinely social unit, as opposed to what were viewed by Marxists as the economic units of family which underpinned capitalism. The fact that it is women's unpaid work in families under both types of organization that keeps the whole system viable is almost always, everywhere, ignored. It could be said that any talk of 'the family' these days is not very helpful, analytically or practically, in that the infinite variety of ways in which people coexist cannot so easily be labelled. Yet notions of 'ideal' families are certainly current in Hungary today, with clear ideas of women's central place within them. Historically, under the old regime, a general social view was that the domestic units in Hungary could be seen to be playing distinct and important roles as counterbalances to the intervention of the state. During the 1980s, discussing this with women across Hungary, I was reminded of the experiences of black communities in Britain.

Given that the state attempted to reach in and
influence every arena of life, the 'personal' became
very closely guarded in Hungary. A friend gave an
example of how children are affected by the state's
influence and intervention. Her daughter drew a
picture celebrating 'Liberation Day' (when Soviet
soldiers 'liberated' Hungary) and forgot to draw the
red Soviet flag alongside the red, white and green
Hungarian one. The kindergarten teacher duly told
her the picture was not good and refused to place it
on the wall with other children's work. My friend
reassured her daughter that the picture was really very
beautiful and they put it on their wall at home. This
is a small example of how children in Hungary had to
learn two ways of behaving – what could be said and
done at school and what was only to be discussed at
home. In this way, mothers passed on their beliefs
and knowledge to their daughters and sons. Adults
also had two ways of judging situations, in terms of
official and unofficial, and ideas concerning the
'personal as political' took on different connotations
within this context.

**Marriage,
divorce and
relationships**

Although marriage is 'popular' in Hungary, the rate
of divorce has markedly increased since the end of
the 1950s. Deteriorating relationships do not always
end in the legal dissolution of marriages. Given the
shortage of available housing, some couples decide
that it is just not practicable to divorce. Others
divorce but continue to live in the same space, with
sections 'curtained off'. The new divorce legislation
introduced within the family law makes this situation
even more difficult for couples wishing to separate, as
terms such as 'living apart' take on a different
complexity in these conditions.

The ages at which men and women marry have
remained relatively stable over the 50-year period,
while the divorce rate can be seen to have soared –
from 113.5 per thousand marriages in 1948 to 440.2
in 1988 (Corrin, 1990a, p. 132).

The dominant family formation in Hungary has been
that of a nuclear family with parents and one or two

children. The two major constraints on the development of large families are the lack of adequate housing and the shortage of money. The chronic shortage of accommodation, as in many other central and eastern European countries, means that young childless couples come very low on the priority list. In 1990 there were 70 000 people on the council waiting list in Budapest alone, for approximately 7000 flats. There are some conditional bank loans by which couples who promise to have a certain number of children are granted loans under favourable conditions. The phrase 'the OTP children' comes from the abbreviation of the Hungarian National Bank – Országos Takarek Pénztar (OTP). Since 1977 couples have been able to acquire apartments at reduced costs providing that they have a certain number of children. Part of the price of their accommodation is children. According to reports in some newspapers, including *Népszava (People's Voice)*, a trade union paper, women are being blamed for 'accepting the role of mother to gain an apartment'.

Often young couples live with their parents and it is quite common for this arrangement to extend over many years, with the couple's room being shared with their first child. Cramped conditions, pressures of noise, cooking, cleaning and child-care can combine with the lack of privacy experienced during this initial marital period to cause both the women and the men involved to 'rethink' their positions. High divorce rates and low birth rates eloquently testify to the substance of such problems. A novel way of solving part of the housing problem is for young people to make 'contracts' with older people living alone. The young people care for the pensioner, often cooking, cleaning, shopping and maintaining the flat, and are able eventually to gain the flat when the older person dies. There are over 5000 young people involved in these schemes at any one time.

During the past 20 years involvement in the second economy has been another cause of marital strain.

The second economy in Hungary is a legalized alternative economy in which those working pay contributions. It may be that a worker uses a state machine at night to fulfil an order for another enterprise, or builds a house at weekends for another person or extends private plot farming to the market-place. People have held more than one job in Hungary not by 'moonlighting' but by taking part in a legally recognized part of the economy. The economic developments brought about significant changes within economic structures so that rather than 'simply' working for the state in a powerless position, some people were able to take control of another area of work and to show their abilities and initiative to better effect.

Yet this involvement with second and even third jobs meant that people often worked very long hours, without holidays or weekends for years. The extent of this second economy can be shown by the amount of people involved – 75 per cent of families in the late 1980s (Eberhardt, 1991, p. 24). Women with whom I have discussed this situation over recent years have told of their loneliness and isolation in their 'concrete boxes' with only their young children to talk to. In such a situation sometimes divorce can seem like the best option as the relationship in which they are involved does not seem worthwhile.

A major consequence for women in terms of divorce is that they often become single parents, at least for a time. Of the 10–12 per cent of households with a single adult, women make up 92 per cent. There are sociologists in Hungary who argue that the single-minded, selfish mothers who choose to divorce their husbands relegate men to a social position in which they suffer. As women tend to get custody of children in most cases, and thereby the flat in which they are living, men do often lose out practically in the process of divorce. Yet it is also true that many men abuse and beat their wives and then refuse to pay the statutory maintenance payments in order to help the women care for the family. Of course there are arguments on both sides, but few women who have had to bring up children on their own on low incomes would countenance arguments concerning their selfish behaviour 'punishing' their ex-husbands.

There is a relatively small proportion of couples 'living together' in Hungary, due mainly to housing shortages but also to some extent due to the non-acceptability of this lifestyle. Marital infidelities are not viewed as scandalous. Some sociologists, such as Cseh-Szombathy László, have argued that the communist regime itself was active in encouraging extra-marital affairs because the 'private' family was viewed as a bulwark against the intrusion of the state. During the 1950s and 1960s married couples were sent on holiday separately to mix with colleagues with the possibility of having an affair. So long as people are discreet about their affairs, it is not a big concern in Hungary. It can be harmful to women, though, when men choose to boast about their sexual conquests and there are quite obvious double standards being upheld. Again men's involvement in extra-marital sex is regarded as something quite 'natural' while women who enjoy sex in this way are regarded as whores. This situation is most certainly *not* unique to Hungary.

Unfortunately, it is true that unmarried women are seen as being in some ways 'deficient' in Hungary, so most women expect to marry. A high remarriage rate parallels the high divorce rate. For women, and feminists in particular, it could be unfortunate that certain ideas of the 'good Hungarian family' are now back in fashion. The argument runs that the Communist Party rule destroyed the ideas of family unity and privacy which are now being restored with the help of the major party in government, the Hungarian Democratic Forum. Ideas concerning the reintroduction of religious education in schools, coupled with traditional notions of the sanctity of the nuclear family sit quite easily with even more fundamental beliefs concerning babies' rights and life beginning at conception.

Young women and youth culture

Young women in Hungary are discriminated against most blatantly in terms of prevailing family ideology. 'Unmarried mothers' and 'illegitimate children' are considered outside the 'good' family framework and such women and children suffer because of the social attitudes which prevent them forming alternative family arrangements. The prohibition of oral contraceptives for those under 18, and the need for parental consent for a woman under 18 years to have an abortion leave young women in a vulnerable position.

There is a great deal of ignorance about sexual matters among young people generally, and juvenile sex has become a subject of serious preoccupation among professionals concerned with demographic questions. Under the communist period there was discussion about helping families and educators to develop a new code of socialist standards of sexual ethics that would fill the gap left by the abandonment of the once dominant religious ethics. The Hungarian Council of Ministers decided that from 1974 onwards all elementary schools should include sex education in their curriculum. However, sex education was often left to 'home-room' teachers – who may have specialized in physics or mathematics – and it was rather optimistic to expect promising results. In the majority of interviews I conducted during the late 1980s, most women who should have had access to such classes either did not have them or had instead general counselling sessions that, while valuable enough in themselves, contained no useful sexual education.

Some 70 per cent of babies born outside marriage are given up for state care as there are insufficient facilities to give assistance to young mothers who wish to raise their children. In 1980 8 per cent of births were 'illegitimate' and a large number of these were to mothers who were still legally regarded as children themselves. Young male attitudes towards their offspring are generally irresponsible and the number of lawsuits to establish paternity has been steadily increasing since the 1970s.

There are several distinct aspects – in political and popular terms – to the youth cultures in Hungary. According to an opinion poll in early 1991, FIDESZ, the Association of Young Democrats, is the most popular political party in Hungary. In terms of breaking with tradition, FIDESZ politicians argue that they represent a new political culture as their policies are independent and free of 40 years of past experience. No one over the age of 35 may be a member of this party, and members are noticed for their different behaviour and style of dress in and outside Parliament. The youngest MP in Hungary is 23 years of age, and Hungary now has 22 of the youngest MPs in the world. FIDESZ was started secretly in 1988 by 37 students. Often during 1988 and 1989 their rallies were broken up by police, and although many supporters were arrested there were no trials. In 1989 one member, Tamás Deutsch, was arrested in Prague for demonstrating and returned to Hungary as a hero before becoming an MP. The FIDESZ symbols are oranges which for them represent freedom and independence. On one of their election posters two eye-catching scenes were depicted – one being two old men (Honecker and Brezhnev) kissing each other in formal communist greeting, and the other a young couple on a park bench kissing. The message was simple – choose us! They have a direct way of doing things and a good rapport with the people. Zsuzsánna Szelényi, their foreign affairs spokesperson, supports arguments for a new campaign on human rights. Their magazine, *Magyar Narancs (Hungarian Orange)*, has offered space for feminist contributions and has reported favourably on the setting up of the National Gay Council in Hungary.

A student rebellion in the Film School in Budapest during June 1990 against old-fashioned teaching methods led to students publishing their criticisms and nominating new tutors. Many of the old staff, including the famous director, István Szabo, resigned. Government funding has now been reduced and the students recognize that they will have to seek commercial funding, which means making films that are more marketable than purely artistic.

In terms of popular culture there are distinct western influences apparent in Hungary. For the pop music fans, the Hungarian version of Kylie Minogue is 'Szándi'. Szándi, a 14-year-old schoolgirl whose records sell in thousands, believes that young people need someone of their own age with whom to relate. Her debut album, *Little Girl*, went 'gold' after selling 100000 copies, with *Teenage L'Amour*, her second album reaching number one in the charts by mid 1991.

The state record company, Hungaroton, manages Szándi and another popular youth group 'Bonanza Bonsai'. EMI recently put in a bid for Hungaroton. Members of Bonanza Bonsai, some of whom are economics students, could be seen as Hungarian equivalents of Depeche Mode, though aiming for a more 'eastern' style.

The two aspects – western and Hungarian – are treated differently by young people, who might name Kylie as their favourite singer but Szándi as their favourite Hungarian singer. Other popular groups include Rock Café, True Blue Box and Tilos As A. One group called 'Bikini' has a song about ethnic Hungarians in Romania called 'Nearby Places', in which Hungarians there are encouraged to try to fight for their rights. In the summer of 1991 Paul Simon, The Pet Shop Boys and AC/DC all played in Budapest. With tickets at roughly £20.00 each, nearly one week's wages, these are definitely special occasions.

Living standards One of the basic differences between living standards in the old 'socialist' regime and in the more open system now developing, is the ever-widening gap between rich and poor. Hungary has one of the most developed market economies in central and eastern Europe, and hard currency can buy almost anything.

Prices have been rising rapidly in the last few years, with subsidies being taken off basic foodstuffs, energy and travel. An understanding of the mechanisms of economic reform in the Hungarian context is important when considering living standards. Basically the reform process begun under the Hungarian Economic Mechanism from 1968. These reforms were planned to ease the transition from a system of central planning to a more market-oriented system – which was vaguely scheduled for 15 years. The barrier was that such change was supposed to be discrete, in other words it should not involve political change. Given events in Czechoslovakia in 1968 it was important for the authorities to stress that economic reform was in no way connected with politics.

By the mid 1970s these reforms had reached a watershed, with the need for either more tolerance or more administration. The latter was chosen and the economic situation worsened. With oil price increases and changes in COMECON prices, Hungary had incurred a loss equalling its entire annual GNP over a period of 10 years by 1983. For working Hungarians both prices and wages were affected. The first price increases in 1980 were shocking for the majority of Hungarians. The price of bread, which had been stable for 28 years as a political price, was raised on average by 50 per cent. Meat increased by 26 per cent, sugar by more than 20 per cent and the prices of dairy products also rose. These rises did not fully cover the subsidies. Energy prices also increased with electricity being raised by 50 per cent and district heating by 40 per cent (which only covered about one-third of its actual cost) (Vajna, 1982, p. 209).

In the 1980s 10–30 per cent of the population fell into the poverty category – made up mainly of those on low incomes, Romany people and families with three or more children. Social policy analysts in Hungary claim that these people are the tip of the iceberg and indeed, with the numbers of homeless people now apparent on the streets of Budapest and other large towns, income inequalities and massive differences in living standards are obviously making an impact within Hungarian society. So for the last 10 years Hungarians have actually been feeling the effects of moves towards a market economy. As women carry out a large part of the domestic budgeting, the search for ways of making ends meet has often fallen to them (Corrin, 1990(a)).

In the first quarter of 1991 inflation reached over 30 per cent in Hungary. Alongside this rapidly rising inflation there has been a decline in industrial production, notably in heavy industry and mining. The number of poor people receiving relief or assistance from state authorities increased drastically in 1990 and early 1991. Women are particularly vulnerable to poverty when economic situations worsen. Given the large numbers of elderly women on low, fixed incomes, and single parents who remain in the lowest income brackets, this is an area to which social policy experts need to turn their attention. It seems sadly ironic that soup kitchens quickly appeared in Budapest after the 1990 elections.

On the other side of the coin in 1990, for the first time, 41 top designers showed their styles in their own clothes show. The average outfit sold for about £400 – to rich Hungarians and foreigners. There are also over 100 000 people on the waiting list for new cars in Hungary, and the Hungarian stock exchange is at least surviving. Many Hungarians wish to become 'good capitalists'; and the famous saying 'only a Hungarian can enter a revolving door behind you and come out first' is quoted at times with pride.

For a large group of people in Hungary, the Romany people – 'cigany', or gypsies, life is very difficult indeed. There are almost one million Romany people in Hungary (1991) and they are officially classified as Hungarian. Unofficially they are viewed as inferior, and suffer from racism. Six out of 10 Romany people are believed to live below the poverty line and are denied opportunities for jobs and education. There are anti-gypsy jokes in Hungary in the same way that there are anti-Irish jokes in Britain: if someone chokes it may be said that something went down the gypsy way ('*ciganyutra ment*'), and 'that's not the way to do it' is translated by 'this is not how they beat gypsies' ('*nem ugy verik a ciganyt*') (Heinrich, 1986, p. 139). Many young Romany women, often from rural areas, become prostitutes to help their families financially. No other work is available to them. Other Romany people are not critical of these girls, as they understand how limited their choices are. Eight out of 10 Romany people are unskilled, and only about one in 200 are able to participate in higher education.

There are now several Romany organizations in Hungary and recently a Romany parliament was set up. Cultural organizations and political groups such as PHRALIPE, which means brotherhood/friendship in Romany, and which is the official organization of Romany people, are now demanding that their race is recognized as a distinct ethnic group in Hungary.

Quality of life

In terms of the quality of people's lives, pollution is a major destructive factor. In Budapest one in 17 deaths is related to air pollution, and oxygen booths have now been set up. Some industrial plants are closed during smog alerts. The air in the city is monitored, and sometimes parents are advised not to take their children out in particular parts of the city. On the streets of Hungary today the old-fashioned, pollutant variety of car runs alongside Mercedes and other luxury models. The beautiful river Danube which parts Buda from Pest is now full of mercury, oil, iron and ammonia, not to mention raw sewage. Over one million cubic metres of untreated human waste are dropped into the Danube each day, and one-fifth of the city's drinking water comes from the river. While swimming is banned, fishing is allowed.

Hungary recently received £18 million from the European Community to promote environmental projects. The first environmental group *Duna Kör* (Danube Circle) was active from 1984 in getting the Danube Dam, or the Gabcikovo-Nagymaros river barrage scheme, stopped. This project has generally become regarded as one of Europe's most absurdly ambitious and unnecessary projects. Many thousands of Hungarians became active in this campaign, and it has been viewed as a major spark to citizens' activity in Hungary during this period. Since 1990 there has been a women's group, *Zöld Nök* (Green Women), that is actively campaigning on environmental issues and making international links.

Women's health

In theory everyone in Hungary can receive free medical treatment whatever the need, as confirmed in the Social Security Act 1975. In practice, as in other countries operating a universal health-care system, there are discrepancies between the supply of service and the demand. Demand in Hungary is far higher both quantitatively and organizationally, than the medical network can cope with. The number of people with a right to free medical services has increased rapidly since the 1950s, yet the amount of money available for treatment has risen only slowly. Statistics on numbers of beds available and doctors in the health system can be misleading, as it is clearly apparent that the whole health system needs overhauling. Almost three-quarters of hospital buildings are over 50 years old, and at least one-third of these need to be demolished and rebuilt. Most of the hospitals use outdated technical equipment. Unfortunately there is much mismanagement. Doctors are expected to see between 80 and 120 patients per day and so even where expensive equipment exists there is no time to use it. The deficiencies have been apparent for a long time and at the end of 1988 the Németh administration attempted to tackle some of the anomalies of the social security and health systems. These plans were upset, however, by the 'overburdening' of the social insurance fund with health service funding. Table 2.5 gives an aggregated overview of general aspects of health care in Hungary.

Table 2.5   **Health care in Hungary (1989)**

	Population 10375000	
	Male	**Female**
Life expectancy (adults)	65.4	73.8
Infant mortality (per 1000)	15.7	8.1
Number of deaths	76 521	68 174
Death rate (per 100 000 inhabitants)	1500	1244

	Most frequent causes of death Per 100000 inhabitants			
	Male	**Female**	**Male**	**Female**
Heart attacks	8461	5710	165.9	104.2
Strokes	9588	11539	188.0	210.7
Malignant tumours	17307	13527	339.3	246.9

	Total	**Per 100 000 inhabitants**
Number of active physicians	31 537	29.8
Number of hospital beds	104 479	98.5

Medical equipment:	
computer tomographs	7
ultrasonic diagnostic equipment	413
dialysators	176
laser instruments	73
Number of days' sick-leave per employee	25
Average duration of hospital care per patient	14.9
Number of in-patient clinics and hospitals	148

(Source: adapted from *The Hungarian Observer*,
vol. 4, no. 3, 1991)

In the area of children's health, there are serious misgivings about the high number of premature births (often blamed on the use of abortion) and increasing childhood neurosis. The infant mortality level in Hungary is one of the highest in comparison with other industrialized countries that have developed health systems.

Because there is insufficient income coming from the state budget, scales of charges are now being considered, as is the introduction of priority criteria in order to limit waiting lists. In practice overworked and underpaid doctors and nurses accept offers of gifts – of goods or services that are in demand. Given that both market and non-market mechanisms are allowed to operate anyway, the question of tipping is a difficult one. In the area of childbirth, for example, the practice has meant that women almost always decide to tip their doctor at the going rate to ensure they get the necessary care. There are great variations in quality of hospital treatment for mothers and children. In some hospitals wards are divided simply by curtains, and children are kept separate from mothers. In some of the teaching hospitals where care is much better, mothers and children are allowed to stay together and relatives can visit more freely. The 'going rate' for tipping doctors in March 1991 was anywhere between 4000 and 8000 forints, with scaled-down amounts for midwives, nurses and so on (author's interviews, 1991)[1].

Women are affected by stress related diseases, particularly in industries such as textiles where the effective length of the working day is often extended by long travelling times. Many older women, unable to survive on their state pensions and forced to look for work in textiles, find that the stress is too much for them to cope with. Factories that employ psychologists note that they are booked for weeks in advance.

There has been evidence in Hungarian medical journals that many school children are seriously affected by stress related illnesses, and alcoholism and suicide are serious problems among young and old alike.

One, perhaps uniquely Hungarian, phenomenon that has emerged during the last 10 years or so is the 'GYES disease', or 'child-care syndrome', which affects mother who are receiving child-care benefit in order to care for young children in the home. GYES was the *gyermekgondozási segély* or child-care grant and this situation was unique to Hungary among the 'socialist' countries at that time because it was the first country in which such provisions were made. Hungary was the first to experiment with loosening the centralization in the economic sphere thereby freeing jobs and needing the 'flexibility' provided by removing large sectors of the work-force (mothers) for up to three, or six or more years at a time. In the cities women describe the lack of adult company, the narrowing of living possibilities and the desire for a job as causes of the syndrome. Symptoms are less apparent in the villages. Dr Mária Szilagyi, a psychologist working with neurosis patients in the eighth district of Budapest, has written of some of the young women under her care:

they are not alcoholics: they only get nervous because they cannot fulfil the desired purpose for which they get the allowance. (Horváth, 1982, p. 62)

Many of the women claiming the child-care benefit cannot cope with the upset involved in the dramatic change of lifestyle. Since the political changes of 1989 women are no longer guaranteed their jobs while they are on child-care leave. As all rights in 'socialist' Hungary have been tied to employment the possibility of unemployment also calls into question women's rights to such benefits as the child-care fee. As child-care institutions close and women's choices concerning working or claiming benefit are constrained the relevance of the child-care fee in policy terms is unclear at present. It is likely that more women will take their third year of allowance instead of attempting to return to work after two years and facing the possibility of unemployment.

This in turn may increase the incidence of their alienation.

Birth control

Abortion was illegal in Hungary in the post-war period, except in extreme cases, yet up to the mid 1950s there were 100 000–150 000 abortions carried out each year (Eberhardt, 1991, p. 30). In 1956 various health measures concerning birth control were introduced, including the legalization of abortion, which, it was hoped, would avoid the harm being done to women's health by illegal abortions. Although the 1956 regulations stated that contraceptives should be placed on sale without restrictions and at low prices, the manufacture of birth control pills was not authorized until 1967. Even then, only one oral contraceptive, Infecundin, was easily available on the market and it was not until the early 1970s that one or two other brands were also made easily accessible. Until September 1973 it was only gynaecologists who were authorized to prescribe them, and women had to pay the full prices, which disadvantaged, if not prohibited, women on low incomes from using this form of birth control. From 1973 district and company doctors were allowed to prescribe contraceptive pills and they were placed in the same category as other medicines. This meant that purchasers paid only 15 per cent of the list price. It was at this time that limitations on induced abortions were announced.

Until the 1973 regulations, effective from January 1974, free abortion on demand had been available to every woman in Hungary. From 1974, women seeking abortion had to appear before a committee that had the right to refuse consent. Although in many cases this was 'just' a formality, young married women who had no children, or only one child, were in practice often refused. As a result some 400–600 children were born each year against the mothers' wishes. Although the regulations still apply today, the committee was abolished in 1989.

There are approximately 90 000 induced abortions each year that are recorded. Given the shortages of

personnel, equipment and facilities generally within
the Hungarian health service, it is hard to imagine
that women would regularly undergo abortions as a
form of birth control if other options were readily
available to them. In 1989 the diaphragm was banned
in Hungary for 'hygienic' reasons. Various studies,
including the longitudinal marriage surveys (Kamaras
et al, 1984), have shown that when men had to take
some responsibility for avoiding unwanted
pregnancies the success rate was very low; when
women shouldered this responsibility the avoidance
of pregnancy became more successful. Effective and
efficient condoms are not readily available in rural
areas of Hungary and are sometimes prohibitively
expensive.

At the present time there is much discussion in the
Hungarian press about the possibility of stricter
limitations on abortion rights. Religious groups
wishing to ban abortion combine with ideological
statements concerning women's 'duty' to replenish
the nation's stock. For every 100 live births there
were 67 induced abortions in 1990. In the 1970s
there were 126 per 100 live births. If the figures over
the years were evened out, almost every woman
between the ages of 15 and 45 would have had an
abortion. Of course, some women have had more
than one abortion and some none, but an enormous
proportion of the population is involved. An outright
ban would not be acceptable within Hungarian
society, yet there are clear moves towards limiting
women's rights to abortion. There have been
petitions on both sides, from the Church and from
the Hungarian Feminist Network.

One danger for women lies in the language in which
the abortion debate is phrased – there is talk of
Nazism, and women as murderesses. The influence of
the Church, while not as gripping ideologically as in
Poland, is nevertheless powerful in Hungary, and the
centre-right coalition has considered giving some
hospitals and schools over to Church control again.
(Before the World War Two 61 per cent of
education was in Church schools – educational and

Church matters came under one ministry until 1948.) On 28 December 1990 (Holy Innocents' Day) pro-life groups in Hungary prayed for 'the almost five million Hungarian children who could not be born in the last 35 years because their environment decided there was no room for them' (Béres, 1991, p. 11). If the sanctity of life arguments are accepted, and some within the medical profession such as the Society of Christian Doctors do accept such arguments, then both intra-uterine devices and 'morning-after' pills will be banned. In such a situation a woman's right to choose for herself how to limit the number of children she wishes to have will clearly be diminished.

Women as decision makers – participation and representation

The arena of decision making often viewed as the most important traditionally is that of political life – the executive decision-making committees, local councils and the National Assembly. During the 'socialist' period participation and representation of women at the lower levels was numerically quite favourable, yet in the higher echelons of the old government structures such as the Council of Ministers and the Politburo it was practically nil. There were no women in the Politburo in 1986.

Since the changes in 1989 there have been several contradictory levels of development concerning women's participation. Women were very active in many of the movements that started to challenge the orthodoxy in the mid to late 1980s. Certainly a group of young women were vital activists in the environmental group that organized large demonstrations against the Danube Dam. Women were also active in the associations and movements that went on to form the major parties such as the Hungarian Democratic Forum and the Free Democrats and Young Democrats. Once these parties had been formed, however, women began to be less prominent.

The contradictory aspects of women's attitudes towards participation include the whole area of distaste for 'party politics' and the belief that the public face of politics, on platforms and in parliaments, is 'men's business'. Of the 3507 candidates in the 1990 election only 316 (9 per cent) were women. Unfortunately gender differences in voting patterns were not monitored during the election but it was apparent that women turned out to vote in great numbers and both during and after the election they visibly supported, with secretarial and administrative work, the organization of party offices. Yet of the 386 seats in Parliament only 28 were won by women – 7.2 per cent. This might be seen to compare unfavourably with the previous regime, but as can be seen in other studies, notably that on the Soviet Union, the 'milkmaid syndrome', by which women were drafted in as token women rather than as political activists with a political education and knowledge of political culture, meant that the representation of women under the old regime was figurative rather than actual. At least the 28 women MPs in Hungary are willing political figures, though not all necessarily champion progressive changes for women. (When I interviewed women MPs and party organizers after the 1990 election it was clear that many did not think women's issues were important, which certainly reflected the predominant political influences at the time.)

In terms of domestic decision making, studies carried out during the 1970s and 1980s (Szabady, 1976; Kulcsár, 1978; Sas, 1977; Valkai, 1986) show that Hungarian women do indeed take a major role where financial and ethical issues are concerned – in matters such as how money is spent and how children's lives may be guided. The other side of this is that they are expected to keep on paying bills and provisioning the home even when money becomes scarce. In the transitional years ahead this burden could become intolerable for women from the low income groups. In terms of encouraging children in their future prospects, this too will become more complicated in a society where the marked differences between richer and poorer, qualified and underqualified underlie people's positions within society.

Women's personal autonomy

Women in Hungary today are paying the heavy price of 'communist liberation'. The former regime made the emancipation of women an official policy, and the rhetoric proclaimed women's gains. In the new climate in Hungary this paternalistic 'emancipation' is disappearing, but the conflicts between domestic work, child-care and paid work have not been reduced. In addition the restyled 'Hungarian family' now being praised by the centre-right government, as an area of life that was oppressed by 'communist rule', is by no means an environment in which women's burdens are likely to be lessened.

The contradictory climate in Hungary at the present time is such that alongside the 'saintly mother' image go the sexually exciting images of women in pornography and prostitution. Such juxtapositions are common in western societies but until the last five years or so there was little direct portrayal of women as sexual objects in Hungary.

Since the lifting of all restrictions on pornography in 1990 over 40 pornographic magazines have become available, both imported and domestically produced (Interestingly, *Playboy* is not considered to be pornographic.) One Lászlo Vörös, who saw himself as a self-styled 'king of porn' claimed that his seven sex magazines helped people to overcome the legacy of communist sexual repression, teaching people about sex and helping those who could not find partners. In June 1991 he was arrested on a charge connected with one of his massage parlours.

By late 1991 one of the biggest new industries in Hungary was the sex industry, with many new clubs opening in which women are employed to strip, dance topless and act as 'hostesses'. Hungarian couples can earn the equivalent of £170 (over two months' wages) to make love on video for distribution. The first sex taxi used by prostitutes for conducting business and the first sex cinema were available in Budapest in 1990.

It is clear from recent discussions with many women in Hungary that some women feel there are forces beyond their control that have been shaping their own images of themselves, and at the most extreme these have been images of failure. In her work on women and alcoholism, Zsuzsa Valkai writes about the sexual role imposed on women by cultural traditions. She writes, 'a woman can only feel herself fully well not when she is a self-developed independent being, but when she lives with a man in a relationship of dependency ...' (Valkai, 1986, p. 131). The notion of a 'sexual role' is not a new one, yet it has generally escaped definition and discussion. It relates to a perceived 'otherness' of women in a male-defined world. Women are seen to have a 'sexual role' or a 'maternal role' or a 'family role' or a 'something else role', whereas men just *are*.

The attacks on women's rights to control child-bearing and the parallel flood of pornography have prompted women to action. The Hungarian Feminist Network (*Magyar Feminista Hálózat*) was set up by about 50 women in June 1990. Initially the intention was to set up a variety of projects, from consciousness raising to homes for battered women and an international information link or library. The major women's paper in Hungary, *Nők Lapja (Women's Journal)*, while now freed from control of the official Women's Council, still promotes a *Women and Home* image. In spring 1991, for example, a typical edition contained a section on the latest bridal outfits and a small profile of Edith Cresson.

Unfortunately when the Feminist Network was founded it was not realized how quickly the group would have to begin work on a concrete task – the campaign to defend abortion rights – and other projects had to be set aside. This level of activity, so soon after the founding of the group, has taken its toll on the women, and 'burn out' within the present anti-women atmosphere is being experienced.

An anti-pornography group meanwhile has had some success. Yellow stickers reading 'PORNO – why do

you only adopt the bad things from democracy?'
were stuck liberally over sexist advertising and
pornographic pin ups, magazines and books. It was
realized that after the oppressive climate of the last 40
years the total prohibition of pornography would not
be likely, but in January 1991 Gábor Demsky, the
Mayor of Budapest, banned the displaying of
pornography from newspaper kiosks near to schools.
Victories such as this boost women's confidence to
carry on with their campaigns.

The question of how to tackle prostitution is
something that is currently being debated by women
not only in Hungary but all over the world. Most
prostitutes in Hungary come from very poor families,
often from rural areas, and a sizeable proportion of
them are Romany. Given the fact that more and
more groups in Hungarian society are facing poverty,
it is hard to see how else some women can make
money. Perhaps one form of protection would be the
setting up of a union, like the British Collective of
Prostitutes, so that women working as prostitutes
could protect themselves.

There are several major barriers against active
involvement in women's groups and organizations in
Hungary today, not least of which is the fact that the
former Council of Women (*Magyar Nök Tanacs
Országos*) was viewed as a purely 'paper organization',
a branch of the communist regime. Anything that
reminds women of this type of organization, which
spoke on women's behalf but did not actively
engage with issues affecting women (other than
occasional pay demands), will be rejected. So too will
most activities concerned with feminism. The bad
press that western feminism received under the old
regime has its legacy in Hungary today in the popular
belief that feminist women are somehow failures as
women, or are man-hating lesbians.

The whole arena of sexual choice has also been
limited by the legacy of the previous regime's
repression. Homosexuals were presumed to be evil
or, at best, sick, so few homosexuals in Hungary were

able to be open about their sexuality. There were always a couple of gay men's bars in Budapest, but few places for lesbians to gather other than underground stations and other outdoor meeting places. During the 1970s and 1980s homosexual men and women used to arrange marriages in order to be seen as 'normal' and to gain access to accommodation. In October 1987 a group called Homosexual Association for Leisure and Health applied for and received recognition. In 1987 it was still legally necessary to apply to become a 'group' of any sort outside the auspices of the communist authorities. For a homosexual group not to apply would have made them an 'underground' group associated with political opposition. In January 1988 a speaker for the Ministry of Health and Social Affairs announced that the authorities would allow the founding of a gay and lesbian organization. The National Gay Council in Hungary now receives support from at least some political parties, such as FIDESZ, towards recognition of the rights of lesbians and gay men in society.

I do not want to give a false impression of the level of activism for women's interests in Hungary. The women's groups mentioned remain small in number and are relatively isolated. Many of the members are intellectuals and professionals. Most Hungarian women are busy ensuring their own situations, which for some means fighting for survival. Women's interests are prioritized within no political party or trade union movement. Anything associated with feminism is treated with suspicion by men and women alike. It will be a long, slow process to get women's rights on to the political and social agendas, and for those women active in this respect to gain the trust of the majority of Hungarian women. Yet the publication in September 1991 of *Nöszemély* (literally 'female person' – an ironic reference to 'women') is a very positive step. This is a feminist magazine compiled by several women's groups including the Feminist Network, Green Women, Women Entrepreneurs, Women in the Trade Unions and other groups participating in the Social Council that was set up in August 1991.

Conclusion

If asked 'what are you?' very few women in Hungarian society would identify themselves as 'housewives', yet many are now looking forward to the possibility of leaving their work-places and spending more time within the home. The shaping of Hungarian women's (and men's) identities by the mediation of policy decisions of the former statist authorities and by the political climate in which they lived is a factor that is recognized within Hungarian sociological debates.

In the coming years it is expected that women will begin to bear more of the brunt of unemployment. Although early figures suggested that men and women are experiencing unemployment in roughly equal terms, the trend towards encouraging women back into the home and offering retraining mainly to men will disadvantage women in their search for future employment, unless positive action is taken to redress this imbalance. Such action does not look likely in the short term. Women are seen as the main carers in Hungarian society in terms of work in the home, and care of children and elderly people, and it seems likely that in the coming years women will be encouraged, possibly by state subsidies and protection of pension rights, to take on the care of those areas of society that the new authorities, like their predecessors, claim are outside the economic possibilities of the state in the present climate. Several prominent figures in Hungary argued during 1991, for example, that it is not possible even to consider the welfare needs of the population 'until the economy is on its feet'. It is precisely the importance granted to welfare considerations that many social policy analysts in western countries view as the core around which a revitalized Hungarian economy needs to be built, in order not to have the depths of poverty and social distress experienced elsewhere following drastic structural changes. Yet though it will take time for women to find the levels at which

they can express their differing needs and aims, they
will not simply acquiesce.

The current competitive market orientation of most
politicians sits awkwardly beside the nostalgic, rural
vision of certain political groups. There are
complaints in Hungary that while the Parliament is
very democratic, it is not very efficient. Pivotal
economic decisions often seem to be decided in
haste, while topics such as the changing of road signs
are debated at length.

The link between economic decisions and political
and social developments was criticized in the former
regime, yet is not problematized within current
governmental structures. Few of the political parties
regard human welfare throughout Hungarian society
as being of fundamental, direct importance. The old
distinction of 'socialist rights', that is equality for all,
came under attack in Hungary when applied to
medical treatment. Equality came to be reduced to
equally bad treatment unless you could pay for it
because of the inadequate infrastructure of the health
service within a crisis stricken economy.

For women the 'right to work' lost any meaning over
the years, associated as it was with the total
exhaustion of working all day in paid work and then
most evenings and weekends at home. In terms of
women's rights over their bodies, being able to enjoy
one's sexuality freely, and to choose whether and
when to have children are basic human rights. Such
rights are not currently recognized within Hungarian
society, nor indeed are they fully recognized in many
parts of the world. Here a change in attitudes is vital.
Even if homosexuality is no longer illegal, while
lesbians and gay men are regarded as deviant other
more dramatic experiences such as beatings and loss
of jobs can and do follow. Traditional (and often
contradictory) notions of masculinity and femininity
need to be opened up for public debate rather than
problematized within personal relationships, which is
generally done at women's cost. Until the value of
the domestic, personal activities of life is elevated to

the level of value accorded to the external, public arenas, a balance cannot be created.

As with all long-term change the process by which women gain confidence and self-respect as citizens and as human beings tends to be gradual. Within these processes choices can be made regarding engagement with state procedures and structures, possibly as they have been in other countries, with women often becoming active in areas concerning welfare and provision. However, it is not to be expected that women in Hungary will follow any particular 'western' feminist route towards gaining access to decision making and changing power structures. In this context collaboration between women in central and eastern European countries may well evolve different, progressive activities towards changing their male-dominated environments.

Notes   1   Note on methodology:

The origins of this work stretch back to 1982 when I first discovered Hungarian sociological writings. My first visit to Hungary was in 1984 when I had overcome some of my worries about 'researching women's experience' given the current debates about women objectifying others in their work or making careers 'off women's backs'. My aim was to privilege women's experience of change, and with close contact with many women in Hungary over the last seven years I am now pleased to be writing about these interpretations so that they can feed back into some of the debates now developing within Hungary.

My way of working was ethnographic in that I spent as much time as I could with women discussing everyday concerns, particular aspects of their lives in terms of work, child-care, money, personal identity and sexuality, hopes and dreams and political change. Sometimes I taped more formal 'interviews' which were always open-ended and included exchanges of information from me about 'western' women and feminism in all manner of different aspects. I also transcribed documentary and other material written by Hungarian sociologists and interviewed people in Hungary who had worked on 'the woman question'. It was relatively easy to spend time with women from various backgrounds and age groups in Budapest, but less easy (because of time, money and access) to get to know women elsewhere. This study is to some extent Budapest focused, but many women now living in Budapest spoke of their lives elsewhere and some women's experience is included from Debrecen, Pécs and Györ as well as surrounding areas of Budapest.

3

Poland
Between church and state:
Polish women's experience

Jolanta Plakwicz

Area   312 683 km^2.

Population   In December 1990 the population was 38.2 million, of
                     which 21.2 million were women. Women make up 51.2
                     per cent of the population (105 women for every 100
                     men). In rural areas there are many more men than
                     women, and in towns this situation is reversed.

Capital   Warsaw (population 1 800 700, 1989)

Urbanization   23.6 million people live in towns and cities and 14.6
                     million live in rural areas (December 1990).

Languages   Polish is the official language and is spoken by
                     approximately 90 per cent of inhabitants. Some German
                     and Russian are spoken.

Races and   Polish 98 per cent plus German, Ukrainian,
ethnic groups   Byelorussian, Slovak.

Religions   Roman Catholicism is the dominant religion in Poland.
                     There are also some Greek Orthodox, Protestant and
                     Jewish believers. In 1983 there were approximately
                     12 000 Jews in Poland (before World War Two there
                     was an estimated 3.5 million Jewish population).

Education   Education is free and compulsory for those aged
                     between seven and 17 years. In 1989–90 girls who
                     finished elementary schools made up 58.7 per cent of
                     children continuing their education at various high
                     schools. Women predominate in certain fields: in 1988
                     women constituted 85.9 per cent of medical service
                     school students, 50.8 per cent of agricultural and
                     forestry students, 59.3 per cent in fine arts yet only 25
                     per cent in technical schools.

                     In higher education women are approximately 55 per
                     cent of graduates, and the majority in humanities (80
                     per cent), teacher training (73.6 per cent), medicine and
                     dentistry (67.7 per cent), mathematics and natural
                     sciences (66 per cent) and economics (55.6 per cent).

                     Women who hold a university degree make up 4.9 per
                     cent of the total female population in Poland; male
                     graduates make up 6.4 per cent of the male population.

Birth rate	Decreasing, at 4.6 per million in 1990. This represents the lowest ratio since 1948. Connected with high death rate, poor health and a constant process of emigration.
Death rate	National average 10.1 (1986). Highest mortality was in the town of Chorzow, in the region of Katowice, where it was 14.9 per 1000 population.
Infant mortality	18.4 per 1000 live births (1984).
Life expectancy	Rural females 75.6 years (males 67.1 years) (1987).
Representation	In the Polish Parliament there are 62 women MPs out of 460 and seven women senators out of 100. There are no women leaders of political parties and no women are heads of divisions within Solidarity trade unions.
Currency	Zloty (20 200 = £1.00 sterling, January 1992).
Women's wages as a percentage of men's	In the highest paid sectors such as law (average pay = 1163 in 1000s zloty) women earn up to 98 per cent of men's earnings. In the lower paid sectors, such as social work (average = 643), women earn approximately 72 per cent of men's earnings.
Equal pay policy	Statutory 'equal pay for equal work' since 1952 constitution.
	At the end of 1990 the government established uniform equal bases for work evaluation, applying to all state employees regardless of sex. If these rules are observed existing pay discrepancies between men and women holding the same posts should be reduced.
Production	Agricultural: grains, potatoes, sugar beets, tobacco.
	Industrial: ships, textiles, chemicals, wood products, metal, autos, aircraft.
Women as a percentage of the labour-force	Seventy-two per cent of women between the ages of 18 and 60 are employed (45 per cent of labour-force). State production employs the highest number of women in various sectors: trade 69 per cent, communication 58.2 per cent and industry 37.2 per cent.
Unemployment	In January 1990 there were 46 000 unemployed in Poland and by the end of December 1990 the number had reached 1 126 100 (8.3 per cent of the work-force). Women represented 51 per cent of this figure.

Background

Poland has compiled very little data on its female citizens. The majority of research (whether by women or men scientists) shows heavy male bias. We appear in statistics as producers and reproducers but data on the sexual politics of our lives is unobtainable. Where evidence is not available I have therefore drawn on my own experience and on the shared experiences of our feminist group in Warsaw during the past 10 years. I will treat the date of the last general elections (4 June 1989) as the turning point in the situation of women in my country.

Women in Poland gained equality of civil rights in 1918 and equal suffrage in 1919, shortly after Poland regained its independent statehood. These legal rights were not translated into practical reality, however, and the situation for women did not really change until after World War Two. During that war more than six million Polish people died, either in battle against the occupants or in the Nazi and Stalinist camps and prisons. After the war women played a large part in the economic development of Poland in the two major areas of industrialization and urbanization, and took on a great deal of the burden of rebuilding normal life.

As in some other countries during this period, economic planning and decision making were controlled by the centralized state. In turn this made it easier for the state to control women's (and men's) participation in various spheres of life, creating conditions based on the Soviet model of five-year plans. Women's needs were often overlooked under communist rule, and the Marxist–Leninist doctrines were used as political propaganda in determining women's rights and duties. Despite the apparent equality of the Stalinist legislative system in the Polish constitution of 1952 the state's policy in this regard remained passive in that no further legislative or other means were undertaken to implement the general principles in practice. The anti-discrimination paragraph of the Polish criminal code has never included discrimination with regard to sex. As regards

Article 3 of the convention, it is worth noting that the Polish People's Republic (1945–89) was a country where human rights and basic freedoms were permanently violated (regardless of sex), and in the period of restructuring the discrepancy becomes more clearly visible.

In 1956, as in other countries, notably Hungary, there were serious disturbances. Workers from Poznan revolted and popular pressure created a situation in which a new party leadership, headed by Gomulka, was elected. Gomulka was seen politically as an orthodox communist yet he believed in a 'Polish road to socialism'. There were other signals of discontent over the years, principally in 1970 and 1976, which were muted by concession and change of leadership, so that the communists held on to power.

It was a woman crane operator, Anna Walentynowicz, who led the strikes in Gdansk shipyard in protest against food price increases. These demonstrations set off a chain of events that culminated in the creation of the first independent trade union in communist Poland. By August 1980 it was clear that the old formulas were no longer working for the current leader, Gierek, as despite concessions the reform movement was growing stronger.

The imposition of military rule in December 1981 was a dramatic end to the year-long negotiations with the new independent trade union *Solidarnösc* or Solidarity. Despite extensive repression Solidarity was able to mobilize over half of the adult population in Poland. Many women became active members of Solidarity and helped to organize support for those persecuted after martial law was declared. They acted as messengers in the underground opposition movement, and as writers, editors and publishers of *samizdat* materials.

Analysts argue that it was the scale of resistance in Poland, along with the economic experimentation going on in Hungary, that led the way to the break-up of the so-called communist rule in central and eastern Europe. A great deal has been written on the activities of Solidarity and I do not propose to add more. From the women's perspective though, the combination of strong Catholicism and protection of men's rights and conditions of work, meant that women again lost out in terms of being able to participate freely and equally in Polish life.

Women as producers and reproducers – workers and mothers

There has always been a general awareness in Poland that the economy is based on production, and that production is based on workers. Thus there has been no recognition of unpaid family workers, who are mainly women, nor has there been acceptance of the fact that virtually all Polish women are 'economically active'. Women's activity outside production has traditionally been taken for granted or ignored totally as an economic contribution. Although it has been admitted that a woman's reproductive role may be equally central to her life, this has always been seen as standing in conflict with her productive role. The Polish labour legislation is the best example of the communist regime's total confusion over women's roles as producers and reproducers.

As industry and construction grew rapidly in the early 1950s many jobs were created. Given that there was a growing recognition that most families needed two wages on which to survive, women were rapidly becoming economically active within Poland. During the years 1945–54, when there were direct labour shortages, the streets of Poland were full of posters showing joyful, smiling women driving tractors, tramcars and working in other 'non-traditional' occupations. It was in 1958 that this trend began to be reversed and the general 'home-coming' of women began to be promoted. From this time until the late 1960s the confusion of women workers–mothers remained an issue. In the 1970s the pro-natal policies and the necessity for women to perform extra duties within the home, in terms of health care and education, resulted in an extra drive to make sure that women would 'recognize and fulfil' their domestic and family responsibilities.

Anna Titkow points to the two centres of power influencing life in Poland – the Church and the state. The combined effects of the unintended co-operation between Church representatives and government officials is the continued exploitation of women:

The Church's influence on defining women's position in Polish society, where 75% of women are faithful and practising Catholics, hardly has to be proven – especially when we constantly hear how woman's domain is home and family while man's world is his job, politics, and all activities outside the family circle.
(Anna Titkow, in Morgan, 1984, p. 566)

This gendered division of the world into the important, external world of men and the unimportant, domestic world of women, is not unique to Poland, but what does appear unique is the fusion of ideologies – Catholicism and communism – which served to confuse and subjugate women's participation within society. In common with women elsewhere at this time, Polish women were subject to guilt feelings about their 'proper' roles as workers–mothers–carers, and it seems that the pressure from the Church certainly added to the strain.

Domestic work and decision making

In the majority of Polish households domestic work is done by women. There has been no change in the division of domestic duties since 1983, and what sharing of family responsibilities does exist concerns decisions on the family budget, rather than domestic chores. Some 82.6 per cent of women undertake such decisions together with their husbands, and the same percentage jointly plan family activities, while 63.7 per cent share decisions on children's upbringing. In their domestic work women are helped by their mothers or mothers-in-law rather than by their husbands.

According to the Polish civil law code (1985) women have equal rights to property and equal status in the family. In reality though, Polish women not only do most of the domestic work but are also the main providers of care of the young, the sick and the elderly.

Equal rights in employment

According to the Polish labour code women have equal rights to work, yet because they are also reproducers there is a ban on certain jobs, listed by the Council of Ministers, 1975. The justification is that these jobs require physical strength and are dangerous to women's health. The list includes 90 jobs in 18 fields of production. Women are not allowed to work as miners, in jobs that require physical strength, such as the building industry, in jobs that carry a danger of poison, radiation, detonation or vibration. Thus women are not allowed to work as tractor or bus drivers. It is pure coincidence, of course, that this list is almost identical to the list of men's top-paid jobs in the field of production under the communist regime.

Because women have also been seen as principal family members there were attempts to introduce the International Labour Organization (ILO) Convention number 89 on night-work with regard to women.[1] The communist regime failed to introduce this, but soon after 1989 elections Solidarity trade unions tried the same thing in the Warsaw steel-works with women working night-shifts, and failed again due to the women workers' organized resistance.

Women as mothers

The concept of women as reproducers is reflected in the Polish labour code in a series of 'protective' regulations for pregnant women and women with children. Pregnant women are not allowed to work at jobs that are dangerous to health, nor are they allowed to work overtime or on night-shifts. Pregnant women have the right to refuse to travel as representatives of their firm.

It is only mothers who can take leave from work because a child is born. The leave is 16 to 18 weeks (depending on the number of children in the family). The justification is that women's bodies need to recover after delivery, and the baby needs its mother during this period when it is most vulnerable to disease. Fathers can take parental leave only if the mother is dead and this provision is granted whether or not the mother would have been entitled to leave. Later, both the mother and the father are entitled to take leave from work for up to two years. Leave is paid at 25 per cent of average monthly wages according to the previous quarter, provided that the family income per capita does not exceed 25 per cent of the average monthly wages of the previous year. Mothers only are entitled to take fully paid leave from work if their child is ill. At the beginning of the 1970s fathers also had this right, but it was cancelled in 1975.[2] Fathers can now take such leave only in cases where both the child and the mother are ill.

Pregnant women and women on maternity leave cannot be sacked except in three situations: when a woman has violated her worker's duties drastically; when her work-place has closed down; and (introduced in 1990) as a result of the so-called 'group reductions' (see page 86).

Unemployment figures are of course based on those persons who have been considered part of the formal labour-force and who are now without work. In mid 1990 a group of housewives who had registered as unemployed was suddenly discovered by the Ministry of Labour. Accused of 'immoral conduct' the women were crossed off the list and sent back home.

Women workers

Women constituted 45.7 per cent of the work-force in 1989. Of the total number of women employed, 59 per cent were employed in production (48 per cent in industry and trade), 26 per cent in agriculture, 13 per cent were on parental leave and 28.9 per cent worked as managers. Educated women were mainly teachers, economists, physicians, lawyers, chemists, dentists, and building and chemical engineers.

Women often want to work night-shifts, which are generally better paid. They also mean that a woman can shop, cook, clean and care for her children during the day. The fact that she may seriously undermine her health by not getting enough sleep does not seem to cause major concern.

The majority of working women aged 34–44 years are professional women (84.1 per cent of women in this age group). In agriculture this percentage can be as high as 92.1. In the state production industries the highest proportion of women work in trade (69.0 per cent), communications (58.2 per cent) and industry (37.2 per cent). The highest percentage of women workers in the manufacturing industries is in textiles and electrical industries. Despite the enormous numbers of women working in these areas the vast majority of higher level posts, from foremen to managers, are taken by men. Women dominate in the non-production areas, and their share in the total work-force here amounts to 70.1 per cent. Those sectors where women's participation is highest are detailed in Table 3.1.

Table 3.1	The proportion of women in non-productive sectors (%)
Finance and insurance	84.2
Health and social services	80.2
Education	76.3
State admin and jurisdiction	63.6
Art and culture	62.5
Tourism and recreation	53.4

(Source: Kuratowska, 1991, p. 16)

In the non-production sector one of the 'feminized' professions in which women predominate is health care. Women also make up the majority of employees in primary schools, banks and post-offices. In government administration and political parties the managerial posts are taken up by men, supported by a large proportion of women clerks and cleaners.

In terms of women's participation in central government during the 1989–90 period, there was one woman secretary of state (6.2 per cent of total), six under-secretaries of state (8.0 per cent), two director generals (11.1 per cent), 25 directors of departments (9.7 per cent), 60 deputy directors of departments (20.7 per cent) and 33 counsellors to ministers (9.9 per cent). Kuratowska (1991) notes that the highest rates of managerial staff are in the Ministries of Culture (35.4 per cent), Health and Social Welfare (34.6 per cent), Labour and Social Policy (30 per cent), Finance (17.7 per cent) and Education (17.6 per cent).

The lowest rates of participation are in the Ministries of Foreign Affairs, Foreign Economic Co-operation, Central Planning Office and Ministry of Justice. With less than 1 per cent (actually 0.5 per cent) of women holding managerial posts in the Foreign Affairs Ministry it is clear that women are not in a position to exercise their rights in terms of representing the state at international level. There are no women holding decision-making posts in either the Ministry of Defence or the Ministry of the Interior.

Equal pay

Differences in pay between men and women vary according to the category of work and the particular area of the economy in which they are employed. However, one thing does not vary and that is that women get paid less for doing the same job as men. On average, based on estimates of family budgets in 1985–88, women were generally paid 30 per cent less than men. Women's wages were 21 per cent lower than men's in 1989. The disproportion is even greater for women blue-collar workers than for white-collar workers. The biggest disproportion is noted in industry, physical culture and tourism, science, technical development, state administration and justice. The smallest disproportion is in forestry, agriculture, trade, finance and insurance. In terms of age the smallest disproportion is at 19 and less. The disproportion is nowhere less than 10 per cent, except in a small number of highly paid jobs such as lawyers (2 per cent difference) and mathematicians (2.9 per cent).

Table 3.2   **Pay scales for women – average highest and lowest pay, May 1990**

Profession	Monthly pay (1000s zloty)	Percentage of men's pay
Highest pay		
Lawyers	1163.0	98
Admin/management experts	1157.0	68
Doctors	1135.7	72
Lowest pay		
Social workers	642.9	72
Store-keepers	674.4	88.8
Agriculture workers	–	–
Technicians	683.6	74

(Source: Kuratowska, 1991, p. 18)

As Table 3.2 shows, there are many discrepancies. It is interesting to note that the discrepancies occur in both high- and low-paid sectors.

In the current climate of redundancies and pressure on women to return to solely domestic duties, it is very difficult for women to press for rights to equal pay.

Unemployment   Women constituted 51 per cent of the unemployed in 1990. In this year some 15.5 per cent of unemployed women were fired due to 'group reductions', or redundancies, which have come about as a result of the restructuring of the economy; in other words state enterprises have dismissed groups of workers in order to make the enterprises more efficient and more profitable in the free market. In this connection, women cannot be sacked from work when pregnant or on maternity leave individually, but they can be sacked as part of a group of unwanted workers. On average there is one job offer for every 37 unemployed women and for every 10 unemployed men.

No retraining courses are available for women. The tradition that it is men who should earn enough

money to maintain families forms the basis of salary
and training structures, despite the fact that many
women work because of economic necessity, and that
13.7 per cent of all families (and the number is
increasing) are headed by women.

**Women's
situation in law
and in fact**

According to the 1965 Polish civil law code, women
have equal rights to property and equal status in the
family. No statistical data on women property owners
are available for viewing. As we have seen, in the
majority of Polish households domestic work is done
by women.

Marriage ratios are high (1989) and increasing, while
the divorce ratio is low. Two-thirds of divorce
applications are filed by women and 75 per cent of
child custodies are granted to mothers (1989).
Women also remarry less frequently than men. More
women than men identify themselves as married.
There are more widows than widowers. The majority
of single-person households are run by women over
60 years of age, of which 28 per cent are invalids.

The number of single-women households is
increasing. Over half of single mothers feel the very
existence of their families is threatened. Single or
divorced mothers are entitled to receive alimony for
their children. Because of men's refusal or reluctance
to pay for their children a state alimony fund was
created and the highest alimony given to women by
the fund now equals parental leave provision. Because
women are seen as mothers and men as providers,
women can marry at 18, but men must wait until 21.
Permission to marry earlier is given by the family
courts if the couple already have a child, if the
woman is pregnant, or if there is evidence that the
couple are practising intercourse.

**Women as
decision
makers –
participation
and
representation**

Women in Poland gained the vote in 1919 and
constitutional equality in 1952 encompassing a wider
set of principles such as citizenship and workers'
rights. However, as in other countries, their
representation was largely nominal under the
communist regimes. During the May 1990 elections
women constituted 15.5 per cent of the total

candidates for local self-governments and the number elected constituted 25.5 per cent of the total elected members.[3] Where young women (under 30) are elected, they are mainly in rural self-governments; no women were elected as members of the Warsaw self-government. The greatest disproportion between female and male self-government members is among the working class – one woman to 83 men. There were no women in the government under Prime Minister Jan Krzysztof Bielecki. At the level of the Parliament in 1991 there were 62 women MPs out of 460, and seven women senators out of 100. The percentage of women in leading government posts is low and decreasing. There are no women at the presidential Council, no women leaders of the political parties, no women as heads of Solidarity trade union divisions. The only exception is the woman head of the Office of Civic Rights – Professor Eva Letowska – who was nominated in the mid 1980s. The Polish elections of 27 October 1991 produced no overall majority for any of the parties. The centre-left Democratic Union had the majority with 12.1 per cent, the Left Democratic Alliance (former communists) secured 11.7 per cent and the Polish Peasants' Party gained 8.9 per cent. The next five parties, all on the conservative right of the political spectrum polled between 5 per cent and 9 per cent. The resulting political confusion with the difficulties of gathering a suitable coalition could mean that President Lech Walesa may try to strengthen his powers. Given the lack of agreement between the various parties and groups over the scope of the free market and social policy, it is difficult to foresee a working coalition which will be strong enough to allay the fears of the Polish people.

Women's personal autonomy

There is a powerful trend in Poland (supported by the Catholic Church) to eliminate the majority of family planning options. The existing abortion bill (1956), already severely restricted by the Polish government in April 1990, is to be replaced with a Senate's bill on the protection of the unborn. The Senate's bill forbids abortion in any case except threat to the mother's life and legally proven rape. Sexuality and family planning issues are excluded from educational programmes in schools.

Contraception is scarce, and relatively little is known of various methods and formulas. What little there is, is seriously threatened by both the constraining legislation and the pro-lifers' attacks against pharmacists selling contraceptives.

Poland has always lacked a strong feminist movement, in the sense of opposition to male political supremacy. During the period 1945–88, while women were officially viewed as 'ideological equals', their energy was channelled into the tightly controlled and conveniently ineffective Women's League, which was the only representative of women's interests. The breaking point came in 1980 when a group of young women established the first feminist group in Warsaw. They were encouraged by the official recognition of Solidarity as an opposition movement, yet at the same time found themselves unable to carry on a dialogue on women's issues with male Solidarity leaders. But it was not until 1989, still under the communist regime, that the male supremacist tendency became openly visible. The first thing to be attacked was, of course, reproductive freedom.

The anti-abortion bill proposed by the Polish Catholic Church and introduced to the Parliament through 78 communist MPs called for a complete ban on abortion under penalty of three years' imprisonment of both the woman and the doctor. It was shelved as a result of protests and in the face of impending elections. The bill was later reintroduced by 35 Solidarity senators, modified with exceptions of no penalties in cases of rape and threats to life, and passed by the Senate in September 1990. A bill can be initiated in either the Senate or the Sejm but must be passed by both to be put into law. In January 1991 the Sejm (Parliament's lower chamber) voted for the creation of a special committee in order to discuss the text of the Senate's bill. The committee duly added a penalty of two years' imprisonment for self-induced abortion. The Sejm also allowed for voluntary consultations on the proposed bill, but these consultations turned out to be an opportunity for the Polish Catholic Church to use its organizational and financial means to 'prove' the people's overwhelming support for the bill. A group of MPs then called for a referendum and in turn the Polish episcopate has already announced its absolute opposition to the idea.

As all this has progressed, women activists in Poland have learnt a lot about how the authorities see us. We learned that the government's decision to abolish rights to reproductive freedom is justified when it is in the 'national interest' such as when the population is declining. We learned that just as women were once seen solely as producers, they can now be seen solely as reproducers. We learnt that just as the 1956 abortion bill (introduced by the communists) was meant to keep women from having wanted children, thus it now turns full circle and they are to be forced to bear unwanted children.

(However, the Polish government's desire to join the European Community means that statements of the European Parliament and the Council of Europe supporting women's rights may be seen as a warning to the government. When Lech Walesa and other ministers travel abroad, wishing to discuss only economic matters, they tend to be asked questions concerning abortion rights in Poland and this emphasizes the realization that abortion is not just an 'internal' issue.)

We learnt also that it is not obligatory to consult women on the question of reproduction. Women have no right to have a referendum on this question. We learnt that because the Roman Catholic Church was supportive of the Solidarity movement, neither the Solidarity Parliament nor the Solidarity trade unions can alienate such a powerful ally on the question of reproduction. In short, we learnt that the woman's place is at home, and that until women constitute a strong political force they will be 'sold out'. We are distrustful of male-controlled left-wing parties, feeling that they capitalize on women's issues and then jettison the feminist movement when it is not needed.

On 20 March 1991 a group of MPs from the ex-communist parties introduced into the Parliament a so-called 'alternative' abortion bill. Although it would have allowed abortion for certain reasons (life, health, rape, difficult financial situation plus personal reasons), the bill gave a woman no right to decide for herself; it also multiplied the bureaucratic obstacles, shortened the period for legal abortion to 10 weeks and increased doctors' penalties for performing illegal abortion to eight years' imprisonment. This bill also proposed to introduce a penalty of up to three years for a woman who causes a miscarriage when the child is viable. Initiated mainly by ex-communist women MPs, this bill could be seen as an example of what women lose if they fail to separate their political struggle from the struggle of their male colleagues.

Women activists are in obvious opposition to conservative right-wing parties, but are often caught between communist offers of reproductive freedom and divorce, and the people's assumption that to defy the Roman Catholic Church is to commit a crime against national integrity. Catholic priests have always used their churches to preach against reproductive freedom. Now they have the mass media and are invited to take part in virtually all state events. They manipulate opinion and legislation according to religious doctrine. Women feel unable to resist such pressure, although they often feel it is a threat to the society's spiritual integrity and to genuine religious feeling in the individual.

Marriage and family

Marriage and family seem to be viewed as the only solutions to women's problems in the near future. The 'sanctity of the family' and the 'Holy Family' image have always been promulgated by the Roman Catholic Church. The myth of the family has recently been restored by the state authorities in order to evade serious economic problems concerning their responsibility to provide care for the young, the sick and the elderly.

Female sexuality is defined solely in the male context. Women have no right to sexual expression, to change partners, to experience erotic pleasure without punishment. Although lesbianism is not a crime against law, in the newly emerging movement a small lesbian group is hardly visible.

The myth of female virginity is now being restored: the press recently announced a prize for female virgins over 21.

A prominent Polish male sexologist, Zbigniew Lew-Starowicz (1988), propagates a theory that there is a 'natural' limit of male resistance to female sexual provocation which, when crossed, results in men (naturally) raping women. Rape is severely punished according to the Polish criminal code if it is proven, but during the investigation the rape victim is likely to be blamed as much as or even more than the rapist, with her 'moral character' and her sexual conduct put under scrutiny. In addition, rape victims are known to encounter violence from their husbands because they have been raped.

Pornography and prostitution

Although the law has not been changed, pornography banned by the communist state is now proliferating. Posters and calendars showing naked women are everywhere, even in the most distinguished institutions. Naked or half-naked women's bodies are used to advertise virtually all kinds of goods, from soap to building equipment. Pornographic films are distributed on video tapes. Sex shops, too, are increasing. The general trend implies that freedom means, among other things, free access to women's bodies.

In theory prostitution did not exist under the communist regime – it was not considered a crime against law, but rather an anomaly within the ideology. There is no prostitution industry, there are no red light districts, no brothels. Prostitutes work in hotels and night clubs in towns and tourist resorts.

The majority of them are self-employed (without pimps), and they pay off hotel and restaurant supervisors and police in order to be able to work. They often use taxi drivers as their chauffeurs and escorts. Because they have no rights they can become linked to criminal underground figures who are their only source of protection against private as well as institutionalized violence against them. Needless to say, there has never been any recognition of their enormous economic contribution to the Polish tourist industry. Because there are so many of them in hotels and restaurants 'unescorted' women are almost always harassed in these places in the evenings, not only by individual men but also by hotel and restaurant workers, and by police.

Women's health
The poor general state of health in Poland is a result of both the economic situation and the high levels of pollution which in some regions – particularly Silesia and Krakow – exceed all accepted norms. The health-care system is inefficient and chronically underfunded, and there is a lack of preventive medicine.

The average lifespan for Polish women is 71 years; 67 years for Polish men. The major reasons for early death are heart and circulatory diseases resulting from arteriosclerosis. There is now a rapid increase in the death rate of women from heart ailments. Although Polish women do not suffer heart attacks as often as men, they die of them in greater numbers. They also suffer more often from strokes, which often result in death. Coronary diseases cause death in 57 per cent of women. In 1988 the death rate of Polish women due to heart attacks and strokes was 59 per cent higher than among the female population in other European countries (Kuratowska, 1991, p. 33).

Polish women often suffer from high blood pressure and diabetes, and weight problems are common, particularly among women over 50 years of age. One in three women in Poland suffers from excess weight, which is a major factor in heart disease and which often exacerbates physical ailments related to spinal degeneration.

Pregnancy and childbirth are major aspects of women's health. Over 60 per cent of pregnant women in Poland suffer from anaemia, for which they are treated with drugs, and the death rate among pregnant women is high – 22 out of 100 000 births result in the woman's death (Kuratowska, 1991, p. 35). Women living in poor economic circumstances and working in harmful environments as well as those who have given birth many times are most badly affected, being prone to miscarriage or to bearing children with inborn ailments. This situation is particularly apparent in Silesia among female workers in the chemical and textile industries. In 1988 8.5 per cent of newborn babies weighed less than 2.5 kilograms. The death rate among newborn babies in 1989 was 18 per thousand.

In terms of violence against women, the idea that battery is practised only, or mostly, by the poor or vulgar still prevails in Poland. There is no data available on the levels of domestic violence against women, and the Polish nation prides itself on male gallantry. Yet, considering even the ratio of male alcoholism in our country, one may expect that the level of battery is high. No shelters for abused or battered women are available. The women's families, or more often their female neighbours, serve as one-night shelters for alcoholics' wives and children. Police intervene only in cases of serious injury.

Women's current activities

There are only two feminist groups in Poland – the Polish Feminist Association, that has about 50 members active in Warsaw and has groups in Kracow, Poznan and Lodz, and the Women's Club. During the last 45 years Poland has been deprived of any genuine women's movement. The two Communist Party linked women's organizations, the Women's League and the Union of Rural Women, are now in retreat. Women in Poland are organizing in different associations around various issues. Some of these are linked to the Catholic Church, some to different parties (mainly the left-wing parties), and there are sections within the two main trade unions. The women's movement has just begun and is as yet too weak to resist the backlash on women's issues that we are now facing in Poland. However as women's issues receive more and more attention there is growing recognition of the fact that women's issues are seriously threatened, and that it is only women who can defend themselves.

Conclusions

Because Polish women are seen as secondary producers they are channelled into part-time, seasonal or marginal jobs that are low in remuneration and prestige. Although Polish women work we tend to control nothing and our work is often invisible. Polish feminists believe that it is because women are regarded mainly as reproducers rather than full human beings that we are viewed in a male-defined sexual context, with violence against women being treated as a purely private matter. Women are objectified, trivialized and commercialized, and feel ignored or abandoned by the new group of men in power. Polish women feel minimalized or manipulated as a political force, but as activists we have learned our lesson well – that the battle for women in Poland should always remain within the area of sexual politics.

The general tendency in Poland is to send women back into the home. What national machinery does exist for the advancement of women is under threat – the women's affairs governmental plenipotentiary is undergoing attempts to change the post into the Ministry for Family, Youth and Women. At the time of writing the post has remained vacant since the change of government in December 1990. Although ineffective, the plenipotentiary was the only women's representative at the level of government.

In the face of serious dangers and the general tendency to resist women's rights, Polish women's organizations have decided to work together towards the creation of both an independent office for equality of status between women and men (an equality ombudsperson) and an equal rights committee in Parliament.

Notes   1   Report on legal discrimination against women in Poland,
               Governmental Plenipotentiary for Women's Affairs,
               Warsaw, 1990.

               2   Regulation of the Council of Ministers, 1 January 1975.
               No reasons given.

               3   *Women in Poland*, Main Office of Statistics, Warsaw,
               November 1990.

4

**Czech and Slovak
Federative Republic**
The culture of strong women in the
making?

Mita Castle-Kanerova

Area	127 900 km^2.
Population	The population recorded in 1989 was 15.6 million, of which 8 million were women.
	Czechoslovakia being a federative republic comprises the Czech, Slovak and Moravian lands. The population census of 1980 gives 10.3 million in the Czech and Moravian lands, 4.9 million in the Slovak lands.
	1988 statistics give a figure of 1043 women per 1000 men.
Capital	Praha (1.2 million in 1989). Other main cities: Bratislava (440 421 in 1989); Brno (391 093 in 1989).
Languages	Czech, Slovak (official), but German, Hungarian, Ukrainian, Romany, and other minority languages spoken.
Races and ethnic groups	1988 census recorded 9.8 million Czechs, 4.9 million Slovaks, 599 000 Hungarians, 73 000 Poles, 53 000 Germans, 48 000 Ukrainians, 7000 Russians and 52 000 other unspecified nationalities.
Religions	Seventy per cent Roman Catholic, 15 per cent Lutheran, and other minority sects such as Czech Brothers.
Education	There is free and compulsory school attendance, which since 1984 has been extended to 10 years (usually from the ages of seven to17).
	The 1989/90 census registered a total of 636 622 nursery school children; 1 961 742 basic education pupils (down from the 1988 census); 153 179 students at the equivalent of A level institutions; 274 298 students at vocational and technical colleges; and 173 547 students at universities and colleges of higher education (of which 77 026 were women).
Birth rate	The birth rate in 1989 was 13.3 per 1000 in Czechoslovakia as a whole; 12.4 in the Czech lands and 15.2 in Slovakia.
Death rate	The death rate in 1989 was 11.6 per 1000 in Czechoslovakia as a whole; 12.4 in the Czech lands, 10.2 in Slovakia.

Infant mortality	Infant mortality in 1989 was 11.3 per 1000 for Czechoslovakia as a whole; 10.0 for the Czech lands and 13.5 in Slovakia.
Life expectancy	Female life expectancy according to 1988 figures was 74.0 years; male 67.5 years.
Abortions	The statistical year book 1988 gives figures of 188701 per year in Czechoslovakia as a whole; 129349 in the Czech lands and 59352 in Slovakia.
Representation	In 1991 there were 8 per cent women in the House of the People (one parliamentary chamber) and 11 per cent in the House of the Nations (the second parliamentary chamber). Women's suffrage and equal rights were established in 1919, with Czechoslovakia gaining its independence from the Austro-Hungarian Empire.
Currency	Koruna (Kcs) or crown = 100 halers. In 1991 the official exchange rate was £1 = approximately 50 crowns.
Women's wages as a percentage of men's	The rate of pay varies according to age and occupation. Among younger women it is 60 per cent of male wages, among older women it is 70 per cent. Among women with university education the rate of pay is about 95 per cent of men's. The average is 65–70 per cent of male earnings.
Production	Agricultural: wheat, barley, sugar beet, potatoes, maize. Industrial: steel, plastics and chemicals, cars and trucks, fertilizers, electronics, cotton cloth, footwear.
Women as a percentage of the labour-force	Seventy-one per cent of all women work. They formed 46 per cent of the total labour-force in 1989. In agriculture women formed 42 per cent of the labour-force. The labour-market is segregated with the highest percentage of women in the service sector and health: 75.7 per cent of the labour-force in home trade, 71.6 per cent in education, 78.8 per cent in the health service and 89.0 per cent in social care, according to 1988 figures.
Unemployment	In 1991 total unemployment was recorded as 3.5 per cent of the total labour-force. No overall figures are available for female unemployment. The higher percentage of unemployment was in Slovakia, with 28 017 recorded unemployed women.

Superwomen and the Double Burden

Background

The Czech and Slovak lands joined together under one state authority after the breakup of the Austro-Hungarian Empire in 1918. Slovakia was always a more rural country with a stronger Catholic influence and with a distinct language that is taught in Slovakia as a first language. Officially the two languages, Czech and Slovak, are equal and used as such in the media. Both are understandable by each other without difficulty. Slovakia's more infamous reputation was established during World War Two when it formed its own independent fascist state. After the war, with some small border adjustments on the eastern side, the Czechoslovak states became joined together again. Slovakia's slower economic and industrial development was a cause of concern and some hostility in 1968, when Dubcek promised the federalism that was later fully implemented by Dr Husak, the Slovak Prime Minister from 1969 to 1988. Husak, together with two other Slovaks in key governmental seats, presided over the period of neo-Stalinist 'normalization'. Slovakia gained ground as far as its development was concerned, and some commentators today argue that it became used to the principle of halving financial resources that is at the root of the current dispute between the Czechs and Slovaks. Slovak nationalism has been threatening the stability of the new independent Czech and Slovak Federative Republic since the revolution of 1989.

As everywhere else in what was once 'socialist eastern Europe', women in Czechoslovakia, formally known as the Czech and Slovak Federative Republic (CSFR) are going through a rethinking of their own past. It cannot be otherwise. Up to now, women's roles have been fixed and defined on their behalf, but one of the effects of the revolutions of 1989 has been an explosion of diverse views. New positive initiatives, particularly in response to the visible perpetuation of male monopolization of political life, combine with chaos and disagreement.

There is a prevalent and tangible cynicism about what 'socialism' brought for women. 'All I am left with is varicose veins,' said one friend of mine. And indeed, the statistics confirm this. Ill health and morbidity among women is higher than among men. In the age category 30–74 morbidity among women is 11–18 per cent higher than among men, reflecting very clearly the type of activity that was assigned to them – the 'hunting and gathering' which came on top of their regular full-time work. Disorders of the spinal column are one-third higher among women, and when it comes to varicose veins, female morbidity overtakes male morbidity by 99 per cent (unpublished internal material (UIM), 1991, p. 5). The socialist past, then, represents a very heavy load indeed for women.

While women in Czechoslovakia are attempting to draw up a 'balance sheet' of their situation, many western writers continue to hold on to notions of the 'advantages' that the past regimes in eastern Europe must, in their view, have achieved and delivered. Most often quoted is the high level of female participation in the labour-market which, while seen as problematic, is nevertheless viewed as having contributed to women's relative economic independence and 'visibility' in the public sphere. The other aspect focused on is the availability of services and provisions such as nurseries and generous maternity leave. Admittedly there is discussion in Czechoslovakia about the poor quality of some of these provisions and the economic pressure on women to return to work (see Heitlinger, 1979; and Scott, 1976). Women had to work, and the choice was minimal.

The drawing up of a balance sheet of advantages and disadvantages does not involve simply looking at the material concerning economic or social policy. What emerges in the current debate among women in Czechoslovakia is how important it is to make a distinction between what was *offered* to women and what it actually *meant* for them; in other words, there was a dislocation between the interests of an overtly patriarchal state and the female half of the population. Some identify the totalitarian past – with its elitist political and social structure that rested on the division between those who belonged to the nomenklatura and 'the rest' – as a form of 'male apartheid' (Cermakova et al, 1991, p. 18). Interestingly, women in Czechoslovakia are more prepared to talk about 'male apartheid' than about patriarchy.

Women undoubtedly gained many formal rights under the old regime. They have equal legal status and their educational level steadily rose in the 1960s and 1970s, although opportunities were more restricted in the 1980s. Yet these rights also meant a form of enslavement. The totalitarian political culture, as it is now called, brought with it a new principle of self-sacrifice for women: to work, to engage in the public sphere, to be a comrade, to be a good worker, became not only a necessity but a form of 'responsibility towards the socialist family' (Cermakova et al, 1991, p. 18). The regime left absolutely no scope for independent activity among women. It was expected that women devote themselves to the new concept of social order, with the family as centrepiece. The authoritarian political culture left nothing untouched, nothing that could be defined 'from below'. The 'totalitarian culture' is a culture of passivity.

Alena Valterova, the founding member of the new Party of Women and Mothers, writing of the situation of gross inequality that is the legacy of the old regime, asks 'what do our women do now?', and replies, 'our women do nothing.' She continues:

They split themselves into married widowed and divorced widowed, the lone parents and married wives, the childless and the ones with children, the rural and urban, the qualified and the unqualified, the healthy and the unhealthy, those with make-up and those without ... There is rivalry and there are hostilities. As in the past, the majority of women wait to see what life will bring to them; they wait for someone to decide on their behalf. (Zena 91, April 1991)

It will take a long time to overcome what one might call the internalized oppression. In the past, the woman's question was presented as solved, as is graphically illustrated by the official 'periods of development' since 1948. Between 1948 and 1959 the question of women's position in Czechoslovakia was being 'installed'; during 1950–66 it was being 'dealt with and solved'; during 1966–68 it was being 'revised and newly defined'; during 1969–71 it was 'normalized'; and during 1972–89 it was 'realistically explained within the socialist framework' (Cermakova et al, 1991, p. 7). Women decided nothing. It was the march of history that decided for them. Women were used by the system, and even their relatively high educational attainment is now seen as a manipulation of the labour-market. Women were thus directed into education from which, in the end, they could never fully benefit as far as their own job allocations were concerned.

Of course, the reaction to all this is huge. Women and men talk of complete social devastation, a crisis of society, and moral and political decay. A coming to terms with the totalitarian past may mean not only a revision of old 'data' on women and the family, but a total rejection of it, as the recent sociological study edited by Cermakova et al suggests. The task of redrawing women's position in society, their aspirations, needs, feelings, and potentials, is enormous. What is becoming clear is that the depth of the effects of the old system on what is now talked about as the 'totalitarian mentality' must not be underestimated. Why is it that women, for example, see their escape from the world of work into domesticity as 'liberating'? Why is it that they shudder at any sign of an organized women's movement? The old regime introduced not only apartheid but also apathy – a form of resignation. It instilled a way of thinking that rendered change difficult, or undesirable – a sense that to organize is to play into the hands of the people at the top. A woman writer, Eva Hauserova, in an unpublished paper in 1991, commented that 'political activism is unfeminine'. It smacks of the old stereotype of female party cadre – eager, ruthless and blind to the world around them; true careerists, with a party card and a uniform. She has also said that 'women's organizations mean admitting that we are a sort of minority'.

Communism wanted to focus people's interests away from politics, and to increase population growth. People were pressured by every possible means to have children: financial bonuses, availability of flats and tremendous propaganda. The authorities were quite successful, in that opportunities to develop other activities, to be creative or to do anything positive did not exist. And so the cult of motherhood developed; a cult that became an 'island of activity in the ocean of boredom' – one way of affirming a woman's role. Yet partners in marriage struggled for dominance, and the anger they felt against the unfriendly, absurd communist world was unleashed in the family. Czechoslovakia has one of the highest divorce rates in the world and an estimated 50 out of every 100 young couples marry because of unplanned pregnancy (Eva Hauserova, 1991).

A study carried out in 1989 (prior to the revolution) among women working at the heavy engineering factory SKODA, in Plzen, reflects attitudes that will be hard to change overnight. The women numbered 12 000 in a total work-force of 34 000; 42 per cent of them employed as shop-floor workers and 58 per cent as administrative staff. Asked whether they were interested in working in a management position, 49.8 per cent of the respondents answered in the negative, and only 3.3 per cent in the affirmative. Asked how many subordinate staff they had, 90.1 per cent answered that they had none. Answers to questions about whether or not wages were adequate were mostly in the positive range, as were answers concerning the facilities offered. Given a chance to express a view about desired changes specifically for women in the plant, most concentrated on greater flexibility of working hours (44.4 per cent), followed by the desire for better services (33.3 per cent), but changes concerning 'equality for women' (in pay or status) were near the bottom of their list of desired changes, with only 16 per cent of women rating this as an option (Hradecka, 1989).

The resignation that the average woman in Prague has had to learn as a strategy for survival must be reflected in some form in her overall attitude to work and to everyday life. The resignation of standing in the long food queues that exist even now, the permanent tiredness caused by getting up in the morning long before other members of the family, the present need to search for cheaper goods (a new phenomenon in a gradually growing market economy), are all part of the harvest of 40 years of communism in Czechoslovakia.

Communism acted on women's behalf – they were never active participants. For some women there is simply no change in the new society; the old patterns, the old duties and the old role divisions between men and women persist. 'What good is the new situation to me?' asked one friend; 'I still get up early in the morning to be pushed around on the bus on my way to work. Now I don't even have enough money to put my washing in the laundry. So whatever I might have gained from the joys of the new democracy is swallowed up by having to do more and more things manually and on the cheap.'

There is a wonderful novel about women and domestic technology by the acclaimed dissident writer J. Smetanova in which she describes her acquisition of a food mixer in a moment of searching for emancipation. The beast consists of so many intricate parts – made somewhere in eastern Europe – that the kitchen is cluttered, leaving no space for anything else. The whole family assists in assembling it, and then watches the ceremonial chopping of the cabbage followed by the mincing of meat and the grinding of the coffee. The pile of dirty bits and pieces, the cutting wheels and spinning adjustments, took so long to wash up that she had serious doubt as to whether this innovation could make any contribution at all to her free time. The food mixer ended up in the cellar. (The novel has been published in extract form by the only pro-feminist women's journal, *Zena 91*.)

While the other central and eastern European countries started to liberalize, Czechoslovakia in the 1970s went the other way. The old regime felt the need to push home the Stalinist rhetoric over and over again, particularly in the aftermath of the events of 1968. The communist ideology contained within itself a paradox: on the one hand it revived the tradition of active women – it talked of emancipating woman from the position of object so that she would become a true subject in history; on the other hand this aspect of the ideology was pure legitimation of the dominant view – of the status quo. A text on the position of women in socialist society published in Czechoslovakia as late as 1984 proclaimed that the 'Marxist–Leninist approach to the woman question meant a turning point in the scientific understanding of women and the family ... this approach did not require a separate movement for women isolated from the revolutionary, working-class movement' (Solcova, 1984, pp. 34, 82). Another text declares that 'The great Russian Socialist Revolution [of 1917] was a force that inspired and changed the fundamental course of human history ... The women's movement without the support of the proletariat is only a caricature of the woman's question ... Industrialization in the Soviet Union removed all the barriers between male and female occupations' (Hanzlova, 1977, pp. 7, 38). Statements such as these, that were used to justify the high visibility of women in the public sphere, namely in the economy, contribute to the reasons why women today do not want to hear about emancipation.

Women as producers and reproducers – workers and mothers

Czechoslovakia today has one of the highest percentages of economically active women, taking into account international comparisons. In the 1980s it stood at 48 per cent, now it is estimated at 46 per cent. Women's inclusion in the labour-market has grown steadily since 1948. In Czechoslovakia today a large proportion of the population lives in towns: 80

per cent in the Czech Republic and 71 per cent in the Slovak Republic. Though there is no legislative discrimination against women living in rural areas, they nevertheless experience particular problems associated with increases in the cost of living and in particular with regard to the increased travelling expenses incurred in getting to their work-places. Table 4.1 indicates the distribution of working women in different work sectors in Czechoslovakia in 1988.

Table 4.1 **Distribution of working women in Czechoslovakia (as a percentage of all workers)**

	CSFR	CR	SR
Total	46.0	46.3	45.5
Productive spheres	41.3	41.7	40.4
Agriculture	39.7	40.0	39.5
Industry	40.8	40.7	40.9
Home trade	75.7	75.2	77.0
International trade	65.4	65.8	63.4
Non-productive spheres	60.0	59.9	60.5
Science, research	38.1	36.8	40.9
Education	71.6	71.3	72.2
Culture	52.1	51.4	53.9
Health service	78.8	79.0	78.3
Social care	89.0	89.1	88.8

(Source: Okruhlicova, 1991)

As Table 4.1 shows, in both the Czech and Slovak Republics women are highly represented in home trade, education, the health service and social care. The lowest participation rates for women are in the fields of science and research, and agriculture.

The average working week in Czechoslovakia is around 42.5 hours, with 15–30 days leave each year. Although women with children can apply for shorter working hours or for different arrangements, in practice these legal rights are effectively unused. Only 7.6 per cent of women worked part-time in 1986, and by 1989 the percentage of women working part-time had only increased to 11.6 per cent (Venerova, 1991, p. 25). Approximately 40000 women return to work after maternity leave each year. While they are on maternity leave they are recorded in the statistics as being economically active, as they retain their claims to work during this period.

In the age group 25–50 the level of economic activity among women is approximately 90 per cent. What is interesting is that 43.6 per cent of economically active women were reported in the official statistics of 1980 to be working in manual, working-class occupations (Cermakova et al, 1991, p. 18). Of all economically active women, 43.6 per cent were working in manual industrial jobs (Navarova, 1989, p. 174). According to a survey carried out in the metallurgy and engineering industries in 1988, only 20 per cent of women working in manual jobs in this field had chosen the occupation deliberately; 60 per cent of them had been forced into these jobs because there were no other vacancies (Kroupova, 1990, p. 15). Herein lies one of the areas of waste in terms of the educational background of some of these women.

Although 'male' and 'female' jobs exist in Czechoslovakia, in other words, labour-market segregation, some of the 'typically' 'female' jobs in light industry carry specific risks and burdens. Not only are the wages lower – approximately 60–70 per cent of the average male wage (Cermakova et al, 1991, p. 5) – with no subsidies, but there are additional health risks due to lack of modernization and lack of good safety practices. Shift-work, too, is a major feature of women's employment:

Shift work is far more current in light industries than in industries employing men ... Every third woman worker in

*Czechoslovakia works shifts. In 1986, Czechoslovak
industries employing a large proportion of women required
48% of them to work overtime ... In 1987, 8.7% of
women employed in those industries held jobs involving
health hazards.* (Kroupova, 1990, pp. 15, 16)

One of the ministers recently reported that in the
period 1970–85 female morbidity per 1000
population was 46 per cent compared with male
morbidity of 30 per cent.

**The effects
of work on
everyday life**

During the 'pre-revolutionary days' the working
woman was celebrated as a permanent part of the
'socialist' labour-market. The 1950 constitution in
Czechoslovakia granted women their equal rights
according to Marxist–Leninist principles. Between
1948 and 1957, women's share in the labour-market
increased from 22 per cent to 42 per cent of the total.
They received 'cadre education', and joined the trade
unions. In the years 1955–59 trade-union
membership among women increased from 24.9 per
cent to 29.5 per cent. Between 1948 and 1971 the
increase in women's participation in the total labour-
force represented four-fifths of the growth in
employment (Hanzlova, 1977, pp. 94, 55, 99). Direct
copying of the Soviet style of industrialization was
totally unsuitable in Czechoslovak conditions, and
would not have been possible without this constant
'bumping up' of the employment figures by drafting
women into the labour-force. It was the regime that
benefited from this situation, not women.

The effects of policies such as these are clearly
reflected in the quality of life. As mentioned above
the average age that women and men in
Czechoslovakia can enjoy is 74.0 and 67.5 years
respectively, according to 1988 statistics. While men
feature badly in comparison with women, the
longevity of women in an international comparison
brings them to thirty-third place in the world's
league. While most industrial countries of the world
have experienced the opposite trend, an increase in
longevity since the 1960s, the situation in
Czechoslovakia has been in decline during this

period. As far as chronic illnesses are concerned, women exceed men by 15–30 per cent in the age category 30–70 (UIM, 1990).

The insensitive inclusion of women in the labour-market has created a situation of unbearable pressure. It has been calculated that on average a family with one child spends jointly something like 23 hours a day in work activity. Paid work constitutes 15 hours. But the ratio of paid work to unpaid domestic labour varies between men and women, with men working outside the home for an average of eight hours a day and in the home for an average 2.5 hours, while women work seven hours outside and five hours at home (UIM, 1990, p. 9).

An international comparison again suggests that Czechoslovakian women spend on average two-thirds more of their time acquiring the basic necessities for the household than do their western counterparts (UIM, 1990, p. 9). An unconfirmed survey from 1988 states that fathers spend only nine minutes per day taking care of their children. For women, this has repercussions on the amount of time they have for sleep, personal hygiene, and even eating.

Lack of services is the most often quoted cause of this continual overloading of women. Up to 40 per cent of women are currently interested in part-time work, yet only 11.6 per cent were thus employed in 1989 (UIM, 1990, p. 11). The greater intensity of work among women is accompanied by lower remuneration. Wages and salaries vary according to age category and the type of employment. In the educational sector, women received on average 77 per cent of the male wage, and in industry 65.4 per cent (UIM, 1990, p. 12). Younger women receive on average 58 per cent of the male wage, while older women receive 68 per cent (Navarova, 1989). Kroupova (1990) also cites average earnings for women in industry as being 65.4 per cent of male wages, with 71 per cent in construction and 66.1 per cent in the health service. In agriculture the figure is slightly higher, at 83.2 per cent.

As in most industrialized societies in the west, women in Czechoslovakia cluster in service occupations. Under the aegis of social welfare between 1970 and 1986 women experienced an increase in employment from 88.9 per cent to 90.1 per cent. In the health service in this period the increase was from 82.4 per cent to 85.9 per cent. At present 99 per cent of nurses are female, while the number of female doctors totals 46 per cent. In banking the increase for women was from 61.1 per cent to 75.2 per cent and in education from 66.9 per cent to 74.9 per cent in the period 1970–86. The percentage of women among agriculture workers was 44.3 per cent and among other manual workers it was 35.5 per cent, with white-collar workers averaging 57.6 per cent. Out of the total female labour-force, 14 per cent held positions in management with 65 per cent in lower-levels, 25 per cent in middle-levels, and only 10 per cent in top management (Kroupova, 1990, pp. 17, 18, 20).

New forms of employment are now being initiated, but are hindered by legislative regulations, particularly by the complicated tax system (the average citizen cannot always find out the details of taxation legislation). According to the results of a public enquiry, only one-tenth of the people in the Slovak Republic are ready to join in privatization, with 56 per cent stating as their reason shortage of money. In the Czech Republic there now exists an association of women entrepreneurs and managers who are active in giving specific education to women and providing consultation (Okruhlicova, 1991, p. 8).

Equal pay It is reported that

> *a professional career does not rank supreme in the scale of values of Czechoslovak women ... Very often, mothers do not conceive employment as a means of self-realization, but rather as an economic necessity to ensure the family's adequate standard of living.* (Kroupova, 1990, p. 21)

At the time of retirement women's earnings average three-quarters of the earnings of men, which puts them at a disadvantage for the computation of their

old-age pension. The law, which is currently under
review, is that women retire at 60, men at 65. In
addition there is the assumption that early-retired
women will take up posts of unpaid child-minders,
with the serious disadvantage that women are pushed
out of the labour-market just at the time when they
may have reached the height of their careers, free
from their own family responsibilities.

Women's earnings differ significantly according to
educational level. In 1988, for women aged 20–24
with elementary education average earnings were 74
per cent of male earnings; for university educated
women, the ratio was 96.3 per cent of male
earnings. The ratio for the age category 25–26 goes
up for university educated women to 99 per cent
but significantly down to 66.6 per cent for those
with elementary education. In the age category
40–44, the figures are 69.5 per cent among those
women with elementary education and 81.3 per cent
among university trained women (Kroupova, 1990,
pp. 25, 24).

Education

The discrepancy between male and female earnings,
and the retention of the traditional pattern of
remuneration is even more surprising if we look at
the level of general education among women.
Czechoslovakia enjoys one of the highest levels of
education among women in comparison with
western industrialized nations. As mentioned above,
this solved a tricky economic situation at a particular
period of time.

The share of women completing the equivalent of
A level education in 1989–90 stood at an average of
62 per cent of the female population. The number of
women completing technical college training rose
from 44.5 per cent of all who studied in these types
of institution in 1948–49 to 58.8 per cent in
1989–90. When we look at women with higher and
university education, their share in this sector
increased from 23.2 per cent in 1948–49 to 45 per
cent in 1989–90. Despite the fact that women at
university level predominate in subjects such as

economics (Cermakova et al, 1991, p. 8), the old regime totally misused this high level of female qualification and instead employed women in the overgrown bureaucratic and administrative apparatus. The extent of the waste of human potential, both female and male, is only now beginning to come to the surface. The old cadre sector, which was a special department in each enterprise, comprising parasitical administrative staff, has now been abolished, but the consequences of the squandering of educational achievement and the stifling of initiative are not as easily resolved. The celebratory presentation of the educational achievement of women by the old regime may serve as a warning that bare statistics should not be taken at their face value.

In 1950, 87.3 per cent of the female population received only elementary education. This had declined to 56.0 per cent in 1980. The ratio of women to men with higher and university education has increased from 1:7 to 1:2 in the same period (UIM, 1990, p. 13). Yet this situation does not compare favourably with indicators of the lower status of female occupations, the growing 'feminization' of poverty among all previous central and eastern European countries, and the pressures experienced by women due to their general overload. The prognosis for the future is not much brighter, though for somewhat different reasons. The emerging reality in all previous central and eastern European countries involves a change in the economy that will very clearly disadvantage women.

Unemployment

The old regime used overemployment as a strategy for full employment and the economic reform of market forces is now based on the cutting down of 'unproductive' labour. The tendency, as in many countries in the west today, is to target the female population as the first sector to leave the labour-market. It is anticipated that in Czechoslovakia women will form two-thirds of all unemployed (UIM, 1990, p. 23). The state budget of Czechoslovakia includes some special reserves for unemployment benefits for the year 1991 these amounted to approximately two billion Kcs. Unemployment benefit applies to the citizens permanently resident in the country who are registered for employment with the appropriate authorities. The state will provide such people with unemployment benefit as one means of assistance. A second form of assistance will be given in the form of help to find suitable employment and the organization of some form of retraining. The conditions by which men and women may claim unemployment benefit will be equal. However women will remain disadvantaged on the basis of inequality of pay, as state benefits (after the statutory unemployment benefit of one year) will be assessed on previous earnings. Unemployed single parents (mainly women) will be the people most badly affected by this situation.

Table 4.2   **Unemployed women in the Slovak Republic, February 1991**

	December 1990	February 1991
Total no. of women	15905	28017
Gypsy women	2823	4669
Qualification structure:		
without qualifications	4346	7702
middle range	8244	14853
higher range	2127	3149
Age structure:		
up to 30 years	7461	12980
up to 40 years	5228	9578
up to 50 years	2404	4246
above 50 years	639	1012

(Source: Okruhlicova, 1991, p. 13)

Unemployment benefit is part of the state assistance within the 'social safety net' scheme that was accepted by the Federal Government in February 1991 (Venerova, 1991, p. 39). Towards the end of February 1991 in the Czech Republic there were 74 753 registered unemployed and 37 978 vacant posts. In the Slovak Republic there were 77 570 registered unemployed and 7563 vacant posts with only 29 per cent of these vacancies for women. Table 4.2 gives further details of this situation in the Slovak Republic.

As is apparent in the table, it is women with the middle range of qualifications who will experience the worst of the first effects of unemployment in the Slovak Republic, and the rate of unemployment for these women is increasing rapidly. In terms of age, it is women in the younger age group (up to 30 years of age) who make up the highest category of unemployed.

Women as decision makers – participation and representation

Such a situation cannot be seen in isolation from the participation of women in political decision making. In the past, women were involved in the political apparatus in purely formal terms, and their inclusion was based on crude quotas. Those women who voluntarily joined the political structures are now seen as having wanted an easy career and having created more harm than good for the cause of women. The statistics here are in direct contrast to the reality, in that the higher the recruitment of women into the official apparatus, the greater was the loss for women. Sources written in the 1980s continue to reinforce the illusion that the situation was otherwise, and that the inclusion of women in the public sphere was one of the positive achievements of 'socialism'. The issue of level of political participation that rose concomitantly with certain women's increased work status remains a difficult one. The old status quo meant, of course, that no position of decision making could be engaged in without membership of the Communist Party. Whilst only 18 per cent of women shop-floor workers were politically engaged, the level rises to 55 per cent among higher levels of management (Solcova, 1984, p. 96). Female membership of the Communist Party, according to this 1984 publication,

was 17 per cent compared with male membership of
33 per cent. Yet women's participation in the official
trade unions was 66 per cent, with male participation
at 77 per cent. Participation in the official Women's
Union was 41 per cent. Office holders in all of these
organizations in 1984 were as follows: the KSC
(Communist Party) 13 per cent male: 5 per cent
female; the ROH (trade unions) 17 per cent male: 14
per cent female; the Women's Union 12 per cent
women (Solcova, 1984, p. 96).

The Women's Union is currently 'under fire'. As a
federal organization it was dissolved in 1990, but the
Czech Women's Union has remained. Although
some women left the organization and joined other
more pro-feminist circles, the old network of female
apparatchiks has remained relatively intact and is
reportedly preventing the rank and file members
from participating in new initiatives by deliberately
misinforming them or by withholding information.
They also remain as a vehicle for the old-style
politics of elitism, and for transmission of subversive,
often clandestine, intentions on behalf of the old
Communist Party. Yet in Czechoslovakia today, in
the 1990s, most political activity seems to be
outside the established political structures. It is
generally accepted, and clearly visible, that the
toppling of the old all-male regime did not alter the
situation for women overall – the new leadership
conserved the masculine model of decision making.
For what it is worth, the figure for the participation
of women in political office in 1987 was 12.4 per
cent, with 51.3 per cent of all working women
having functions in voluntary organizations
(Kroupova, 1990, p. 20).

In the first free elections in 40 years, women
candidates were only 13 per cent of all political
parties in the two houses, that is the House of
Nations and the House of the People. The actual
percentage of women elected to Parliament was even
smaller – 8 per cent to the House of the People and
11 per cent to the House of Nations. The proportion
of women representing regional bodies stands at

16–20 per cent. There was one woman in the Czech Government and there were no women in the Slovak Government. In the Slovak Republic a Government Committee for Women and the Family was established in June 1990 as an advisory body of the Slovak Government, but at present this seems to be inoperative (Okruhlicova, 1991, p. 7).

Today the issue of women's participation is concerned not so much with numerical representation and the 'co-opting' of women into the political sphere (something that has been, and perhaps still is, characterized by nepotistic tendencies) but with the absence of a basic political infrastructure from which women can filter into leading decision-making offices. The old fragmentation persists. What is now in place is another, perhaps softer form of dictatorship. There is no democracy. Men still make the decisions.

It is important to stress that the removal of the nomenklatura does not mean an improvement of the situation for women. Some may say that the same applies to the situation for men. Although the current political developments in Czechoslovakia contain many positive features, such as civic freedoms, freedom of expression and freedom of organization, some women talk of a 'hidden aggression' in domestic politics, whether of nationalism or of the fast-moving 'back into Europe' policies, not to mention the neo-classical economic reform with its emphasis on the 'self-made' individual. One of the more positive features of the current changes, is that women have been less compromised by their past deeds, though this meant that the majority of women have emerged from the past with very little political experience (Cermakova et al, 1991, p. 17).

Women's personal autonomy

There are several features of family life in Czechoslovakia that need to be taken together. The most frequently quoted characteristic of all eastern European families is their traditionalism. The family acts as an economic unit, able to obtain goods through informal contacts; without these and without family back up, life can be hard. In a dictatorship, the family has a dual role. It can become an effective hiding place; an escape route from the all-pervasive forms of public authority; internal emigration as a form of dissent. One woman friend even mentioned that it was thanks to the family being able to keep alternative values ticking that 1989 could occur at all. Yet, of course, dictatorship also relies on the traditional family as a key institution. It is affluent democracy that creates the right conditions for a more liberal family structure and for greater openness in relationships generally. One of the features of the current debate about the family in Czechoslovakia is the way in which conservative functionalist theories were applied in conditions of so-called socialism. What was attractive to the 'socialist state' was the functionalist emphasis on a view of society as a collection of separate parts: the family fulfilled a social role but could otherwise be treated in isolation, and the needs of its members mattered least. The search for independence and escape in a society where scope for the development of personality was limited led many young people into early marriage. Czechoslovakia has reportedly one of the highest rates of marriages of all developed countries – 85 per cent of all women marry, and they marry young (UIM, 1990, p. 5). The average age at which women marry is 21.5 years; for men it is 24 years. Although the reason most often given for these early marriages is the economic, financial and housing situation, there is another factor that plays a role and that is not sufficiently discussed. This concerns the lack of sex education, and poor family planning and contraception. Some 60–70 per cent of all young couples in the younger age category marry because of the pregnancy of the bride (Navarova, 1989, p. 158). Although western sources have created an image of eastern Europe in which contraception is in a desperately short supply, this appears not to be the case according to women in Czechoslovakia. Condoms are freely available in chemists and even in some underground stations in Prague, and apparently Czechoslovakia overproduces condoms, so much so that they are now being exported abroad. Yet men, in particular, have not been educated to use them. Other means of contraception, such as the IUD and the pill do not have good reputations and are not so frequently used because of their associations with health problems for women.

Social policy generally was aimed at reinforcing the institutional standing of the family. It was made financially advantageous to marry, for example, as new couples received interest-free loans. On production of three children one-third of this loan would be written off. To be married also allowed a couple to jump the housing queues.

Abortion

The rate of abortion in Czechoslovakia is high, as is the rate of childbirth among women aged 16–19, and this rate is apparently characteristic of Czechoslovakia and what was previously East Germany. In an international comparison it was found that women in Czechoslovakia give birth some two to three years earlier in their lives than their western counterparts, where the age of child-bearing is shifting towards the late twenties and early thirties. Only 6 per cent of women in Czechoslovakia are childless (UIM, 1990, p. 6).

The number of abortions has increased in recent years, particularly since the passing of a more liberal Abortion Act in 1987. Before the Act, a woman had to receive permission for a legal abortion within the first 12 weeks of pregnancy, and had to go through a humiliating interview in front of a commission.

It is estimated that in the Czech Republic the number of abortions is equal to the number of live births. In 1985 the total number of abortions was 144 232; in 1986 it had gone up to 149 576. The rate of abortions per 100 live births increased from 61.3 per cent in 1984 to 67.6 per cent in 1986 (Czechoslovak Statistical Bureau, 1989).

Table 4.3   **Breakdown of abortions according to age, 1986**

Age	Total number of abortions
up to 15	44
15–19	11 234
20–24	35 383
25–29	37 432
30–34	34 675
35–39	22 962
40–44	7241
45+	563

(Source: Czechoslovak Statistical Bureau, 1989)

The rate of abortions per 1000 women is highest in the age category 25–29. One of the explanations for this is that it is the working women who already have one or two children who cannot afford another child. Yet the general situation concerning sexual attitudes and the lack of open discussion about sexual matters, preferences, forms of contraception and so on, also comes into play here. Some of these problems are reflected in the dissatisfaction expressed by women, and the most telling indicator of the fact that the family is not 'working' is the high rate of divorce. Every third marriage ends in divorce. Again, the economic situation and especially bad housing are to blame in large measure, yet the personal dimension of family life is insufficiently researched or understood. There were 32 divorces per 100 marriages according to 1985 statistics, compared with 9.8 divorces per 100 in 1960, 19.7 in 1970 and 28.7 in 1980 (Navarova, 1989, p. 174). Dissatisfaction within marriage grew as Czechoslovakia was reaching the higher stages of 'socialism', in the language of the old propaganda. What needs to be understood by western writers is that the current revival of the family has a specific dimension that goes beyond crude revival of the cult, the institution, the 'pillar of social order' so often

debated in western literature. The political
atmosphere now, in 1991, cannot be separated from
the devastating heritage of the past 40 years. There
has been a visible decay in the sphere of human
relationships – in the civic sphere. To talk about the
revival of the family is not, therefore, necessarily to
play into the hands of the traditionalists; it is also part
of an effort to regenerate a society whose personal
dimension has been so much forgotten and neglected
in the reduction of relationships to duties. The moral
revival of society is seen as an essential starting point
for a new democracy. Now is the time to talk, to
play, to review the past. Openness about family
matters, about sexual roles and relationships, belong
positively to the sphere of society that is coming alive
in its own way in Czechoslovakia as in other former
'socialist' societies in central and eastern Europe.

Judgements on these developments from western
perspectives are not always useful, then, and may lead
to blind alleys. Clearly a lot needs to be done to
address the issues of women's autonomy, but what
we see as refreshing is that the Czech and Slovak
women consider their liberation mostly as a society-
wide issue. The ground is ripe for their own brand of
feminism, though this label is still strongly objected
to. This is not to say, of course, that women have an
easy time in stating their case – the latest abortion
law, for example, is being debated in an atmosphere
of crisis across society as a whole. Attempts are made
towards preventative measures such as educating
people, women and men, girls and boys towards
respect for life, for parenthood, to take responsibility
for conception, etc. The moral arm of the state is
back in action, so it seems.

Women today   The level of women's activity in the 'revolutionary'
days was high. They participated and were visible.
This does not seem to be the case now, and indeed
the statistics about their political representation are
very disappointing indeed. One might conclude that
though some women have re-established 'normality'
by returning to a more passive form of coping with

new economic circumstances, others have been
forced underground by 'male apartheid'.

Most inhabitants of Czechoslovakia were shocked by
the experience of the economic reforms. From
December 1990 to February 1991 prices were raised
by 31.5 per cent without parallel increases in wages.
The term 'feminization of poverty' is currently used
to point out the negative effects that the economic
reforms have had on women. In fact the liberalization
of the prices of foodstuffs has raised some prices to
inaccessible levels. According to a public opinion
survey of March 1991, 11 per cent of households in
Slovakia find that their incomes do not cover even
their basic needs, and 44 per cent live 'from salary to
salary'. Another 40 per cent were described as living
'pretty well', although in a plain manner, and only 5
per cent of families felt no need to retrench. Fifty-
one per cent felt that reform should proceed more
slowly, and only 8 per cent agreed with its rapid
course (Okruhlicova, 1991, p. 12). The highest price
rises are expected in the second half of 1991, due to
the raising of energy prices and rents.

In terms of women's activity, some women have
started to organize anew. The number of registered
women's groups and parties in 1990 stood at 37.
They are widely disparate, embracing Women in
Management, Gypsy Women, the Political Party of
Women and Mothers, as well as the Prague Mothers,
and the Christian Democratic Union of Women and
the old Women's Union. Two of the best organized
groups are reported to be the Single Mothers, and a
caucus of women within the Social Democratic Party
who are aspiring to take the centre-left position in
the current nationwide political development.

Most of the activities of these women's groups seem
to be single-issue campaigns, apart from the growing
coalition comprising around six women's groups who
are addressing the political hierarchy. This grouping is
led by the vocal and active Political Party of Women
and Mothers, which aims to gain women's
representation at the top, to encourage and educate

women to become politically active, to protect the
weakest and the socially disadvantaged in society, and
to provide the information about women's rights that
most women, particularly in small towns and villages,
do not have. They now have a nationwide network
of contacts and are the only federal women's
organization. Their main problem is financial, and the
publication of their new journal, *Zena 91*, for
example, is funded purely through the personal
resources of the founding member. At the time of
writing there is a dispute with the old Women's
Union concerning funds and resources in the region
of millions of koruna that the Women's Union is
unwilling to release, and the 'apparatchik' mentality
(80 per cent of the old membership of the Women's
Union are reported to have been Communist Party
members) is evident in the ill-feeling between the
two groups. The first issue of *Zena 91* was not even
allowed to be distributed among the Women's Union
rank and file. *Zena 91* carries information that was
previously taboo, such as statistics showing the high
ratio of morbidity among women, and women's low
political representation.

Yet a more optimistic situation exists among the
many 'anonymous' women who simply take
initiatives into their own hands. As described earlier,
networking is spreading but forms of officially
organized activities still carry the stigma of top-down
authoritarianism. Also, women generally no longer
want to have their activities defined on their behalf.
They have been heroines of labour or of motherhood
for far too long, and prefer to start to define what
women want and how best to get it from a less
pompous position. It will take time. Women have to
find their own feet, their own strength. Czech and
Slovak women have never lacked strength; now they
are learning to use it in a different direction. Disputes
about which direction is the right one will continue,
but a new sharpening of politics is on the horizon.
Women in Czechoslovakia will not be silenced. And
they will not be pushed into the home either – such
is the verdict of a recent survey taken at this time of

mounting unemployment and economic tensions as 1991 draws to a close.

The author would like to give special thanks and acknowledgements to Hana Navarova, Sociological Institute, Prague.

5

German Democratic Republic
Emancipated women or
hardworking mothers?

Barbara Einhorn

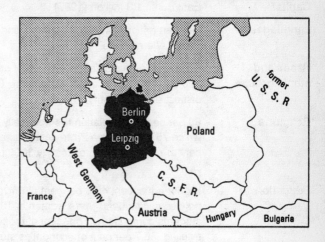

The GDR is now the five new länder of the united Germany (the Federal Republic of Germany: FRG, Bundesrepublik Deutschland: BRD)

Area

108 333 km^2.

Population

1980–88: 16.7 million, of which 8.7 million or 52 per cent were women.

Population density

154 per km^2.

Capital

East Berlin 1.3 million (1987)

Languages

German (official language of instruction), also Sorb, Polish, Vietnamese.

Races and ethnic groups

German, Sorbs plus small number of others comprising 190 000 or 1.1 per cent of population. The Sorbs are a distinct ethnic minority.

Religions

60 per cent of population are nominally religious, of which 75 per cent are Protestant (Lutheran) and 25 per cent are Catholic; approximately 3000 registered Jewish.

Education

Higher education: 48.6 per cent of university and polytechnic students were women in 1989; women students comprised 73 per cent of those doing teacher training, 66.7 per cent of economics students, 55.2 per cent of medical students and 46 per cent of maths and science students. At technical colleges in 1989 women accounted for 95.5 per cent of those in nursing and health related occupations; 88.6 per cent of teacher trainees, 85.9 per cent of economics students. Figures for vocational training show a concentration of girls in traditional female occupations throughout the 1980s.

Birth rate

(Per 1000 pop.) 1988: 12.9; 1989: 12.1.

Death rate

(Per 1000 pop.) 1988: 12.8.

Infant mortality

(Per 1000 live births) internationally low and declining. 1980: 12.1; 1989: 7.6.

Life expectancy

1989: female 76.4; male 70.1 years.

Currency

Mark der DDR (January 1990: 3M = 1DM = £1.00).

After 3 July 1990 currency union with West Germany eliminated mark der DDR.

Number of women in workforce

78 per cent or 91 per cent if including female students and apprentices.

Women's wages as a percentage of men's

1990: on average women earned 76.9–91 per cent of men's wages in industry; they tended to be employed in lower paid, low-status female or feminized occupations or sectors of the economy, for example wages within industry were highest in the metallurgy and energy sectors, both with a majority male work-force, and lowest in food processing, light industry and textiles, all three sectors employing a majority of women.

Equal pay policy

The principle of equal pay for equal work was implemented by the Soviet military administration in 1946, and confirmed in the first constitution of the GDR at its foundation in October 1949.

Production

Industry: the most important sectors were mechanical engineering and vehicle production; chemicals and metallurgy.

Agriculture: over half of the arable land is devoted to grain crops and feed grains for animals.

Women as a percentage of labour-force

Total (1988) 48.9 per cent; with women accounting (in 1989) for 41 per cent of the work-force in industry; 37.4 per cent in agriculture and forestry; and an unknown percentage of clerical and other service workers in the military.

Employed women's occupational indicators (1988)

17 per cent of construction workers were women; 35 per cent of workers in transport, post and telecommunications; 36 per cent in agriculture and forestry; 72 per cent of wholesale and retail trades; 77 per cent of teachers; 83 per cent of health service; 92 per cent in restaurants/hotels (1986); and 99 per cent of commercial cleaners. Women formed the majority of industrial workers (1989) in: light industry 55 per cent, textiles 66.9 per cent and a high proportion of workers in food processing (47.1 per cent) and electronics (48.4 per cent).

Unemployment

The transition to a market economy has produced the first unemployment in the history of the GDR. The percentage unemployed rose from 1.6 per cent for the first six months of 1990 to 272 017 or 3.1 per cent of the work-force in July 1990 with further steep rises predicted in 1991. The proportion of women among unemployed people rose from 41.3 per cent in February to 51.6 per cent in July 1990.

Women as producers and reproducers – workers and mothers

The central contradiction of state socialism as far as women were concerned was that it viewed emancipation for women as something that could be given to women without taking anything away from men (Scott, 1978). This had a double-edge implication. On the one hand women's involvement in social production, that is, their labour-force participation, was seen as the single necessary and sufficient condition for emancipation. On the other, the dual burden that emanated from a woman's role as worker and mother was structurally enshrined in all legislation promulgated in the GDR, without any similar classification of men as workers and fathers.

Gender issues such as sexual harassment at work, the domestic division of labour, sexuality and autonomy, and violence against women were not addressed in public discourse, nor did they appear in official statistics. They were simply excluded from the parameters of the official canon as adopted from Marx, Engels, Bebel to the exclusion of Kollontai. It was mechanistically (and somewhat simplistically) assumed that all forms of violence against the person would automatically disappear with the elimination of private ownership of the means of production.

Equal pay?

Within the logic of this limited definition of women's emancipation there were multiple contradictions. In the GDR women had the right (and, some felt, the obligation) to work, and in 1988 83.2 per cent (or 91 per cent if one counts those in higher education and training) of women of working age were actively employed in the labour-market. On the positive side of the balance sheet, the GDR boasted some of the earliest legislation on equal pay, with the Decree of the Soviet Military Administration in 1946 and the 1949 constitution both predating by several years the earliest comparable UN legislation. In reality, however, one of the disillusioning realizations that dawned at the end of 40 years of dalliance with the socialist experiment was the revelation that women had earned on average 12–25 per cent less than men.

This gap existed even in industry, the most privileged sector of the economy, due to the concentration of women in jobs requiring lower levels of qualification and responsibility. Hence in 1989, 56.7 per cent of all women employed in industrial production were concentrated in the two lowest income brackets, whereas only 13.8 per cent of them held demanding jobs in the top two income brackets. Of the total work-force, women made up an average 72 per cent of the lowest three income brackets, but only 16.4 per cent of the top two (Winkler, *Frauenreport 90*, pp. 86–92).

Occupational segregation

Female workers in the GDR were heavily represented in industry as a whole, but there was a high level of occupational segregation. Women tended to be concentrated in certain traditionally female-dominated sectors of the economy, in retail and in the service sector, all of which paid lower wages than did the prioritized heavy industry and construction sectors. Most nurses, crèche and nursery school teachers, secretaries, cleaners, shop assistants, and hotel and restaurant workers were women. This clearly illustrates the notion, widely held to be true for western Europe, that women's labour-force participation tends to parallel their domestic roles. Put more crudely, it seems that in the GDR, as in non-socialist countries, the majority of working women tended to be concentrated in occupations involving care for and cleaning up after other people.

Table 5.1   **Female employment by industrial sector**

Female participation rates expressed as percentage of total employment in that sector

Industrial sector	1970	1980	1989
Industry total	42.5	43.3	41.0
Light industry			55.7
Textiles			66.9
Food processing			47.1
Electronics			48.4
Construction	13.3	16.2	17.2
Agriculture/forestry	45.8	41.5	37.4
Transport	25.5	27.4	26.4
Post/telecomm	68.8	70.0	69.0
Retail	69.2	72.8	71.9

(Source: Winkler, 1990, Tables 3.11 and 3.12)

Feminized
professions

It should be acknowledged that women in the GDR had made considerable inroads into previously male-dominated occupations and professions. In 1977–79, 45 per cent of judges and 30 per cent of lawyers in the GDR were women (while only 5 per cent of West German (FRG) lawyers were women). In 1983, women accounted for 57 per cent of dentists and 52 per cent of doctors in the GDR (compared with only 20 per cent of dentists and 23 per cent of doctors in the FRG in 1987). Nevertheless, there was a diminishing representation of women towards the top of career pyramids, such that medical consultants tended to be men, as did head teachers or university professors. Although 77 per cent of teachers in the GDR in 1985 were women, only 32 per cent of head teachers and 7 per cent of college and university lecturers, including full professors, were women. Relativities are important, however, so it should be borne in mind that this 7 per cent figure was already valid for 1977–78, when the corresponding figure for the FRG was 0.6 per cent (Einhorn, 1989, p. 290; Shaffer, 1981, p. 76).

Women in leading positions

In GDR industry too, this under-representation of women at the top was characteristic even of those occupations and sectors of the economy that remained female-dominated. The average female share of managerial positions in industry as a whole was 21 per cent in 1988. However, this relatively favourable proportion is misleading, since it is made up of disparate figures. In light industry, and post and telecommunications, for example, women held 44 per cent and 41.7 per cent of leading positions, whereas in the coal and energy, machine building, construction, and electronics sectors they held only 13.2 per cent, 14.2 per cent, 11.2 per cent and 15.9 per cent of leading positions respectively (Winkler, *Frauenreport 90*, Table 3.33, p. 95).

Women in education and training

Education in the GDR was uniform for girls and boys throughout their 10 years of compulsory schooling. There was no curriculum choice, hence no gender segregation or gender-biased choice of subjects. Despite this, statistics for the GDR show a persistent and, during the 1980s, even increasing trend for girls to choose traditionally 'feminine' occupations. In 1987, 60 per cent of female school leavers entered training for a mere 16 out of a possible 259 occupations (Nickel, 1990, p. 40). This would tend to belie both the GDR's own officially proclaimed equality of educational opportunity and the widely shared view that education will overcome discrimination on the basis of gender.

It is also worthy of note that where women had made some inroads into formerly male-dominated occupations there appears to have been a reverse trend during the 1980s. It appears to be the case that especially where the introduction of new technology requires skill rather than manual dexterity and hence involves higher levels of pay, women tend to be displaced by men.

Table 5.2   Occupational training

Female participation expressed as a percentage of all school leavers entering training in selected occupations

Occupation	1980	1985	1989
Secretary	99.8	99.7	99.8
Clothes factory worker	99.9	99.5	99.4
Textiles worker	96.6	94.7	95.3
Salesperson	98.2	97.1	95.6
Postal worker	94.8	93.1	90.9
Data processor	82.8	77.8	70.0
Electronics worker	49.8	33.0	19.5
Machine builder	8.3	5.8	5.8
Toolmaker	11.9	9.0	5.2

(Source: Winkler, *Frauenreport 90*, Table 2.9)

Child-care facilities

Again on the positive side of the balance sheet, the GDR went to considerable lengths to mitigate the impact of the double burden: it was the only one of the state socialist countries to turn universal rhetoric on the subject of child-care facilities into an increasingly and, by the end of its existence, almost universally available reality. The massive increase in provision between 1970 and 1980 parallels a whole package of sharply increased measures designed to encourage women to have more children, the measures later derided as *Muttipolitik* (Mummy policies) – policies with no emancipatory thrust.

Nevertheless, it cannot be overlooked that while in Poland such measures were accompanied by neglect of child-care facilities on the assumption that mothers would stay at home with their children, in the GDR the availability of child-care gave women with small children real choice about whether and when to return to work. Both crèches and nursery schools were free, with parents paying a nominal 35 pfennig (approximately 10p) per day towards the meals provided for their children.

The 'Hort' was an after-school care programme in which children aged 6–10 had their homework supervised and could engage in hobbies, thus alleviating the problem for working parents caused by the East German school day ending after the midday meal.

Table 5.3

Child-care provision

Availability of child-care expressed as the percentage of children in the relevant age groups looked after in child-care facility

Year	Crèche	Nursery school	Hort
1950		20.5	
1955	9.1	34.5	
1960	14.3	46.1	
1970	29.1	64.5	46.6
1980	61.2	92.2	74.8
1985	72.7	94.0	84.0
1989	80.2	95.0	81.2

(Source: Winkler, *Frauenreport 90,* Tables 4.27, 4.28, 4.29)

Socializing domestic labour

The system of work-place canteens, and the availability of pre-packed or frozen foods, of dry cleaning, mending and other services, while deficient, were by no means as lacking as in the other countries of central and eastern Europe. In many of these, women spent, and still spend, two hours or more each day simply standing in queues for scarce services or sufficient foodstuffs to put together any kind of meal. In Czechoslovakia for example a recent survey revealed that as a result of travel to and from work and shopping, fully employed women spent 9.5–10 hours daily away from home (Kroupova, 1990, p. 12).

The initial dream of 'socializing' domestic labour in order to 'ensure that women can reconcile the demands of their job still more successfully with their duties towards child and family' faded (Programme of the Socialist Unity Party (SED), ruling party of the GDR, quoted in Einhorn, 1989, p. 292). It must be said, however, that this resulted not merely from an inadequate availability of goods and services, nor from bureaucratic inefficiency. Another factor was people's rejection of the collective ideal. Hence early attempts in the GDR to install shared washing machines in the basement of each block of flats were unsuccessful – every family (or every woman?) hankered after its own washing machine, competing not with the Joneses, but at an individual level with the capitalist west, as represented by their relatives in West Germany.

The ironic heritage of the old devotion to collective ideals persists even today in quite recently built apartment blocks. The GDR building industry was based on prefabricated wall sections and standard plans for the mass building programme originally designed to house or rehouse the entire population of the GDR by 1990. These plans include a bathroom neither large enough comfortably to house a washing machine nor with washing machine connections plumbed in. As a result, plumbers and other tradesmen have long formed the affluent 'ruling class' in GDR society according to popular wisdom, and going to the toilet in most GDR bathrooms requires the skill of a Houdini to negotiate the confined spaces made yet more constrained by the inclusion of an unplanned washing machine.

In 1988, 67 per cent of young married workers in their twenties owned automatic washing machines, while all households owned some form of washing machine and a refrigerator. Approximately 54 per cent of all households of employed people also owned a freezer, 60 per cent possessed colour TV – as opposed to black and white – and 59 per cent owned a car. These figures make clear the GDR's relative affluence as expressed in terms of consumer durables, especially in relation to the Soviet Union and the other countries of central and eastern Europe. Despite their washing machines, and as a result of the lack of drying facilities, most GDR households gave their sheets and towels to the communal laundry for washing once a month, an expression of the sort of service that was readily available in the GDR but not necessarily in all the state socialist countries. The element of choice cannot be overlooked therefore, when considering issues of the dual role. Despite the fact that most children and adults enjoyed a hot meal at midday at their place of work or school, most women chose to cook again in the evening, not believing somehow that the institutional meal would be sufficiently nutritious for their family.

Reproductive rights

Real choice was also a reality for GDR women in relation to reproduction. The combination of universally available contraception, generous maternity leave provisions and the right to abortion on demand within the first three months of pregnancy meant that women could choose whether and when to have children, and whether, or more often when, to return to work after childbirth. Maternity leave comprised 26 weeks at full pay, with a second six months on 70 per cent of pay, together known as the 'baby year', during which time a woman's job must be kept open for her. As of 1986 the 'baby year' can be regarded as parental rather than maternity leave, since it can be taken by mothers, fathers or grandmothers.

Contraception was free and available to all women over the age of 16, regardless of marital status. The most favoured method was the contraceptive pill. In addition, women had the right to abortion on demand within the first three months of pregnancy. The 1972 Abortion Law, while rather paternalistically begrudging in tone, was in fact very progressive in terms of its espousal of the principle of choice:

The equality of women in education and vocation, in marriage and family makes it necessary to leave it to the discretion of women themselves to decide whether and when

*to have a child ... Women have the right to decide on their
own responsibility on the number and timing of children
they bear and shall be able to decide upon this through a
termination of pregnancy.*

At the same time it was the case that while abortions
were free and women had the right to paid sick leave
for this purpose, social stigmatization was such that
many women chose to give fictitious reasons for their
absence from work. In Brigitte Martin's short story
'Im Friedrichshain', the narrator says that her child is
ill, and goes to the lengths of getting a doctor's
certificate to this effect. This story also documents the
patronizing and didactic treatment to which women
were often subjected by the doctors who had the
responsibility of advising them on contraceptive
methods. And apart from this advice, there was little
follow-up – as in Britain – in terms of counselling for
the possible emotional or psychological after-effects
of abortion.

The number of terminations in the GDR was high
until after the introduction of the Abortion Law in
1972. In 1973 there were still two abortions for every
live birth, almost equalling the situations in Poland or
the Soviet Union where the widespread use of
abortion as a method of contraception may be
explained by the lack of availability of other
contraceptive means. In the European part of the
former Soviet Union and Czechoslovakia for example,
the number of abortions still equals that of live births.
There has been a fall in the number of abortions in the
GDR since 1973, with the lowest level – 2 per cent of
all women aged 15–45 – registered for 1977–78. The
slight increase since then has been attributed to what
the Germans call 'pill weariness', or worries about the
health side-effects of the contraceptive pill (Winkler,
Frauenreport 90, p. 167; Kroupova, 1990).

**Welfare
provision**

One of the positive achievements of the GDR is
reflected in the achievements of the health service.
Life expectancy for women was 76 years in 1989
(improved from 70 in 1952) as opposed to 70 for
men, a gender gap comparable to but not as great as

that in some other central and eastern European countries. The number of women who died in childbirth was 1.4 per 10 000 live births compared with 13.7 in 1955. And the infant mortality rate of 7.6 per 1000 live births in 1989 compares favourably with the lowest rates elsewhere in the world (Winkler, *Frauenreport 90*, pp. 159, 165–6). In social welfare terms, then, these few examples serve to demonstrate that the GDR provided a high level of care, even if the quality of care left something to be desired. Many GDR women felt, for example, that the unfavourable child–carer ratio in crèches and nursery schools made for impersonal or over-regimented care. And the long working hours in the GDR meant that children had to be woken very early and spent long hours away from home.

Women's rights and population policy

Despite some positive discrimination in education and training, welfare rights and social provisions enjoyed by women in the GDR, it was striking that the first publicly aired views of the new independent women's movement (*Unabhängiger Frauenverband* (UFV)) after the 'turning point' of 1989 expressed derision at what they interpreted as *Muttipolitik*. Some rejected official measures for women's emancipation as little more than pro-natalist policies pursued by a government concerned with its declining population and with an eye to the need to reproduce its labour-force (UFV Programme, 1990).

It is therefore an open question whether women felt there was, as has been previously asserted, a real commitment to emancipation for women, or whether, as the cynics would have it, women's labour-force participation was simply driven by economic demand with women's rights subsumed under this. At first glance the GDR would appear to provide a prime target for the accusation that it instrumentalized women, in the sense that it is perhaps the only state in history to have had a constantly declining population throughout its entire history. In the context of a male population decimated by World War Two and the pre-Wall losses of skilled and professional workers to West

Germany, female labour-force participation could be interpreted as a matter of sheer economic necessity.

Hence, this steady population decline was the result first of the GDR's unique geo-political location bordering the 'capitalist west' (the 'other' Germany), and second, of the very low birth rate. The number of live births per 1000 of the population dropped from 17 in 1960 to 12 in 1989 (Winkler, *Frauenreport 90*, p. 24). Although this was paralleled in West Germany, it was compensated for there by the importation of foreign 'guest workers', who in the 1970s were allowed to bring their families with them and settle in the FRG, albeit without voting rights. Extended maternity leave and other measures were introduced in 1976 (following a drop to 10.8 live births per 1000 population in 1975) with the express aim of raising the birth rate. Nevertheless the one-child family continued to be a very common response in the GDR to the stresses of the dual or triple burden.

The GDR-specific cause of the declining population was the constant leak through the border to the west. It is a historical irony that just as this population drain prompted the building of the Wall on 13 August 1961, so the single most important factor in what some saw as the Wall's overly hasty demise on 9 November 1989 was the huge numbers of GDR citizens who poured out of the country via Hungary from August 1989. According to the programme 'report' of the West German TV station ZDF on 5 December 1989 for example, a total of 4500 or the equivalent of 11 per cent of all GDR doctors left that country during 1989, 1500 of them after the mass exodus began in the summer.

Nor have the opening of the Wall and German unification put a halt to this population drain. On the contrary, rising unemployment and delayed investment in the restructuring of the former GDR (the five new federal 'länder') reached a level in early 1991 where potentially serious demographic distortions began to occur, with the young and skilled 'getting on their bikes' and going west to where the jobs are, while the old and socially weak remain behind.

The socialist family

The existence of the nuclear family, rechristened the 'socialist' family – seen as the basic cell in society with the duty to rear the 'socialist' citizens of the future – was never questioned. The traditional patriarchal family structure was addressed in the progressive Family Law of 1965 which provided for both partners to make compromises in the interests of furthering the other's career, in addition to taking equal responsibility for housework and child-care. Yet a survey carried out in 1988 revealed that 37 per cent of women and 43 per cent of men believed that when the children are young, women should make career compromises. Only 3 per cent of women and a miserable 1 per cent of men believed that men should at some time compromise their career when there are children in the family (Winkler, *Sozialreport 90*, p. 274).

There have been changes in the traditional domestic division of labour, especially in the area of child-rearing. Nevertheless it is still overwhelmingly women (78 per cent of cases) who take time off work to care for sick children. And while 66 per cent of women and 60 per cent of men asserted in 1988 that domestic labour was shared fairly equally between them, a 1985 survey revealed that women were still responsible for at least 60 per cent of the work (albeit an improvement on surveys conducted in 1970, according to which women were responsible for 80 per cent of domestic labour). Nevertheless, in 1988 both women (55 per cent) and men (64 per cent) expressed satisfaction with this arrangement (Winkler, *Sozialreport 90*, pp. 269–73).

Not only did men contribute much less towards the household in terms of their labour than women, but it seems that children also did very little work, especially boys. In part this may have been the expression of traditional attitudes about sex role divisions, in part it also reflects the guilt of overstressed parents who tended to indulge their children, overwhelming them with material benefits – clothes, toys, cassette recorders, videos – to make up for their own absence as carers or companions. This meant that children were not required to contribute their share to the collective enterprise one might expect the socialist family to constitute. A short story by Angela Stachowa gives a moving evocation of the desperate loneliness felt by an only child of two overstressed working parents (Stachowa, 1976, p. 197). The vandalism and violence of young people that has become visible since the 'turning point' in late 1989 in fact surfaced much earlier. It can be interpreted as another symptom of the way the GDR's prioritizing of economic goals with long daily working hours undermined the 'socialist' family unit by leaving children and young people to their own devices for many hours every day.

Beyond this, the 'socialist' family itself, consisting of two parents and two children, was an ideological construct which bore less and less resemblance to reality, to social relations as actually lived in the GDR. One-third of all children and a very high 52.7 per cent of all first children were born to unmarried mothers, although some of those would have been living in stable relationships. Of all families with children, 18 per cent were single-headed households. By the end of 1989, the one-child family still constituted 50 per cent of all families in the GDR (Winkler, *Frauenreport 90*, pp. 29, 103). While the institution of marriage did not seem to be questioned (with 75 per cent and 70 per cent of young people interviewed in 1982 and 1988 respectively declaring their intention to marry), the divorce rate (38 per cent of all marriages) was fifth highest in the world after the USA, the USSR, Cuba and Britain. In 1989, women petitioned for 69 per cent of all divorces (Winkler, *Frauenreport 90*, pp. 109, 111).

In addition, the scarce housing in the GDR resulted in a system of priorities in the allocation of flats, with married couples, especially those who already had children, taking precedence over young single people or unmarried couples. This meant that there was scarce opportunity for young couples to live together on a trial basis before marriage. Nor did the small prefabricated apartment units which were standard in the GDR allow for extended family or alternative shared household patterns. In other words there was a certain structurally determined pressure to get married. This was reflected in the attitudes of young people who gave as their motives for marrying: love, tradition and the possibility of getting a flat (Winkler, *Frauenreport 90*, p. 105).

Education for equality? The so-called 'measures for the promotion of women' ('*Frauenförderungsmassnahmen*') were a form of positive discrimination enabling women in employment to take paid time off for courses or training to improve their level of qualification. This resulted in the percentage of working women who were unskilled falling from 44.4 per cent in 1971 to 12.3 per cent in 1989 (as opposed to 23.3 per cent and 7.1 per cent of men in each of those years). The number of women without any formal qualifications is highest in the age group over 30, in particular among rural women (Winkler, *Frauenreport 90*, pp. 38–41).

With the younger generation, however, it was assumed that equality of educational opportunity would raise women's educational standards to equal those of men. This had interesting consequences, in that from the beginning of the 1970s, girls constituted more than half of the pupils going on to sixth-form level (*abitur* – the equivalent of A level) education (Winkler, *Frauenreport 90*, p. 41). As a result, some degree of positive discrimination for boys was instituted. Despite their uniform curricula and girls' high educational achievement, gender stereotypes persisted in occupational choice, as indicated above. GDR studies established that by the time children started school at six, preconceptions about which sex was cheekier, better behaved, tidier, wilder and so on were well entrenched (Edwards, 1985, pp. 39, 60; Einhorn, 1989, pp. 288–90, 303, notes 13, 19).

This raises the question of the degree to which educational practice was non-sexist. While some studies suggest (see Edwards, 1985, pp. 54–6) that great efforts in this direction were made at the crèche and nursery-school level, perusal of a standard pre-school text and the first reader used in GDR schools in the late 1970s reveals very traditional images of the family and gender stereotyped career roles. The only time Daddy is actively involved is in preparing with the children a gift for Mummy on 8 March, International Women's Day. (It is interesting to note that by 1991, although newspapers carried exchanges of letters on the pros and cons of celebrating International Women's Day, the tokenist manner in which it had been an official day of celebration in the past, with women being given flowers, and men making the tea at work for this one day, meant that even the independent women's movement ignored it.) Mothers and grandmothers do the shopping, serve the dinner, supervise play, and pick up children from school. In a scene depicting children helping with domestic chores it is of course the daughter who has taken Mum's place. Road awareness is taught with stores about Stefan who falls off while learning to ride a bike, Jutta who teaches her little sister how to cross the road safely like a little mother, and Sabine who is crying because she is lost, but impresses the friendly policeman with her knowledge of her address (*Unsere Fibel*, 1978, pp. 5, 6, 8, 18, 51, 60–3, 79; Witzlack et al, *Bald bin ich ein Schulkind*, 1977, pp. 17, 42–3, 66–7).

In the sections of both books dealing with the kinds of job done by adults, women or mothers appear as dairymaids, doctors, primary school teachers, textile workers, draughts 'men' and supermarket cashiers. (A revealing aspect of public discourse was that the GDR ignored the linguistically available feminine ending espoused by the West German Green and women's movements for women in certain occupations and professions.) Men and fathers appear as architects, engineers, construction workers, brigade leaders, steelworkers, machine tool operators (*Maschinenschlosser*), bus drivers, performing artists, scientists, and soldiers of the National People's Army (the NVA). Both books praise the 'workers' in the NVA, and didactic user instructions in the pre-school text encourage parents to introduce their children to the peace-keeping role of the army, while the first school reader encourages classes to 'adopt' and correspond with a member of the NVA (*Unsere Fibel*, 1978, pp. 22, 29, 43, 71, 105–107; Witzlack et al, *Bald bin ich ein Schulkind*, 1977, pp. 28–9, 64–5).

There is no encouragement of alternative role models, even for women, and certainly men are not depicted in any kind of caring profession or child-rearing role. Crèche and kindergarten teachers in the GDR were 100 per cent women, as were 77 per cent of all school teachers. There was some rhetoric but no positive discrimination in terms of material incentives for men to enter such traditionally female occupations.

Neither heterosexuality nor stereotyped images of female beauty and self-presentation were questioned. Already in the late 1970s, many ironic or satirical short stories by GDR women writers rejected the 'superwoman' image of the media in which a woman manager of a factory, shown in lab coat and hard hat, was also photographed in her immaculate flat with her model children, beautifully dressed – and still smiling (Einhorn, 1989, pp. 293–97).

Transition to the market: gains or losses?

All the problems and contradictions outlined above do not alter that fact that women in the GDR enjoyed a degree of real choice in terms of reproductive and welfare rights, motherhood and career. One of the ironies of the situation following unification, with adaptation to the 'social market economy' and democratic system of the Federal Republic, is that it is precisely these rights that women in the former GDR now stand to lose.

Contraceptives now have to be paid for. Under GDR law women were entitled to 26 weeks' fully paid maternity leave followed by up to 12 months' paid leave (the 'baby year') for a first child and 18 months for a second child at 70–90 per cent of salary. This has been replaced by the West German provision for 10 weeks' maternity leave followed by child-rearing leave up to a total of 12 months on DM600 per month, a sum it is not possible to live on in any part of Germany, East or West. The five weeks of annual paid leave in the former GDR to care for sick children shrinks under Federal German law to eight days per year, and that only until the child's eighth birthday (Dölling, 1991, Kolinsky, 1989, p. 71).

Pre-school facilities that previously cost parents a nominal 35 pfennig per day for meals (approximately 7 marks or £2.50 per month, depending on whether one uses the then official GDR exchange rate) are either being closed or rising sharply in price. As of 1 July 1990 the price had already risen to DM250–300 (approximately £80–£100) per child per month. The monthly paid 'household day' to which GDR women had a right if they were married, had children under 16, or were over 40, while it was open to criticism as perpetuating the gendered division of household labour, was abolished altogether on 1 January 1991.

Reproductive choice especially in terms of the right to terminate an unwanted pregnancy is in doubt, as outlined below. Women were considered 'unreliable' workers precisely because of their absence from work due to maternity leave and caring for sick children. State enterprises faced with the need to shed labour in the attempt to survive have leapt at the opportunity in the new situation to sack their female work-force first. Women formed 54 per cent of those unemployed in the former GDR as of March 1991, and with the closure of child-care facilities many will find it difficult to find alternative employment or to participate in retraining courses.

Women as decision makers – participation and representation

In the past the GDR could point to impressive statistics for the political representation of women: 45 per cent of judges (1979), 25 per cent of local mayors (1986), and 32 per cent of members of the Volkskammer, the GDR's Parliament (Einhorn, 1989, pp. 287, 289). Much of this representation was, however, of a rather token nature in that the Volkskammer representation, for example, was the result of a system of fixed quotas for the German Democratic Women's Federation (DFD), the official semi-governmental women's organization, and within the political parties. In addition, the real decision making took place within the structures of the Socialist Unity Party (SED), rather than in Parliament.

Women were seriously under-represented in the upper echelons of the Socialist Unity Party. While they comprised 35 per cent of ordinary members, only 13 per cent of Central Committee members were women in 1986. In all the 40 years of the GDR's existence, not a single woman entered the Politburo. Two women held non-voting 'candidate member' status for over 15 and 25 years respectively (Einhorn, 1989, pp. 287, 302). Neither were renowned for partisanship on women's rights. Indeed when the Modrow government proposed to instate one of them, Inge Lange, as a Minister for Women, a spontaneous demonstration by women successfully demanded her removal from the post.

Despite the tokenist nature of the high female representation in the Volkskammer it was noteworthy that the first free elections in March 1990 produced a much lower level of representation for women. Only the newly formed Green party and the Party of Democratic Socialism (PDS) (the successor to the previous ruling Socialist Unity Party) responded to women's movement demands for quotas for female representation. The Independent Women's Association (UFV) together with the Greens achieved only 2.7 per cent of the vote, but the women received no seats in Parliament due to a misunderstanding about the placements on electoral lists. The former official women's organization, the German Democratic Women's Federation (DFD) received only 0.03 per cent of the vote, despite its membership of 1.5 million. This trend was confirmed in the May 1990 local elections and the October

1990 elections for the governments of the five new states (länder) (Dölling, 1991).

The role of the DFD had been positive in the early days of the GDR in terms of pressing for legislation that guaranteed women's equal status at work. Beyond that, it also encouraged women to participate in social production and to widen their horizons by attending lecture series on political as well as social issues and household 'tips'. Yet it outlived its own usefulness in the sense that it continued to focus these activities on rural areas or full-time housewives who, in a country where 91 per cent of women were in education or worked outside the home, constituted a tiny minority. Its advice centres for young couples setting up a home and its focus on domesticated hobbies in rural communities earned it the derisory label after the 'turning point' in autumn 1989 of the 'knitting and crochet circle'.

The DFD's subsequent attempt to re-form itself and re-legitimize its role was both misguided and doomed from the outset. It had become too bureaucratized an institution, too remote from women's actual needs in dealing with the contradictions between officially proclaimed equality and the reality of the dual or triple burden. Attempts to open itself up to the public in its central Berlin offices, making meeting rooms available to newly formed independent women's organizations, or running 'open days' with crèche facilities, were seen as too little too late. The organization's efforts to run for the first free elections in March 1990 in coalition with the Independent Women's Association (UFV) were rebuffed, despite the potential campaigning advantage the DFD could offer in terms of a still functioning network of local and regional groups with paid workers in situ.

Women's personal autonomy

It has already been pointed out that the problem with the Marxist notion of emancipation as adopted by state socialist countries was its exclusive focus on women's labour-force participation as the necessary and sufficient condition for emancipation. Although there was periodic talk of the goal of socialism being the development of the full potential of each of its citizens, this limitation meant that the parameters of official discourse did not include issues of autonomy, sexuality, sexual harassment at work, pornography or violence. Indeed there was a rather simplistic or mechanistic assumption that with the elimination of private ownership of the means of production, all forms of exploitation would be eradicated, including all forms of violence against the person.

The current transition period in central and eastern Europe is perhaps best characterized by paradox. One, with bitter consequences for women, is the sharp increase in violence, mugging and rape since the revolutions of autumn 1989. The reasons for this are not well established, and the common, rather glib, assumption that repressive authoritarianism and state control in the past successfully suppressed these symptoms does not seem to provide an adequate explanation. For women this means that the democratic freedoms won by popular pressure out of the long-repressed desire for individual autonomy and – in the GDR case – for the freedom to travel, have led to a sudden loss of freedom of movement. The demand of many western feminist movements that women should 'reclaim the night' was a mystery to women in the GDR. They took it for granted in the past that they could walk the streets at night with impunity. Now one receives constant admonitions about the dangers for women of being out alone at night in Berlin and the other large cities of the former GDR and other central and eastern European countries.

Another ironic twist to the notion of freedom can be seen in the proliferation of pornography as the first visible evidence of freedom of the press. GDR women were enraged by articles in respected newspapers and journals justifying the appearance of pornography as a sign of liberalization, as opposed to the rather repressive and puritanical nature of Stalinist state socialism with regard to sexuality.

Sexuality was for a long time not a topic for public discourse in the earlier years of the GDR. Indeed it was always assumed that 'sexuality' implied heterosexuality, and that 'homosexuality' was a kind of unfortunate social and medical disease. All literature on the subject of homosexuality referred only to gay men, as if lesbians did not exist. Since it might be infectious, in social terms, it was better to avoid contact with homosexuals. The late 1970s saw the issue surfacing, like so many other issues for which there was no public forum, in literary guise. Many short stories by young women writers dealt ironically with the contradictions experienced by women in their daily lives, ranging in theme from the reality of sexual harassment at work, through the patronizing homilies given to women by doctors or professionals, to the impossibility of 'mastering' the legally enshrined dual role of worker and mother without being superwoman, a feat possible only with the help of totally non-socialist supernatural or magical means. Christine Wolter in 'I've Remarried' gives a wonderfully humorous twist to the lesbian theme in her deadpan account of her fantastically supportive, sharing new partner. The reader fantasizes about the 'new man' until the last line of the story which reveals that the new partner is, like the narrator, a woman (Wolter, 1978).

The gay movement, like the peace and women's movements in the GDR, developed under the roof of the Protestant Church, somewhat to the Church's embarrassment, during the 1980s. In fact it was lesbians who were the first to come and form groups, along with the peace movement, in the space provided by the Church. In the late 1980s several gay bars flourished in Berlin and there were open discussions in *Junge Welt*, the youth newspaper, and other journals, about the discrimination gays faced in employment. Such gay bars and gays, along with African students, squatters and Jews, became, during 1990, targets for the many neo-fascist attacks, watched helplessly by the old discredited GDR police force, and apparently – according to reports of the

Black Unity Committee in Berlin – tolerated by the newly merged joint Berlin police squads.

One of the most prominent groups, which became active in 1982, was 'Women for Peace'. The group's protests heightened against the revised Law on Conscription of March 1983, which provided for women to be conscripted in times of emergency. As a result two of the leading members were imprisoned for six weeks without trial on charges of treason. Bärbel Bohley and Ulrike Poppe went on to become leading figures in New Forum and Democracy Now, two of the groups instrumental in the autumn 1989 'turning point' (Einhorn, 1984; Einhorn, 1989, pp. 297–300). Vera Wollenberger, who was expelled from the GDR for peace movement activity at the beginning of 1988 (together with Bärbel Bohley and others), has gone on to become a founding member and representative in the Bundestag (the all-German Parliament) for the Green Party of the five new federal länder (states).

Women speak for themselves

In a historic public meeting in December 1989, over 1000 women came together in an East Berlin theatre to form the Independent Women's Association (UFV). This was conceived as an umbrella organization to represent the many women's groups that had mushroomed throughout the country both before and after the autumn of 1989. Some of the oldest groups, like Lila Offensive (Violet Offensive), a radical feminist group, had existed since the early 1980s under the shelter of the Protestant Church. Other groups had existed for 10 years as academic feminist discussion groups.

At its inception, the UFV encompassed a wide range of groups, from the Socialist Women's Initiative (SOFI) to single-issue groups focusing on campaigns to establish women's centres, refuges, and cafés for women. It demanded genuine equality of opportunity rather than the economically driven *Muttipolitik* of the late 1970s and 1980s, equal pay for work of equal value, equal representation in political structures, and freedom from exploitation as sex objects. Its demands reflected the desire to extend the agenda from the parameters of previous official discourse on emancipation to encompass gender issues such as the domestic division of labour, sexual harassment at work, violence against women, pornography, sexuality and autonomy. Rapid success was achieved in the early days of 1990. Dr Marina Beyer was appointed as government spokesperson for women, and all localities in the then GDR comprising more than 10000 inhabitants were obliged to appoint such a spokesperson. Almost every local council was persuaded to let women take over former state security buildings in order to set up women's centres, cafés and refuges. The UFV looked like a potentially mass movement with a national network of groups.

Unfortunately, the acceleration of the process of unification during the first half of 1990 and the imposition of West German norms in that process meant that many of these successes were short-lived. On the eve of German unification on 3 October 1990 Dr Beyer, as the government spokesperson for women appointed by the recently dissolved GDR Parliament, was dismissed from her post in the Ministry for the Family, Youth and Women. The optimistic hopes of autumn 1989 of extending the agenda in relation to women's rights very quickly dissolved into the necessity to defend what rights women already enjoyed. So, for example, the demand for the right to part-time work quickly became commuted to the demand that the previously taken-for-granted right to work itself should not be jeopardized. The GDR has, apart from Poland, suffered perhaps the most severe shock treatment in the economic transformation process. However, far from being a 'short sharp shock' such as that proclaimed in the Polish and discussed in the Czechoslovak cases, GDR women are experiencing a long drawn out prolongation of the shock, with large-scale redundancies being carried out in defiance, during 1990, of the terms of the then still valid GDR labour code.

In the first half of 1991, many women in administrative or academic posts were still in their jobs on short-time work – 'zero hours' – a makeshift arrangement many saw as designed to mask the true extent of mass unemployment until at least after the December 1990 all-German elections, and meant thereafter to cushion the traumatic effects of the transition to the West German labour-market. Nevertheless, the generally accepted prediction as of February 1991 was that 50 per cent of the work-force in the five new länder would be unemployed by June 1991. Similarly, maternity leave stipulations that a woman's job be kept open for her while she was on the 'baby year' were ignored. By February 1991 54.7 per cent of the officially unemployed were women (Beyer, 1992). With many firms sloughing off their child-care facilities to near-bankrupt local authorities who felt unable to take them on, prospects for finding alternative employment were sharply reduced. Newspapers reported sharp increases in the number of women seeking shelter in refuges as the experience of unemployment took its toll in higher levels of domestic violence.

The most clear-cut attack on women's rights came in the debate around the abortion law. For a brief period in 1990, disagreement over this formed the single most important stumbling block to agreement between the two German states on the terms of unification. The GDR law had provided (since 1972) for legal, free termination within the first three months of pregnancy on the decision of the woman alone. Under West German law, the notorious paragraph 218 of the federal basic law (the equivalent of the constitution) makes abortion fundamentally illegal, with some exceptions on economic or medical grounds, to be decided by a panel of doctors. A compromise agreement provides for the relevant laws of each German state to remain operative in the territories of those former states for a transitional two-year period. During 1990 the West German Free Democrat or Liberal Party (FDP) put forward a draft for a joint new law which seeks a formulation

acceptable to all parties including the strongly
Catholic ruling Christian Democrats (CDU) and
especially the Bavarian Christian Socialists (CSU). It
involves a compromise between the two existing
laws, providing for legal termination within the first
three months of pregnancy on condition that the
woman first undergo a compulsory vetting and
counselling process. This compromise is fiercely
resisted by the UFV in the former GDR. They view
compulsory counselling as representing a fundamental
attack on women's autonomy and rights. At the time
of writing the outcome is still uncertain.

The potential or actual losses for women of rights
they enjoyed under the old state socialist GDR
would suggest that there is a need for a strong
women's movement to articulate and to defend
women's needs and rights. However, the UFV and its
constituent organizations, which looked in early 1990
like a potentially mass movement, with a
countrywide network of groups and spokespersons at
all levels of government, has now declined in the face
of the gross attacks on living standards, and the
material insecurity being faced in the former GDR.

As Christiane Schindler, UFV spokesperson, put it in
March 1991, the previously unknown experience of
unemployment does not mobilize women; on the
contrary, it demoralizes them. A national meeting of
the UFV in March 1991 also faced internal
disagreements. During 1990 there had been
widespread feelings that the organization was too
intellectual, or that it was dominated by socialists or
younger women at the expense of older women or
those of other political views. At the March 1991
meeting differences over strategy surfaced. There was
disagreement over whether questions of lifestyle, the
articulation of women's needs in terms of personal
autonomy or the right to reproductive choice were
paramount, or whether the need for welfare support
during unemployment, the establishment of more
retraining schemes, and campaigns to maintain child-
care facilities were more pressing in the current
situation.

In addition, women are discovering that access to the media to make their demands heard is not so easy under the new market-dominated conditions. *Für Dich*, the main women's magazine which had become, in the first nine months of 1990 a campaigning forum for the issues of the new women's movement, was involved in a take-over of the massive Berliner Verlag publishing house by Robert Maxwell and the Hamburg-based Gruner & Jahr. The latter presented the editorial collective with a revised concept for the magazine, based on the assumption that 'women all over the world are the same' and that therefore the needs and aspirations of GDR women could be catered for by a magazine identical in content to western women's glossies. The *Für Dich* editorial collective felt that this represented a move to use the market as a veiled form of censorship, since *Für Dich*, with its inferior paper quality and colour reproductions, could not possibly compete with West German women's magazines. Subsequently, in mid 1991 *Für Dich* was closed down, confirming this view.

This fundamental elision of an independent 'voice' for the specific interests of women in the former GDR facing the total economic, social and political transformation of their society, together with the relatively weak and potentially divided women's movement, the low female political representation and the demise of former GDR laws and social policy measures, means that women in the five new German states are not, for the moment, in a position to defend existing rights, let alone extend the agenda of demands.

Perhaps the effects of unification and the extended opportunity to work with existing West German women's groups and trade-union women's sections will alter this balance in the future. Many GDR commentators are also convinced that women in the GDR, who did enjoy some degree of autonomy, choice, and economic independence from men, will not take kindly (unlike women in some of the other central and eastern European countries) to an enforced return home, and will therefore begin to speak out on their own behalf.

The author would like to thank the John D. and Catherine T. MacArthur Foundation in Chicago for their support of this research.

6

Yugoslavia
The transitional spirit of the age

Milica Antic

Area   255 804 km^2.

Population   23.6 million, including 11.3 million women (1981).

Capital   Belgrade is the capital of Yugoslavia (population 1 087 915) although each republic has its own capital.

Languages   Serbo-Croat, Slovene, Macedonian (all official), Albanian, Hungarian.

**Races and
ethnic groups**   The 1981 census showed 24 nations and ethnic groups, eight of which constitute major ethnic groups (over half a million population) although data is usually given only for nationalities with republic status. The single largest national group are the Serbians 36.3 per cent, then Croatian 22.1 per cent, Arab 8.4 per cent, Slovene 8.2 per cent, Albanian 6.9 per cent, Macedonian 5.8 per cent, Montenegrin 2.5 per cent, Hungarian 2.3 per cent, Turk 1 per cent. Albanians (1.73 million) and Hungarians (426 900) are two major national minorities. Muslims are registered as a nationality.

Religions   There are 10 different religions with their own associations. The largest is the Serbian Orthodox Church (approximately 50 per cent, with the Catholic Church primarily in Croatia and Slovenia (30 per cent), and Islam (10 per cent).

Education   Free universal primary school education and eight-year secondary education. In 1990 the total enrolment of women in colleges was 49.1 per cent ranging from 34.9 per cent in Kosovo to 54.8 per cent in Slovenia.

Birth rate   The all-Yugoslav birth rate was 14.3 in 1990 per 1000 population. A breakdown of figures for republics shows that the fastest growing population is in Kosovo (27.8) and the slowest growing populations are in Slovenia (12.5) and Croatia (11.9).

Death rate   The all-Yugoslav death rate was 9.1 in 1990, encompassing a range of 11.3 per 1000 in Croatia to 4.7 per 1000 in Kosovo.

Infant mortality   Infant mortality per 1000 live births calculated as the number of children dying up to one year of age, is 24.3 in Yugoslavia. The highest rate was found in Kosovo (40.6) and the lowest in Slovenia (8.9) in 1990.

Life expectancy   Female life expectancy was 74 years in 1988–89 and
male life expectancy was 69 years.

Currency   Yugoslav dinar (Jan 1992 38.70 = £1.00 sterling)

**Women's
wages as
percentage of
men's**
Women's wage level per 100 dinars of men's wages
was on average 86.9 per cent in 1986. This varies
across republics and sectors of work, with the highest
figure at 93.7 per cent for managerial and administrative
workers in Kosovo (the number of such workers is very
small) and the lowest at 69.3 for manual women
workers in Bosnia and Hercegovina.

**Equal pay
policy**
Statutory since 1946, but lack of literacy limits progress.
Women predominate in lowly paid and low-skilled work
in the service, education and cultural sectors.

**Average
personal
incomes**
In 1990 the Yugoslav average in the state sector was
5603, ranging from 3778 in Kosova to 6702 in Slovenia.

Production   Agriculture: grain, corn, tobacco, sugar beets.

Industry: steel, chemicals, wood products, cement,
textiles, tourism.

**Women as a
percentage of
the labour-force**
Women comprise 39.3 per cent of workers in the
Yugoslav economy. This percentage varies across
republics, from 34 per cent in Slovenia and 31 per cent
in Croatia to 14 per cent in Kosovo.

**Employed
women's
occupational
indicators:**

Percentage of women in various activities in 1988

Industry and mining	37.5
Textiles – as part of industrial sector	81.2
Trade	51.1
Education	59.1
Catering	60.9
Communal services	16.9
Financial services	52.3
Health	74.6

Unemployment
In 1974 unemployment was 9.4 per cent. By 1990 it was
20.7 per cent. In 1987 unemployment was highest in
Kosovo at 57.2 per cent, and lowest in Slovenia at 1.8
per cent.

The 'Age of Transition' is a suitable description of the present-day so-called 'post-socialist' regime in Yugoslavia. This ex-federal state consisted of six republics (Croatia, Bosnia, Montenegro, Macedonia, Slovenia and Serbia), and until 1990 there were two autonomous regions within Serbia (Kosovo and Vojvodina). The complexity of the ex-state makes any representation of Yugoslavia difficult, not least because the political and social divergences between these groups have been increasing at a rapid pace. Serbia and Montenegro have been in favour of a modernized federal system but Slovenia and Croatia have argued for recognition of their own independent states.

Prior to the current political divisions, Yugoslavia had three separate major religions, its inhabitants speaking four main languages, and many ethnic and other minorities with their own distinct languages and religions. The differences between north and south have been easily discerned and richer and poorer parts represent almost separate societies.

On 15 January 1992 the European Community recognized the independence of Slovenia and Croatia. But EC recognition was not given to Bosnia-Hercegovina or to Macedonia, who have also declared their independence, although Macedonia has been recognized by Bulgaria, an act strongly condemned by Greece.

As this work goes to press a fragile ceasefire between Serbia and Croatia has lasted for two weeks.

Despite the current political upheavals there are some trends general to the whole of ex-Yugoslavia that have specific relevance to the position of women. It should also be said that there are difficulties in obtaining specific statistics on women and citing those that are available with confidence.

Background At the end of World War Two the communist-led government of Tito took over the administration of increasingly large areas of liberated territory. The war had taken a massive toll, with over one million of Yugoslavia's 16 million dead. The Federal People's Republic of Yugoslavia (FPRY) was proclaimed on 29 November 1945 and made up of the six federal republics. The elections of 11 November 1949 resulted in a victory for the People's Front, which immediately abolished the monarchy. Later, following the new constitution of 1963 and the Self-Management Law (the name we gave our attempt to make a society without social differences) the state was given a new name – the Socialist Federal People's Republic of Yugoslavia (SFRY). The constitution of 1974 would give autonomy to the regions of Vojvodina (with many ethnic minorities) and Kosovo (with a predominantly Albanian population) as part of the republic of Serbia. Of all these republics only Slovenia was ethnically homogeneous. Immediately after World War Two Yugoslavia modelled its constitution on the federal constitution of the USSR, together with USSR's centrally planned economy.

The split between the USSR and Yugoslavia in 1948 has been seen as one of the most dramatic breaks with Stalin's desire to ensure unquestioned acceptance of his political and ideological authority throughout the communist world. The Yugoslav leadership gave up trying to prove itself truly Stalinist after the failure of the 1949 collectivization. In time, it was decided that the Yugoslav path to socialism lay in the workers' self-management, with some elements of market competition. These changes meant that in principle the commitment to full employment ended. In fact preferences were given to the highly skilled as international competitiveness was introduced in investment and pricing policies.

At the end of the 1960s there was increased decentralization of both economic and political power from the federal authorities to the republics and from the republics to the enterprises. At the beginning of the 1970s there was an attempt to introduce more liberal attitudes between republics and the federal state authorities, but this was brutally stopped, with the leading figures being accused of nationalism and 'technocratic deviation'.

Problems arising from the desire for self-determination on the part of the peoples within Yugoslavia occurred from this time on. The Yugoslav constitution appears to give the republics the right to secession: Article 1 of the first federal constitution of 1946, repeated in a similar form in the 1963 and 1974 constitutions, states that 'Yugoslavia is a community of equal people which, on the basis of self-determination, including the right of secession, have expressed their will to live together in a federal state.' In 1989 the Slovenian Assembly approved an amendment to the Slovenian constitution asserting 'the lasting integral inalienable right of the Slovenian people to self-determination, which includes the right to secession'.

Before the war, Yugoslav communists had placed great emphasis on women working, to prepare them for resistance and revolution. The Anti-Fascist Women's Front (AWF) was established at the end of 1942. During the war this organization helped partisans with food, clothes and other essentials and continued after the war to work under the auspices of the Communist Party. Although these women were partisan and did not look towards feminism, the atmosphere of freedom within the Party generated a mood of self-confidence and optimism about the future. Rada Ivekovic points out that it was during this period that many active women who had previously belonged solely to feminist organizations that focused on women's suffrage, civil rights, rights to work and equal pay, joined the Communist Party (Ivekovic, in Morgan, 1984, p. 737). The rhetoric of 'bourgeois feminists' with contradictory interests to those of 'working class women' was temporarily quietened. It was evident that women from different classes had problems and aims in common. However, although women remained active in political life in the years following the war, the situation did not actually allow for permanent changes in the consciousness of what was, after all, the patriarchal Balkan mentality. Women were again eased back into the home and had increasingly less impact on politics.

The AWF was dissolved in 1953 and the Conference for the Social Role of Women's Activity came into existence. This was a constitutive part of the Socialist Alliance of the Working People (in theory all social organizations had to be within the alliance – a means by which the Party could secure complete control over organizations) and as such was simply a channel for the dissemination of state measures by paid professionals. On the outside of the official organization there were some activists from the old anti-fascist movement with feminist backgrounds who now emerged once again as socialist feminists to become active among progressive women, struggling particularly for freedom of abortion rights.

Political developments

At one time the only subject recognized by the state was the proletariat. It was considered that there were no differences – of interest, party, or class – there were only the interests of the working class. And within this group there were no declared differences. The group was, of course, genderless. Legally women and men enjoyed equal rights, though in practice women had few rights, especially in the field of politics. This is not to decry the social rights women did have (welfare provision, health insurance, close-to-full employment), but all of these rights arose from work; there were almost no rights of citizenship. The dictatorship of 'work and workers' was a sacred institution that veiled the communist party-state.

In the last few years, in the process of changing the old regime, many different political and social groups (national minorities, representatives of conscientious objection, peace movement activists, ecologists, women, writers and poets, punk subculture, youth, etc) arose to demand their particular rights. In 1989 – known as the Slovene Spring – it seemed that the coming period would also bring liberation for many groups. It was a time when many people thought that we were on the best route to establishing a truly modern state. The old system had been outgrown in most parts of Yugoslavia. So we hoped that by establishing democracy we would win the rights of citizenship without further conditions.

The 'new men' who grasped the emptied places of power very soon showed us that these spaces of liberty, scarcely achieved, were in danger again. The new state-power would have liked to narrow the field of what was 'acceptable' and introduce merely a different kind of totalitarian rule. They would have liked to homogenize the people into one nation and one political subject. But, as outlined above, the biggest problem in Yugoslavia has been the diversity of the republics in terms of nationalities, religion and language and the different agendas and demands of different groups. The people of different nationalities are now in conflict because they are not happy with the subjection of their individual or group rights under the rights of the larger 'nation' if that 'nation's' rights do not happen to coincide with their own. Some are unhappy with the subjection of their rights to any nation at all. One of these groups is women.[1]

Women as producers and reproducers – workers and mothers

One unusual feature of post-war Yugoslavia was a labour surplus. This, coupled with the more market oriented economy and no commitment to full employment, meant that women were not encouraged into the labour-market at the same high level as women in neighbouring countries. Yet the Yugoslav, and especially the Slovene, authorities were proud to point out the high percentage of employed women during the socialist period. Although the share of women in the social sector of the labour-force actually fell during the 1950s it gradually grew after 1957. The proportion of women employed in the social sector in Yugoslavia increased from 24 per cent in 1954 to 30 per cent in 1989 – less than most of the other ex-socialist countries.

The percentage of women in the total number of employed persons in 1989 shows that women are employed mostly in health and social welfare, which becomes heavily feminized (75.4 per cent), catering and tourism (60.3 per cent), education and culture (54.7 per cent), and governmental and political organizations (53.5 per cent). A much smaller percentage of women are employed in other sectors such as civil engineering (10.9 per cent), water management (11.2 per cent), forestry (11.9 per cent), housing and other utilities (18.7 per cent) and in industry and mining (37.7 per cent). If we compare republics, Slovenia always had the biggest share of women in the work-force: 33.3 per cent in 1955 and 46.5 per cent in 1989.

As Table 6.1 shows, the proportion of women employed in the social sector differs across republics, from those that are more developed to those with fewer opportunities. Slovenia has the highest percentage, though this figure is increasing only slightly, and Kosovo has the lowest rate.

Table 6.1

Share of women employed in the social sector according to republics and provinces (%)

Republics/provinces	1986	1987	1989	1990 (Mar)
Bosnia–Hercegovina	34.6	35.5	36.2	36.7
Montenegro	35.8	36.8	38.7	39.2
Croatia	41.2	41.7	42.7	42.9
Slovenia	45.9	45.9	46.5	46.7
Macedonia	34.9	35.5	37.3	37.4
Serbia:	36.2	36.9	37.7	38.2
Serbia proper	37.2	37.9	38.9	39.5
Kosovo	22.3	22.6	23.4	23.7
Vojvodina	38.7	39.3	40.1	40.2

(Source: Pesic, 1991, p. 26)

It is apparent that the old division of labour still exists
and there is a concentration of women employed in
'traditional' female activities such as education and
culture, social care, medicine and administration.
This is paralleled by women's employment in
'typical' female sectors of industry such as textiles,
leather, tobacco and printing, which are labour
intensive and low paid. The share of women in
textile production and finished textile products, for
example, was 75 per cent in March 1990, but 69 per
cent in 1973. Similar increases in women's
employment are apparent in the leather, fur and
footwear industries where the percentage rose from
59 per cent in 1973 to 69 per cent in March 1990.
This trend has continued during the 'reform' period,
as the data for 1989 shows.

The socialization of housework

In the early period the planners aimed to take care of
women's work at home by socializing it. They built
big restaurants so that people could have meals
outside the home and so that women would not need
to cook. They established the so-called 'whole-day'
schools and built kindergartens and nurseries.

Table 6.2   **Number of children attending kindergartens and nurseries**

Year	Buildings	Children
1960	942	69915
1965	1236	89316
1970	1756	123215
1975	2436	191427
1980	3430	305735
1985	4242	405396
1986	4397	418191
1987	4481	430378
1988	4491	432494

(Source: author's calculations)

During 1987–88 10 kindergartens/nurseries were
built in the whole country.

Unemployment   During the 1970s and even the 1980s, technically,
unemployment did not exist. We were all so-called
'working people', from doctors to factory workers, or
better still, we were working as part of the Yugoslav
nation. Yet by the late 1970s women's employment
in the social sector had increased only to levels
comparable with western European averages
(approximately 33 per cent) rather than to those of
the high participation countries in eastern and central
Europe and Scandinavia. Statistics on unemployment
collected by the government from the early 1950s
show that since the mid 1960s women have been
more likely than men to be unemployed and less
successful at finding work. As countrywide
unemployment rates rose it seemed that work
associations did not like to employ women:

*Newspaper advertisements for jobs began to specify
'military service completed', to signal that both women and
youth need not apply.* (Wolchick and Meyer, 1985,
p. 245)

As in the Soviet Union, so in Yugoslavia, the
'protective' legislation enacted during the 1970s (the
Associated Labour Acts of 1976 and 1978) was
double edged in its effects on women's lives.
Pregnant women were indeed protected by such
legislation but at the same time the exclusion of
women from a wide range of jobs and activities was
sometimes almost arbitrary, in that they were allowed
to continue to work at other (lesser paid) jobs that
were equally dirty, dangerous or potentially damaging
to their health.

The 1974 constitution recognized the need to
legislate against any discrimination on the basis of
maternity, and from 1978 extensive maternity
benefits were created. Parental leave of between 105
and 210 days (for women or men) is available,[2] along
with free dental and medical care for pregnant
women, and the reduction of an eight-hour day to a
four-hour day on full pay. Women or men can ask

for additional paid leave to care for children. Family allowances continue to be paid if schooling continues.

In practice, with high unemployment rates, it is men rather than women who tend to gain jobs. High unemployment figures among women show that it is often the educated women who cannot find work – those who stay at home for a while after having children find it difficult to get a job to return to, which can mean the end of their career. Similarly, girls tend to be trained into the 'female professions' which are now in less demand. Despite the fact that levels of education are equal for men and women, the rate of girls opting for 'female schools' has not changed in many years. Data on women job seekers shows the effect of this, in that women with a secondary school diploma account for 78.4 per cent of the unemployed. Of these, graduates of secondary librarian school account for 77 per cent, nurses for 86 per cent, those in the catering profession for 71 per cent, teachers for 69.9 per cent, administrative post-secondary school graduates for 59 per cent, social workers (post-secondary) for 83.7 per cent and medical nurses with post-secondary education for 81.7 per cent (Pesic, 1991, p. 15). A similar list can be given for women with university education. Yet such figures often mask high levels of 'hidden' unemployment in rural areas where women's opportunities are less varied and have become even more restricted in recent years.

Marriage and divorce

Marriage is recognized as a secular practice under the protection of the state. Among more highly educated people there are exceptions, but marriage remains traditional in most part of the country. Since 1956 both husband and wife have had the right to a choice of surname, but women generally take the husband's surname.

Divorce is legal. The 1974 constitution and family legislation created divorce by mutual consent and eliminated most 'guilty party' suits. The last available figures are from 1988, when there were 160 419 marriages and 23 127 divorces in Yugoslavia. More divorces occur in the more highly developed republics: in Slovenia 22 per cent of all marriages in 1988; in Serbia 18 per cent; in Croatia 17 per cent. There are fewer divorces in underdeveloped republics: in Montenegro 9.5 per cent; in Bosnia and Hercegovina 5.8 per cent; and in Macedonia 5.2 per cent. Statistics shows that divorce is more frequent both for men and women among the younger generation, those of 20–29 years of age. Divorce tends to happen with the greatest frequency among couples who have been married for between five and nine years or for more than 15 years with either one child or no children. Women generally obtain custody of children.

Women's position in society

Attitudes towards women's position in society have been shifting since the late 1980s. In the revised division of labour women's place is not now considered to be the public work-place. During the period of 'socialism' the term most frequently used to describe a woman was 'working woman'; nowadays it is 'wife' or 'mother'. Suddenly the term 'working woman' has almost entirely disappeared and it is not hard to understand why. The economic situation is fast deteriorating and with the closure of factories many women have lost their jobs. Their exclusion from employment is also occurring in more indirect ways, for example via the introduction of split working hours in branches employing mostly women, or via the so-called 'European working time' (nine to five) without the back-up of social institutions for the performing of domestic tasks. More importantly, the living standards of lower middle-class and working-class people are in constant decline, so that they cannot afford private child-care or help in the house, nor can they afford to eat lunch in restaurants. The worsening economic situation, combined with the new ideology, has led to a situation in which more and more women now stay at home or are attempting to find work in part-time jobs in the private sector.

The exclusion of women from paid employment is only one of the many different routes by which women are expelled from the public sphere and forced once again into the private one – to economic dependence on men and, in the end, to political passivity.

Controlling the family

The family is a very important social institution not only for individuals but for society too. It is, of course, an important ideological apparatus, and it is not difficult to realize why the family has become a political focus. Almost every political party in Slovenia in their election campaigns for the first free election, in April 1990, stressed the importance of the family, and individual parties competed to promise more for family welfare. Of course every new policy needs the support of the family[3] and in the newly arising nation-states in Yugoslavia we can see the attempts of political organizations to have an influence on the family, to determine family shape and to put families into a framework. In Slovenia and Croatia the family is a constitutional subject with its own rights. The draft of the Slovene constitution is written using the male pronoun. Women are mentioned only as mothers, and motherhood is protected by the state.

The creation of a nation-state requires that:

- the family is a natural and moral foundation of the society, and motherhood is a value (exclusion of women from work is therefore normal);

- more children are needed to protect the state from dying out, so the sanctity of life is declared, and accordingly abortion is seen as acting against the sanctity of life;

- members of the nation need to be morally healthy, so that the state does not recognize other patterns of life as equal (the one-parent family, couples without children, lesbian and gay couples, etc).

The family is seen as a homogeneous, unproblematic, monolithic entity which, because of the uncertainty of the economic situation and widely different social circumstances, needs help from society. Political debates go on under the mask of helping children and families but at the same time they impose definite models of family life. It seems that in Slovenia, for example, there is a model of the monogamous nuclear family with two or three children based on the paid public work of men and the unpaid, invisible housework of women.

The family is usually connected with reproduction or population policy and this is one of the reasons why the new ideology is in favour of families. Another reason is that the economically weak state will be unable to provide a full range of social care and must rely on strong family units to provide this in its place. The traditional family pattern is seen as a 'morally pure' pattern of life, and that is exactly what the new nation-state needs. In this view one-parent families, couples without children, lesbian and gay couples, are something unnatural and immoral, and the state will neither encourage them nor treat them equally in legislation.

It has long been apparent that the family can become a site of violence, generally violence against women and children. Independent women's groups started SOS telephone lines for women and children who were victims of violence in order to help those suffering and to 'make violence visible'. The first of these started in big cities like Zagreb, Ljubljana and Belgrade. In Ljubljana the first shelter for women and children experiencing domestic violence has now opened. According to the Belgrade line, a woman is beaten or molested every 15 minutes – in 80 per cent of cases by her husband, former husband or common-law husband. One in four women who called this line complained of being sexually molested by their partner. More than half of the women stated that violence was daily, while 75 per cent claimed that it had gone on for several years.

Controlling the reproduction of the nation

Attitudes towards abortion changed with the 1974 federal constitution in which Article 191 stated that: 'It is a human right freely to decide on family planning. This right may only be restricted for reasons of health.' The individual republics accepted this position and made their own laws in which abortion was available until the end of the tenth week, after which special permission was needed. Despite the law, abortions were often carried out in awful conditions – sheets changed only once a day despite several appointments per bed each day. When, in the mid 1980s, the economic problems started to worsen there began to be a shortage of anaesthetics. Most women had just a local anaesthetic and went back to work after 15 minutes' rest.

As in most of Europe, birth rates are decreasing throughout Yugoslavia. For politicians attempting to establish a nation-state this is a worrying fact, since the establishment of a nation-state requires members of specific nations: Slovenes, Serbs, Croats, Albanians, etc. So politicians in Slovenia try to influence people to increase the numbers of Slovene children, while Serbs or others are undesired. Meanwhile, in Serbia they try to influence the birth rates of Serbs and even to reduce the birth of Albanians. In these circumstances national politicians attempt to encourage 'their women' to give birth to more and more children. Motherhood has thus become highly valued again, as was the case at the end of the nineteenth century, or just at a time when women's reproductive activity had begun to decrease (see Saraceno, 1981).

When in 1989 pro-life campaigns started in Serbia, Croatia and Slovenia it seemed that they were less linked to the dominant religion, although it was clear that the Catholic Church (in Croatia and Slovenia) was still much more concerned with this issue than the Orthodox Church (in Serbia and Macedonia). In Slovenia this is primarily due to the intention to restore 'good old values' such as the home, family, religion, and of course the rise of nationalism. But elsewhere the concern was centred on the nationalist question. One of the basic assumptions of the Yugoslav pro-lifers is that it is necessary to have more

Serbs, Croats, Macedonians, Albanians and so on if, as they put it, we 'want to resist those others' who are 'endangering our very existence as a nation'.

Mothers are valued mainly in terms of intermediating, instrumental values. The 'right nationality' of a woman is likely to result in a new 'citizen' but all children are not equally important – they have to be of the decisive nation whatever that might be. Difficulties with nationality are demonstrated by graffiti in Ljubljana: 'How good it is that I'm not a Serb'; on the walls in Croatia: 'An unborn Croat is a Croat too.' Children are associated with the nation to the extent that they are valued first for the nation, and second as human beings in their own right. The Croatian Democratic Union (a right-wing nationalist party that won the elections in Croatia) ended many of its pre-election meetings with the appeal to its sympathizers to go home and 'make a new Croat'. One of the leaders of the Serbian conservative nationalist party insisted that Serbian women ought to have at least four children, while another leader of the Serbian National Renewal argued during a television discussion that the new Serbian constitution was advocating a 'special war' against Serbs because they had equalized marital and extra-marital relationships. The new Act on the Social Protection of Children passed in Serbia on 26 January 1990 has as its primary purpose the achievement of certain population policy goals. Similarly the Croatian Programme of Economic Policy for 1991 promises the right of early retirement to parents with three or more children, while financial aid is to be given to all families (*Danas*, Zagreb, 9 March 1991). Women's individual rights to decide their own fertility have become subsumed under the individual nations' population goals.

Abortion rights and the sanctity of life

Tied in with these questions is the right to abortion. As noted, women gained the right to abortion with the federal constitution in 1974. Today it is considered as part of the too-liberal socialist legislation of the past, hostile to the new notions of life. According to the author of the preamble to the draft Slovene constitution, every life is 'sancta' and the sanctity of life should not be directly connected with the abolition of abortion rights but should mean a new context of the question of life as a whole (and therefore also the status of the foetus). It is not difficult to see that within this concept the total abolition or certainly the narrowing of the right of abortion is only a question of time. Pro-life movements in Slovenia with Catholic traditions are as strong as they are in Croatia, where their constitution has a clause concerning the provision of the conditions for promoting the right to life of every unborn child.

All this opens large possibilities for the state to intervene directly in this sphere of women's autonomy. It is likely that abortion will be allowed only in certain cases, for medical or social reasons decided upon by a committee of doctors and social-policy workers. So the issue of abortion is inextricably linked both with nationalists' desires to keep their own population growing, and with religious beliefs.

It is pointless to argue that the economic collapse, increasing unemployment and attendant poverty are not ideal conditions in which to encourage women to give birth to more children. In Yugoslavia the long-lasting economic crisis, combined with a strong, and sometimes completely uncritical drive towards marketization and privatization, puts women in a terrible economic situation. As previously outlined women are employed in low-profit industries, such as the textile and garment industries, leather and shoe industries, and in the lower levels of administration. These areas of employment are the first to suffer from the economic changes not just in Yugoslavia but in all the former communist countries. The percentage of women among the so-called 'technological surplus' is much higher than their percentage in the total employee population, and women were among the first to lose their jobs.

However, the return of women to the home fits well
with nationalistic desires for more children and with
the prevailing notion that this absence of women
from the home has engendered a moral crisis that
can be resolved by a return to the traditional
family.

**Women as
decision
makers –
participation
and
representation**

In all the republics there were the first 'democratic
and free' elections in 1990 and in all parts the winners
were nationalists – in Serbia and in Montenegro
communist nationalists and in other parts non- or
anti-communist nationalists. And in each case the
leaders wanted to establish nation-states.

What has happened with women in the transition
from the central communist leadership to the nation-
states? In certain parts it seemed that the coming
period might bring liberation for many social
minorities and marginalized groups, not least women.
But a widespread fascination with the process of
democratization turned into disappointment with
democracy, which barely yet exists. The interests of
so-called 'social minorities' were proclaimed to be
less important than the interests of the newly-arising
nation-state. Women's issues are considered to be, yet
again, less important than questions about the survival
of the nation, national protection and security, the
need for armies, and other such issues. Therefore, the
problems of women, the 'largest minority', within
the establishment of a new democracy have been
ignored. Women's marginalization as political
subjects jeopardizes the 'process of democratization'.

Political parties in general have barely given women
any attention. They did nothing to become more
attractive to women members, nor did they
strengthen the position of women in party
leaderships. In quite a number of their manifestos one
can find no sections about women's issues, and there
are no policies regarding equal opportunities or equal
status. Women figure only as an electoral body and
are not seen as political subjects but as apolitical
beings who do not have their own opinions about
politics and are too emotional to be involved in

policy making. This is despite the fact that a recently conducted survey in Slovenia revealed that women mostly have their own opinions about politics, are informed about political affairs, and are very rational about political life.

In the first 'democratic and free elections' women were losers. Formally, there were no obstacles to the participation of women in the elections but neither the parties nor the electoral law incorporated any mechanism to enable or encourage the greater involvement of women as candidates. They were very poorly represented in the lists of candidates: in Slovenia 18.4 per cent were women, in Croatia 6 per cent, in Montenegro 6.4 per cent, in Bosnia 5.5 per cent, in Macedonia 5.4 per cent and in Serbia 5.0 per cent. Even fewer were elected. Throughout the whole of Yugoslavia there are now 63 (4.4 per cent) female and 1272 (95.6 per cent) male MPs. It is clear that politics is still considered to be a man's affair and there is very little concern about the inequality of this so-called democratic representation. In Slovenia and Serbia there were independent women's lists but no women were elected.

Women's activity in present-day Yugoslavia

Many women in Yugoslavia were far from satisfied with this train of events and some have decided to become more organized, particularly in the bigger cities such as Ljubljana, Zagreb and Belgrade. Campaigns vary from women's aid groups, to women in Belgrade whose dissatisfaction with the elections has encouraged them to create their own parliament. Different women's initiatives in Serbia, Slovenia and Croatia have taken a stand against nationalism. And a Yugoslav-wide umbrella organization of women's groups has been co-ordinated, replacing that of the former Party. What follows is a regional survey of these activities.

Zagreb There are various groups in Zagreb including a feminist group which emerged from the earlier feminist initiative launched in 1978 at a meeting in Belgrade with women from all over Yugoslavia. The Sociological Association of Croatia has its women's section called Women and Society, which is very active. Women in Zagreb have had an SOS telephone for four years and their experiences were very useful for women in Ljubljana and Belgrade in starting their own SOS service. There are several unique groups in Zagreb, including the Independent Women's Association started in April 1990 as an all-Yugoslav umbrella group. The political situation, however, has made it extremely difficult for the association to work on all-Yugoslav issues, so it has now become more centred on Croatia. Issues taken up range from the problems for women wanting to start small businesses to 'pro-choice' campaigns and the advocation of abortion rights in an area where these are becoming increasingly restricted. There was an important event in Zagreb in spring 1991 when a *zenski sabor* (women's gathering) took place with more than 500 women in Zagreb protesting about the policy towards women as outlined in the new constitution. This was the first time that such a large group of women had got together to question the democratic character and policies of the new government.

Belgrade In October 1989 a group of concerned citizens, mostly professionals – sociologists, physicians and lawyers – with some activists, tried to organize a campaign against the 'pro-lifers' to keep freedom of abortion for women. The feminist group 'Women and Society' also launched a campaign. These groups then started to work together and formed the basis of the Belgrade Women's Lobby, created in the spring of 1990. The lobby included women from different progressive political parties and groups including the Association for Yugoslav Democratic Initiatives, the Social Democratic League for Serbia-Yugoslavia, and the Green Party. Approximately 20 to 30 women gathered each week and organized discussions about reproductive rights, political representation, the different party programmes and how to relate these to women's issues. The lobby also included women from the SOS telephone (founded in March 1990). (The whole issue of violence against women is very important and phone lines are now being set up in smaller towns modelled on those in Zagreb, Belgrade and Ljubljana.) This lobby then made two petitions to the Serbian Parliament against the new restrictive laws and regulations on demographic policy which made explicit differences between Albanians and Serbs, discriminating against Albanian women wishing to have more children, and encouraging Serbian women to have more. The lobby succeeded in stopping the legislation and both proposals were 'frozen'.

On 8 March 1991 the first session of the Women's Parliament of Serbia was called. Fourteen parties were invited to take part by the initiators, the feminist group, women's lobby, Women's Party (ZEST) and the SOS telephone organizers. There were 150 women at the first Parliament and a praesidium was constituted with independent representatives and one representative from all parties and groups involved in its formation. A number of initiatives were decided on, dealing with the social and economic position of women, their rights, and reproductive rights. The SOS telephone lines were able regularly to publish information for women and a feminist group co-ordinated the publishing of a small journal, *The Feminist Newspaper*.

Ljubljana Again there are many women's groups. The first one emerged at the beginning of the 1980s as part of the Sociological Association. This was followed by the establishment of a women's club, 'Lilit' that fostered an active lesbian group. A few years ago the club started an SOS telephone line which has grown to three different SOS telephones and a refuge for women and children. Very soon after the election a group called 'Initiative', campaigning for equal opportunities, emerged from the women's list. This group has repeatedly advertised the unequal treatment of women and men in legislation and in other social organizations. Women are trying to organize inside certain oppositional parties to improve women's position within them, such as the ex-Communist Party in Slovenia. In April 1990, a pressure group 'Women for Politics' was formed and their programme is written in the form of demands addressed to relevant institutions and political leaders. The group organized, in June 1990, a well-attended colloquium with the theme 'Women–Politics–Family'. The participants pointed out the unacceptability of the idea of families as natural social cells and exposed the ways in which the new political rulers want to impose a 'suitable family pattern', the traditional notion of public men and private women. They criticized the draft of the new constitution favouring the family based on marriage and the disregarding of other social units. Finally they opposed the claims for the abolition of abortion and joined the demands for the equal treatment of homosexuals within the constitution. A group of women with some help from certain oppositional parties managed to establish a parliamentary committee for women's issues. The committee members include women MPs as well as professionals on women's issues (sociologists, psychologists, philosophers, historians) and representatives from different women's groups. This committee does offer some opportunities for the political articulation of women's specific issues but, despite all requests, there is no women's ministry to which the committee can address initiatives, demands, or suggestions concerning women.

Conclusion

The new 'democracy' in Yugoslavia has not succeeded where women's rights are concerned. The election results were the first real reflection of what is actually going on. The low rate of engagement of women in political life is due to well-known factors: besides having little time, women are now much more afraid that they will lose their jobs; and it has always been difficult to reach peasant women, not only because they lack education, but because the patriarchal culture in which they live discourages them from being involved in politics.

Often women see politics as a male activity and men do not discourage this view. Politics in this transitional period, with fierce struggles for power, has been a very dirty business. Women find this alien and have remarked that the women's meetings have been much less tense, with higher levels of discussion, than meetings of the political parties. It is important to remember that it is not only in Parliament that women are marginalized but that very few women are members of any party's leadership. Women involved in women's groups are seldom prepared to get involved in 'dirty' party politics, quite apart from the fact that they are given little incentive to do so.

The worsening of the economic situation means women have already begun to lose any gains they may have achieved in previous decades. They are among the first to lose their jobs and they are being pressurized by their individual state governments into having more children in circumstances of increased poverty. Their rights to work, to be represented, to control their own reproduction, are under threat. The significant rise in unemployment for women is convenient for the nationalists, providing a 'convincing' ideological cover story, that is (as one feminist commentator has put it):

women have to stay at home, be good mothers and raise children. The society is living in not only an economic but also a moral crisis. One of the main reasons for this is that women were outside their homes. A moral renewal is only possible if we turn them back where they belong. (Licht, 1991, p. 3)

Sometimes it is difficult to believe that on the threshold of the twenty-first century this conservative attitude prevails in central and eastern Europe, but we have to face the truth.

The author would like to thank Chris Corrin and
Sonja Licht for added help with this chapter. A
shorter version first appeared in 'Shifting Territories:
Feminism and Europe', *Feminist Review*, no. 39,
autumn 1991.

Notes

1   Women are not a homogeneous, unproblematic subject or
     category, as D. Riley writes (1988).

2   It would be useful and interesting to be able to present
     figures here about this process, but as events are shifting
     daily so the data is hard to collect.

3   For further details about ruling with the family see
     Donzelot (1979).

7

Russia and the former Soviet republics
Behind the mask of Soviet unity: realities of women's lives

Hilary Pilkington

Figures are for 1989 unless stated otherwise.

Area
2 403 000 km^2, of which the RSFSR (Russian Soviet Federal Socialist Republic) covers 17 075 400 km^2.

Population
285.6 million including 151.4 million (52.8 per cent) women.

Population density
0.78 per km^2.

Capital
Moscow was the capital of the USSR although each republic – except the RSFSR – had its own capital. Minsk has become the formal centre of the current Commonwealth of Independent States although it is unlikely that this state of affairs will be long lived and Moscow effectively remains the centre of power.

Urban population
In 1989, 66 per cent of Soviet citizens lived in towns or cities (as compared to 48 per cent in 1959). Levels of urbanization differ regionally, ranging from 74 per cent in the RSFSR to 33 per cent in Tadzhikistan. In general the Slavic and Baltic republics are more urbanized than the all-union average while the Transcaucasian and Central Asian republics (except Armenia) are less urbanized than average.

Languages
Over 200 languages are spoken by the peoples of the former USSR, with 39 being used in education as the primary means of instruction. Russian remains the official language of international communication but most republics have now adopted the language of their titular nationality as the official language for government business.

Races and ethnic groups
The 1989 census showed 102 nations and ethnic groups, 22 of which constitute major ethnic groups (over 1 million population), although data is usually given only for the 15 nationalities with Union Republic status. The single largest national group is the Russians who constitute 50.78 per cent of the total population. Ethnic tension is exacerbated by the fact that the federal structure of the USSR provided for a union of *republics* not *peoples* and that the assignation of territorial status (republic, autonomous oblast', autonomous area, etc) was not coincident with the size of the national

population. The new Commonwealth of Independent States has as yet addressed few of the outstanding problems of population and territory and future disputes are likely to emerge over issues of borders, territories and the rights of ethnic minorities in the newly independent states. Russia was referred to as the RSFSR in the Soviet Union because it contained a number of autonomous republics and territories within its borders. Although now the RSFSR has become 'Russia', these territories remain and are already beginning to demand their independence.

Religions

There is no state religion in the USSR and atheism has been promoted by the state since the revolution, so precise statistics on religious believers are difficult to find. There are over 40 different religions with their own associations in the former USSR. The largest ones are: the Russian Orthodox Church; the Muslims, the majority being Sunnite followers; the Catholic Church, primarily in Lithuania but also in the western Ukraine, Belorussia and Latvia; Judaism – the Jews are considered a national group in the USSR and so appear in census figures – currently about 1.5 million Jews; Evangelical Christians, or Baptists, over half a million; and Buddhism – a variant of Tibetan Buddhism is practised in the Buryat, Tuva and Kalmyk autonomous republics.

Education

Free, universal primary school education was introduced in the Soviet Union in the 1930s, universal eight-year education in the 1950s and universal secondary education in the 1970s. Generally women are slightly better educated than men: women currently constitute 61 per cent of specialists with higher or secondary specialized education (1988) and 54 per cent of students in higher educational establishments.

Birth rate

The all-union birth-rate is 17.6 births per 1000 population. This is a growth rate of 7.6 per 1000 population. A breakdown of figures for national groups (as opposed to republics) shows that the fastest growing nationalities are the Tadzhiks, Kirghiz, Uzbeks and Turkmenians (all with a natural growth of over 30) and that the slowest growing nationalities are Latvians,

Ukrainians and Russians (natural population growth of 1.5–2.5).

Death rate The all-union death rate is 8.8 per 1000 population encompassing a range from 12.1 per 1000 in Latvia to 6.0 per 1000 in Armenia.

Infant mortality Infant mortality is calculated as the number of children dying up to one year of age per 1000 live births and the average rate in the former USSR is 22.3. The highest rates are found in the central Asian republics (with Turkmenia recording the highest rate at 54.2) and the lowest rate is in Lithuania at 10.7.

Life expectancy Female life expectancy is 73.6 years (for rural women it is 72.8 years and for urban women it is 73.9 years). Male life expectancy is 64.8 years.

Currency The official currency of the Soviet Union has been the rouble which until recently exchanged with the pound sterling at an official rate of 1:1. Since its flotation by the Russian President Boris Yeltsin its value has plummeted and at the time of going to press (January 1992) it was exchanging at 160:1. It is expected that during the course of 1992 most of the former republics will introduce their own currencies.

Equal pay policy Since 1917 women have had the right to receive equal pay for equal work and this right is embodied in Article 35 of the constitution.

Women's wages as a percentage of men's Women on average earn around 70 per cent of what men earn although this figure rises to 80–85 per cent for professional women and decreases to around two-thirds for manual women workers.

Production The Soviet Union was self-sufficient in food and energy production. It was the world's largest producer of oil, gas, steel, iron and non-ferrous ores, metal-cutting, machine tools and tractors, and 80 per cent of its hard currency export earnings came through the export of oil and gas. Principal crops produced by the USSR were grain, sugar beet and potatoes. The USSR traditionally conducted most trade with other members of the Council for Mutual Economic Aid (socialist countries) although it steadily increased trading with western countries. Although the former Soviet republics are now actively seeking trading partners outside the former Soviet bloc they are likely to remain highly dependent on Russian trade, especially in the area of raw materials and energy supplies.

Women as a percentage of the labour-force

Women comprise 50.9 per cent of workers and white-collar workers in the Soviet economy. This percentage varies across the republics from 54 per cent in Estonia and Latvia to 39 per cent in Tadzhikstan and 41 per cent in Turkmenistan. Women also comprise 45 per cent of collective farm workers (from 38 per cent in Kazakhstan and 40 per cent in the RSFSR to 55 per cent in Uzbekistan). It is estimated that 4.5–5 million women are unpaid family workers usually looking after children at home.

Employed women's occupational indicators

The percentage of women in various branches of the economy

Communications:	69
telegraphists	99
postal workers	88
Trade and public catering:	82
shop-workers	91
cooks	86
waiters/waitresses	84
Public service workers:	71
cleaners	94
Industrial workers:	44
seamstresses	99
weavers	98
assemblers of electrical goods	84
Construction:	14
painters and decorators	72
plasterers	63
auxiliary workers	44
Information, computing and accounting workers	81
Cultural sphere workers	72

Unemployment

The traditional definition of 'unemployment' (*nezaniatnost'*) includes all those who are capable of work but not employed in social production. Such people currently number 13 million, and it is estimated that more than one-third of these are women involved in housework and bringing up children. There is, however, growing concern over structural unemployment (*bezrabotitsa*), which is nearer to the western definition. There are as yet no reliable figures broken down according to gender, although figures from newly formed labour exchanges suggest that up to 80 per cent of those registering with them as unemployed are women.

Introduction: the politics of equality

Since this chapter was written the disintegration of central power in the USSR finally led to the formal dissolution of the Soviet Union when Mikhail Gorbachev resigned on 25 December 1991 and the Soviet Parliament voted its approval the following day. The formal end of the so-called Soviet system makes even more timely a study of the social, political and cultural relations which underscored the Soviet period, the changes which led to its collapse and the prospects for women in the new independent states.

There has been no vacuum of information on the position of women in the Soviet Union. On the contrary, a significant amount of important and interesting work has already been done, and will be referred to throughout this chapter. The problem for those studying the experience of Soviet women is using this large body of information in a way that will really aid understanding of just what this experience has been. In particular, readers of the existing material on Soviet women should bear in mind that the aim of those writing has generally been to explore the 'politics of equality' by looking at the 'Soviet model'. What is meant by the 'Soviet model' is the existence of a number of socio-economic and political conditions which are seen to be different from those pertaining in modern capitalist societies. These are: social or state ownership (as opposed to private

ownership) of the means of production; state mobilization or intervention, as opposed to *laissez-faire*, in the social sphere; and utopian rather than pragmatic world outlooks. Scholars of the Soviet Union have tried to illuminate our understanding of sexual equality by comparing and contrasting the experience of women living in very different social conditions from those in which they, and the majority of their readers, live. The 'politics of equality' project itself has been a lesson in the politics of 'equality' for a number of reasons.

First, 'equality' must, by nature, be relational, yet it is rarely stated against whom the equality of Soviet women is being measured. The emphasis on the specifics of the Soviet 'model' or 'system' often suggests a comparison with women in other developed societies, and the position of women is seen as a category that can be used to analyse what is perceived to be an alternative modernization model. This in-built notion of what a modern society looks like means that there is a tendency to use indicators such as women's conformity or non-conformity to traditional gender roles to define the degree of women's emancipation, or the level of 'modernization' achieved by Soviet society. This is clearly dangerous, since it ignores the cultural context in which women act and pre-defines what 'emancipation' is for all women.

Official Soviet publications have approached the equality debate by comparing the position of Soviet women to the relative position of women in traditional societies. Here the emphasis is laid on the gains made by women thanks to the modernization programme of the Soviet state and, therefore, once again pre-judges what constitutes social 'development' or 'progress', and tends to focus on the benefits reaped by women from a benevolent state rather than viewing women as makers of their own history.

Another variation has been to measure the degree of women's equality in relation to the position of men

in the same society (Holland, 1985). This demands a more contextual exploration of women's experience in Soviet society and in so doing raises two important questions that have been underplayed in existing work. First, it raises the problem of the gap between the formal rights of women and their actual experience. We are then forced to consider, how can we measure equality in society? Second, it raises the problem of the relationship between the politics of gender and the politics of class and race. In other words, when we compare the position of men and women in Soviet society, which women are being compared to which men?

That 'equality' itself is a political term is revealed, secondly, in the emergence of a fourth measure of Soviet women's equality that is not generally applied in other societies. This is the 'ideological yardstick' used to measure the position of women in Soviet society against the claims made by the revolutionary project. Gail Warshofsky Lapidus, for example, makes it her explicit aim to show how the Soviet effort to alter women's roles was just one dimension of an overall strategy for facilitating the seizure and consolidation of power by a revolutionary movement and for enhancing the economic and political capacity of the new regime (Lapidus, 1978). This premise is shared by Mary Buckley in her detailed exploration of ideology on women in the Soviet Union. She concludes that Soviet ideology on women has been tailored to the needs of different periods of Soviet history, as defined by their political leaderships (Buckley, 1989). Crude or reductionist examples of this approach assume a single, ideologically consistent policy around which women have been mobilized or manipulated throughout Soviet history, but even sophisticated approaches, such as those mentioned above, tend towards viewing women as objects of state ideology and policies which lends the state too great a role in the definition of gender relations at the expense of other crucial sites of oppression.

The third and final question that must be raised when using existing material on women in the Soviet Union concerns the category of 'women' itself. In western work on Soviet women, the assumption that women form a cohesive social group has largely been a result of the fact that 'women' are taken as a case study for the exploration of social relations in a different 'political system' (Scott, 1976). In Soviet work the unitary concept of women has traditionally stemmed from the ideological refutation of the existence of other specific and conflicting interests, such as class or ethnic interests, which might either cut across or reinforce common interests between women. In Soviet work women have been seen to have specific interests as a result of their peculiar position in society as well as their peculiar psychology – which may be expressed through gender-specific strategies to draw women into the general movement for the common good. Women are not seen to have separate end goals. This is inevitable unless some notion of patriarchy is employed. The absence of this explanatory tool is often also a failing of western approaches and can lead to extremely economistic readings of the oppression of Soviet women. By this is meant an explanation of women's oppression arrived at by referring to women as the victims of state mobilization policies which move them in and out of the labour-force according to the demands of the Soviet economy. One such example is the approach taken by Richard Sakwa, where this end result is particularly ironic since the intention of the author is precisely to critique traditional Marxist (and economistic) approaches to the 'woman's question' (Sakwa, 1989). In fact, of course, women are not a unitary category: the 'Soviet model', if we can talk of such a thing, has been experienced very differently by women depending on their ethnic origin and their social and economic background and position.[1]

This chapter sets out to provide an account not of the 'Soviet model' focusing on the state (and its policy towards women), but of women's lives and experiences. These experiences are gathered by women in their daily lives as producers, reproducers and decision makers. Although these spheres will be explored in isolation, individual women will rate their experiences in each area differently, and each area will be more or less important to how they perceive the whole of their life. In the final section the focus will be on how women construct their own identities as women on the basis of their life experiences and the images of women with which they are confronted. Women are not taken to be a unitary category, but the confines both of space and of cultural and linguistic expertise inevitably mean that the term 'Soviet women' in fact will signify women of Russian or other Slavic nationality, and the experiences referred to will be largely those of urban women. Where cultural specificities, urban–rural divides, and 'class' differences are particularly prominent, however, attention will be drawn to them.

Women as producers and reproducers – workers and mothers

Women and men have equal rights in the USSR. The implementation of these rights is ensured by granting women equal opportunities with men to receive education and professional training, equal rights at work including payment and promotion at work, in social and political and cultural activity as well as by special measures to protect the labour and health of women; the creation of conditions allowing women to combine work and motherhood; legal protection, material and moral support of motherhood and childhood, including the granting of paid leave and other privileges to pregnant women and mothers, the gradual reduction of working time of women with young children.

This is how the equality of women and men is set out in Article 35 of the Soviet constitution. But how have women experienced this 'equality'?

It has often been observed that workers in the Soviet Union are guaranteed the right to work by Article 40 of the constitution, but that they are also obliged to work (Article 60). Those who do not fulfil their obligation become liable to prosecution for 'parasitism'. In this way, for the individual, the 'right' to work cannot be separated from the 'obligation' to work and is thus experienced not as a freedom from unemployment but as a duty imposed from above. For women, the merging of rights and obligations is even more explicit, and is qualitatively different. As we see from Article 35 of the constitution above, women's 'rights' and 'duties' extend beyond the productive sphere and into the reproductive sphere. Women's equal right to work is established not in Article 40, which guarantees all Soviet citizens the right to work, but in a separate article which links their rights and obligations as workers with their rights and obligations as mothers. Unlike in western capitalist countries, therefore, women's participation in the work-force has confronted a high politics of combination, not of choice. For individual Soviet women, this has meant that the realization of Engels's first condition for the emancipation of women – the bringing of women into social production – has been experienced not as liberation but as a dual oppression. It is aspects of this experience that are outlined below.

Women at work in the national economy

The Soviet Union has encouraged women into the national economy more successfully than any other nation-state. In 1989 women comprised 50.9 per cent of the work-force in the national economy – even in Central Asia where 'vestiges of the past' have been most resistant to the Bolshevik modernization programme, women now constitute around 40 per cent of the work-force. The Soviet Union has also been successful in promoting the education of women. In 1988, 61 per cent of specialists with higher or specialized secondary education were women and 54 per cent of the student population were women: this is double the percentage in 1928 and in world terms it puts the USSR behind only Mongolia (63 per cent) and Sweden (56 per cent), and significantly above Britain (40 per cent) and the USA (51 per cent).[2]

Women have experienced their involvement in social production as unliberating, though, for two main reasons. First their work itself has been of a nature which demands little personal involvement and initiative. Women have been integrated into the labour-force in a way that has allowed them to become ghettoized in low-pay, low-prestige areas of the economy traditionally referred to as the 'non-productive' industries. These areas of work have tended to be those posited to be closest to 'women's nature', e.g. public services, textile and garment-making industries, communications and the 'caring' professions such as nursing, teaching and nursery-care. This process is referred to below as the 'horizontal structuring' of the labour-market. Second, women's experience of the 'combination' of roles of mother and worker has not been a liberating one in which they might choose different life patterns involving either or both of these 'roles'. On the contrary, it has been an oppressive experience, obliging women to perform both roles with little help from either the state or their partners. This can be seen, to some extent, as a result of the failure to implement Engels's second condition for the emancipation of women, i.e. the socialization of child-care and domestic labour. It is also due to the failure to promote a re-evaluation of traditional male roles so that home-based labour might be equally shared between parents/partners. The effects of this can be seen in the psychological and physical exhaustion of women in Soviet society and is reflected in the labour-market in the relatively low achievement of women in progressing to work that is either better paid, more suited to their training, or that has better working conditions. This is referred to as 'vertical structuring'.

Horizontal structuring of the labour-market

Despite images of women tractor drivers defying gender stereotypes, in fact the horizontal structuring of the Soviet labour-market by gender is very familiar (see Table 7.1).

Table 7.1   **Percentage of women in the national economy by sector**

Sector of the economy	Percentage of women in 1989
Industry	44
Agriculture:	
State farms	36
Collective farms	45
Communications	69
Construction	14
Transport	20
Trade and public catering	82
Municipal housing	41
Consumer services provision	71
Credit and state insurance	82
Health, physical education and social insurance	81
Information and computing	81
Public education	75
Culture	72

(Source: *Statisticheskii Press-biulleten,* no. 13, Informatsionno-izdatel'skii Tsentr, 1990, p. 13; and *Narodnoe Khoziaistvo SSSR v 1989,* Goskomstat SSSR, 1990, p. 54)

Even within branches of the economy there is a second-level process of horizontal structuring that channels women into specific jobs, such that virtually all cleaners, telephonists and sales staff are women, whereas there are very few women fitters and machine operators (see Table 7.2).

Table 7.2 **Percentage of women in specific occupations**

Occupation	Percentage of women in 1989
Telephonists, telegraphists	99.3
Textile workers (seamstresses, weavers)	96.9
Cleaners	93.4
Shop workers	90.6
Packers	80.2
Cooks, waitresses, bar workers	84.8
Accountants, information technologists	73.7
Assemblers	71.3
Painters, decorators, plasterers	68.1
Casual labourers	43.7
Machine operators	18.3
Fitters	7.3

(Source: *Statisticheskii Press-biulleten*, no. 13, Informatsionno-izdatel'skii Tsentr, 1990, p. 29)

These figures clearly indicate that the gender division of the labour-market is as strong in Soviet society as it is in other industrialized and industrializing societies. Although Soviet women's experiences have differed in as much as they have been wholeheartedly encouraged to participate in social production, nonetheless they share the experience of women elsewhere in the world in seeing the transposition of the supposed 'natural' sexual division of labour from the private to the public sphere. This is not to suggest that this division of labour does not also continue to exist within the home – even opening a bottle of wine can cause serious disruptions of such norms, since this is apparently *muzhskoe delo* ('a man's job').

The failure to disrupt the gendered division of labour is not surprising since, despite the Bolsheviks' undoubted commitment to women's participation in the labour sphere, Bolshevik ideology was infused with essentialist misconceptions about the form such participation should take. Post-revolutionary state policy, based as it was on the work of Marx, Engels and Lenin, emerged as a combination of: paternalism – that the state should protect women by prohibiting their work in industries specifically injurious to their health or reproductive capacity; and the gender division of labour – that women should be especially encouraged into production and distribution of food and state-run child-care facilities since this would be, according to Lenin, a 'continuation of motherhood' (Lenin, 1965).

The horizontal structuring of the labour-force along gender lines cannot then be reduced to a return to conservative role models under Stalin, but began in the immediate post-revolutionary period. Women were drawn into the labour-force most actively in the areas of medical and cultural services, children's nurseries, trade enterprises and restaurants – indeed the increase in employment in the sphere of direct servicing of people was accounted for almost solely by women (Gruzdeva and Chertikhina, 1987). While this in itself need not deny the possibility of 'equality through difference', the prioritization of heavy industry (Group A industries) during the first five-year plan also established a differentiation in remuneration between branches of industry (see Table 7.3).

From this it is evident that in those areas where women were under-represented wages were higher than the average, but where women formed the majority of the work-force wages were below the national average. Furthermore it is clear that this trend, already evident by the beginning of World War Two, was to become even more solidly entrenched in the post-war period. A new importance was accorded to the 'feminized' service and consumer industries, the so-called 'non-productive' spheres of the economy, in the switch from the extensive to the intensive economy. By 'extensive' economy is meant an economy which is growing by expanding its material base (and thus requiring more inputs in order to increase output) and by 'intensive' is meant an economy which is improving its output by making more efficient use of the given inputs through technical innovation. The Soviet Government officially declared its intention to switch from the former to the latter type of economic strategy in the mid-1970s. As a result, in the period 1970–80, the wage rates and salaries of workers in a number of non-productive branches of the economy were increased, and by the mid 1970s wages began to grow faster in a number of branches of the economy where female labour was concentrated.[3] Despite this, the gap between the average wage of workers in industry and those in the non-productive sphere is not narrowing but growing – in those branches of the non-productive sphere, which are characterized by the greatest concentration of female labour, the absolute growth in the average monthly money wage has been accompanied by a relative decline (Gruzdeva and Chertikhina, 1987).

Vertical structuring of the labour-market

The second problem confronted by women workers concerns even more directly the demands made on them to combine their roles as producers and

Table 7.3 **Wages as a proportion of the national average wage in feminized and non-feminized sectors of the economy**

Branch of economy	Percentage of women in 1940	Wages (100 = national average)	Percentage of women circa 1985	Wages (100 = national average)
Industry as a whole	38	103	44	111
Transport	21	105	19	117
Construction	23	110	15	124
Trade, catering	40	75–100	82	71
Public health	76	75–100	81	73
Education	59	75–100	75	79

(Source: adapted from Gruzdeva and Chertikhina, *Narodnoe Khoziaistvo SSSR v 1987; Statisticheskii Press-biulleten,* no. 13, Informatsionno-izdatel'skii Tsentre, 1990, p. 29)

reproducers: women's additional obligations mean that they do not progress in their careers at an equal rate to men. This vertical structuring of the labour-market by gender manifests itself in two principal ways: the absence of women in top management positions, and the unequal proportion of women involved in manual work. Although in 1988, 61 per cent of specialists (workers with higher or specialized secondary education) were women, it is estimated that 40 per cent of male specialists are employed in the highest grades compared with only 10 per cent of women specialists. Furthermore whereas 48 per cent of men with higher education hold managerial jobs, only 7 per cent of women do. Indeed, under perestroika, the tendency appears to be towards a worsening of the situation. In 1989 women comprised just 5.6 per cent of directors of enterprises and organizations – marking a reduction from 6.9 per cent in 1985. In the Transcaucasian republics the number of women directors is virtually negligible – less than 1 per cent in Armenia and between 1 and 2 per cent in Azerbaidzhan and Georgia. Even in the industries and professional areas dominated by women the vertical occupational structure ensures that women always remain at the bottom of the ladder. In the teaching profession, for example, in 1988–89 women constituted 74 per cent of teachers but only 39 per cent of secondary school head teachers. While at the very top of the academic ladder, of 309 academicians there are only three women. At the other end of the employment ladder women are also left to do the most menial and physically demanding tasks. Although the Soviet Union has had a long-term commitment to the mechanization of labour – the aim is to phase out the lowest class of work (purely manual labour) and increase the number of workers employed in mental work or mental/manual labour – this process seems to have been weighted primarily towards the ending of male manual work (see Table 7.4).

Table 7.4   **Proportion of women and men involved in manual labour**

Sector of economy	% workers using machinery	% workers doing manual work	% workers repairing machinery
Industry:			
women	55.0	43.3	1.7
men	50.7	26.4	22.9
Construction:			
women	25.5	73.9	0.6
men	49.6	44.1	6.3
Agriculture (state farms):			
women	21.3	78.6	0.1
men	37.7	54.6	7.7

(Source: *Statisticheskii Press-biulleten*, no. 13, Informatsionno-izdatel'skii Tsentre, 1990, p. 29)

Although much recent discussion has concerned the continuation of women's work in professions seen as injurious to their health such as road-laying and repairing, dock work, cement work, etc, it is the plight of women agricultural workers that is probably the most acute. Since the late 1950s women have never formed more than 1 per cent of Soviet agricultural machine operators and so dairying remains the archetypal form of women's work on Soviet farms. Much of this work is still done by hand, and the work is highly unsocial – since milking is done in the USSR three times a day, women are on call from before dawn until late at night. Although the wages are high, workers in dairying have less free time than any other category of employees in either agriculture or industry. Soviet agricultural labourers are almost exclusively female: in arable farming, market gardening and fruit farming 98 per cent of manual workers are women. Field workers are employed for long hours in monotonous, arduous jobs and at the lowest wages. In addition, the poor provision of basic amenities and services makes housework considerably more complicated and time consuming than in the towns. The lack of mains water supply and public transport combined with a long working day as well as additional private allotment work, necessary in order to provide basic foodstuffs for family consumption, mean that rural women have less than half the free time of women in the towns (Bridger, 1987).

Women's experience of the labour-market

If we bring these statistics down to the level of women's everyday lives their significance becomes apparent. First, the horizontal and vertical structuring of the labour-market in the Soviet Union makes a mockery of the formal commitment of the Soviet Government to equal pay. Surveys in the city of Taganrog showed that the ratio between the average wages of men and of women is approximately 3:2. It was calculated from this that any wage differential due to differences in the sphere of employment (horizontal structuring) accounted for 15 per cent of the discrepancy, the rest being the result of women's unequal opportunity for promotion as a result of their worker–mother role (vertical structuring). The root cause of unequal payment for labour, though, is not uniform for all women. For those women working in occupations involving auxiliary, unspecialized manual labour of the industrial type such as unskilled labourers and cleaners, the cause was identified as men's higher 'material compensation premium' which is awarded for the greater physical difficulty of the jobs being performed. This is a general problem for women working in industry – women are concentrated in non-priority industries where both basic wages and bonuses for arduous conditions are lower than in the male-dominated heavy industries. Generous bonuses for plan fulfilment, often accounting for almost one-third of the average male wage, also discriminate against those who work in non-productive, service-based work such as nursing, teaching, clerical and accounting work – again heavily female-dominated areas. In graduate occupations the differential between men and women is generally smaller (women earn about 80–85 per cent of men's wages) and is attributed to the fact that occupational and career growth take place primarily in the first six to 10 years of work, i.e. when women are most likely to be establishing a family and having children (Rimashevskaia, 1988).

Second, the horizontal and vertical structuring of the labour-market means that women work in jobs where they gain little satisfaction and thus develop negative attitudes towards themselves as workers. At both the top and bottom of the ladder women find their paths to more fulfilling and better paid work blocked: graduate women find it hard to get top management positions and often end up doing monotonous clerical work outside their specialism, while women who have few qualifications remain in unskilled, manual and casual work where they earn little respect for the work they perform. A survey conducted in Moscow region enterprises in 1987 found that women were not only paid on average 40 roubles a month less than men but that they also did the least attractive work. For example, 32.1 per cent of women and only 16.1 per cent of men were employed on conveyor-line work and single-operational benches. Conversely, men predominated in highly qualified manual labour – 32.5 per cent compared with 15.5 per cent of women (Golodnenko and Strakhova, 1990). Although women are concentrated in the 'light industries', this does not mean that the work they perform is any lighter or easier. Textile workers in the city of Ivanovo, for example, work in factories built before the revolution with miserable sanitary conditions and equipment designed for the average male physique. The work is classed as highly arduous, yet 90 per cent of work time is taken up in actual production (higher than any other profession) and there is a high proportion of night-shift work, despite this being officially illegal for women. In fact, some of the worst working conditions pertain in these industries precisely because they are non-priority industries, and under glasnost there has been considerable discussion in the press about the connection between women's working conditions and health problems such as abnormal rates of high blood pressure, nervous, cardio-vascular and respiratory illnesses, chronic hearing deficiencies, complications during pregnancy and infertility (Telen', 1988). Although female life expectancy is significantly longer than that of men, Rimashevskaia concluded from her data that women's health was worse than men's (women scored 3.6 points compared with 3.9 for men) as a result of: the high female employment rate in workplaces with hazardous and difficult working conditions, and women's double burden at work and at home (Rimashevskaia, 1988).

Women's experience of their activity in social production is characterized by stressful work for low pay, resulting in a quality of life that is materially and psychologically poorer than that of men. It is not surprising that women develop very negative images of themselves. It is fashionable among Soviet scholars and journalists to attribute this negative identity to women's lack of access to cosmetics, quality clothes and perfume which are seen as the tools with which women construct positive images of themselves. Such interpretations, though, pay too little attention to the psychological effect on women of their treatment as second-class workers and the way in which this encourages women to see work as materially necessary but undesirable, and thus to favour options to 'return to their womanly mission' in the home (see Gorbachev, 1987).

Sociological explanations of inequality at work

Given the premise upon which the state's policy on women is based – that women must combine their roles as workers and mothers – it is not surprising that attempts to explain women's lack of actual equality have been couched in terms of the problems of combination. Women are seen to be disadvantaged in the competition for promotion because their training is interrupted by taking time off to have children and

by having little free time to spend on furthering their
qualifications because of their 'second shift' in the
home. Both these arguments are essentialist since they
attribute women's inequality in the labour-market to
their additional 'natural' role as child-bearer, child-
rearer and home-maker. That discrimination against
women at the work-place does indeed start with their
role as wife and mother is born out by sociological
data. Although women start off equally, if not more
qualified, than men they quickly lose their
advantages. Sociological studies have shown that
83–87 per cent of working women do not continue
their education after marriage or upgrade their skills.
Furthermore, children tend to follow quickly after
marriage – 78 per cent of first children are born
during the first two years of marriage. Women either
give up work temporarily – one-sixth of women stop
working for an average of four years after the birth of
a child – or, more frequently, change jobs to places
where they can work part-time or more flexibly.
This means that more and more women move into
less-skilled jobs during the period of childbirth and
child-raising. Surveys of women's career patterns
show similar findings: a survey in Leningrad showed
that in childless families women actually did better
than men: 97 men were promoted for every 100
women promoted. In families with three children, on
the other hand, men did considerably better: 122
men were promoted for every 100 women. In
monetary terms this means that although at the age of
20 average male wages exceed average female wages
by only 15 per cent, by the age of 30 the difference
increases to a ratio of 3:2. As women look to the
future, therefore, they can expect not gradually better
paid work in better conditions, but to move
sidewards into jobs to which they are unsuited or
which are undemanding, in order to minimize travel
to work and maximize their chances of access to
better housing.[4] Although the socialist project has
brought women into the sphere of social production,
therefore, women very often continue to see that
sphere of life as the secondary one and look to the
private sphere for self-fulfilment.

But why do women find it so difficult to combine their 'roles' as mothers and workers? The argument generally advanced by Soviet sociologists is that women's 'duties' in the home mean that they are left with little time to study in order to improve their qualifications. Surveys show that women do an average three hours and 13 minutes housework on a working day, and about double this on a day off, while men do an average 58 minutes and two hours 44 minutes respectively. On an average working day this leaves women with just 18 minutes for reading, 11 minutes for sport, 17 minutes for educating the children and 11 minutes for studying to raise their professional qualifications, participating in social work or undertaking the community work that is obligatory for Party members (*Zhenshchiny v SSSR*, 1988). On the birth of the first child the weekly domestic labour burden of women increases from around 26 hours to 36 hours. The result is that women do not study for higher qualifications and remain in relatively unskilled occupations.

Under glasnost a third explanation for women's unequal position in the work-force has been tentatively advanced – direct discrimination against women at the work-place. This discrimination, it is suggested, is primarily against women with small children because directors assume that they will take a considerable amount of time off in order to look after sick children. Men were favoured by management, it was argued, because: men are stronger physically than women and so can be used for all kinds of work; men can more easily be sent on business trips, do overtime, etc; women take more time off to look after sick children and relatives; and men are traditionally seen as the breadwinners of the family.

State protection of women: the role of legislation

The paternal state, though, has not abandoned all its perceived obligations to women workers. In particular legislation has been employed in order to guarantee the rights of women workers. This legislation has simultaneously perpetuated the paternal and protective role of the state. Legislation has had two main concerns: the protection of women's health, and the improvement of possibilities for women to combine their 'roles' of workers and mothers.

Legislation on working conditions for women is very comprehensive. The 1970 Labour Law stipulated that: women's labour could not be used in heavy or dangerous work or in underground work, except for some non-physical work or sanitary and public service work underground; women should not work night-shifts, except in those branches of the economy where it is 'essential' and then only as a 'temporary measure'; that women who are pregnant, breast-feeding or have children of one year or younger are not allowed to be asked to perform night-shifts, overtime work on non-working days or be sent on business trips (*kommandirovki*); that pregnant women are to be moved during pregnancy to lighter work, retaining their level of pay; that pregnant and breast-feeding women or women with children under one year cannot be dismissed except in cases of complete liquidation of the enterprise. Nevertheless at least four million women still work in conditions that do not conform to the existing norms of labour protection and 3.8 million women work night-shifts, i.e. two to three times more than men, and in certain industries six times more than men. Consequently new legislation has been introduced to strengthen that which already exists. In 1990 additions and amendments to various Acts concerning women, children and the family provided for the extension of the exemption from night-shifts to women with children up to three years of age and an additional paragraph was included to the effect that while lighter work is being found for pregnant women these women should be freed from work, retaining pay, at the cost of the enterprise. There has also been some attempt to address the discrimination against women with children: amendments to existing laws now mean that all women with children who are refused work must be given a written explanation of why work has been refused, which may be protested in the Peoples' Court.

The chief thrust of legislation on women, however, has been directed towards the extension of maternity benefits. This has entailed not only the statutory right to paid maternity leave, but the gradual extension of a subsequent period of partially paid and unpaid leave to care for small children. In 1990 these benefits were also made available to fathers, grandparents and other close relatives of the child.[5]

Looking to the future: women and the market

The fact that the legislative protection of women workers has been raised so prominently in recent times does not merely reflect the extent of the spotlight of perestroika, but the fears of women for the future. Despite claims that 'the market is ... gender-neutral' (Piiasheva, 1991), a public opinion survey of women's views on current changes showed that one in three associated transition to the market with a lowering of their standard of living and rising unemployment (Sillaste, 1991). Such fears reflect the new social reality. It is estimated that about 60 per cent of labour shed between 1989 and 1991 has been female labour, and where jobs have been lost as a result of the contraction of the administrative apparatus the figure rises to 80 per cent (Bodrova, 1991). The lack of detailed statistical evidence means that it is as yet impossible to say whether it is the case that women are being laid off before men in all spheres of work, or whether redundancies are primarily affecting the already feminized areas of employment. Perestroika, after all, should primarily benefit the stratum of highly skilled workers, which for the reasons explored above, means primarily men. It is certainly true, however, that women, especially working mothers, are beginning to feel themselves to be 'second-class workers' (Piiasheva, 1991). One young woman in Moscow reported to me that when, at a job interview, she admitted that she had recently married she was told that the employers were no longer interested in her application.

Women as reproducers

The provisions for the protection of women enshrined in the Labour Law, however, indicate very clearly that it is not women but mothers who are being protected. Women's health is protected in order that their reproductive capability is not harmed, and benefits are granted in order to allow women to combine work and motherhood. In areas where women need protection against men, such as the area of sexual harassment, there is no legislation. In addition to legislation, the state has prided itself on the provision for mothers and children. In 1988, 5321 million roubles was allocated in payments to women during pregnancy and birth and in benefits to women looking after children at home. This is more than double the figure in 1980 and quadruple the sum in 1970. There are 256 500 ante-natal and post-natal clinics throughout the Soviet Union and around 8000 million roubles is allocated annually to maintaining kindergartens, nurseries, after-school work with children and pioneer camps. The provision of these services together with the glorification of the 'mother' through medals for mothers with large families were considered by the state to be its part of the bargain – women's rights had been materially guaranteed, their duty was to replenish the nation.

In this way the state felt that it was fulfilling its side of the 'rights and duties' bargain. By the mid 1970s, though, it seemed that the bargain was breaking down. Women were not conforming to the assumption at the heart of state policy since the revolution – that in 'socialist' society women would naturally want to have children. Policy makers began to talk of a 'demographic crisis' and the need for the development of a 'demographic policy', and the latter was declared at the twenty-fifth Party congress in 1976.

Demographic policy

The demographic crisis in the Soviet Union consisted of a decline in the net population increase from 18 per 1000 in 1960 to 8–9 in 1976. Demographers were predicting a further fall, to 5.8, by the year 2000. The reasons for the perceived crisis were twofold: first there had been a decline in natural population growth in the late 1960s because of a relatively small number of mothers in prime child-bearing ages; and second a decline in fertility rates among these women (Helgeson, 1982). While the first factor was temporary, the second has persisted and it is this that has caused concern among Soviet policy makers. The fears are both economic and social, and are related less to net population falls than to demographic dislocations and imbalances. The population in Central Asia is growing at around three times the all-union rate, while the growth in Slavic and Baltic republics is growing significantly more slowly than the all-union rate (see Table 7.5).

Such a demographic imbalance means that much of the labour-force growth will take place outside the regions where industrial production is most developed. This has already led to serious localized unemployment and there is a fear that ethnic tensions arising from this could spread into western areas as young workers, from the Central Asian republics in particular, migrate into Russian cities in search of work. (The problem of migration between areas of the former Soviet Union is likely to be a source of serious tension between the newly independent states and in conditions of economic shortage race relations in large cities are likely to deteriorate. If current attempts by the Russian President to preserve some kind of unified armed forces fails and independent armies are raised by the former republics, it is clearly the more aged Slavic republics whose military potential will suffer.)

In order to explain why women appeared not to want to have children, or to have only one or two children, the state turned to 'objective circumstances'. Policy became focused around improving such circumstances (inadequate housing conditions and child benefits) in an attempt to create the material conditions for reproduction. Increasingly, though, Soviet society came to be seen as similar to developed western countries where urbanization and higher living standards meant the financial burden of

Table 7.5: Birth rate, mortality rate and natural growth in the populaion by republic (calculated for every 1000 population)

Republic	Births				Deaths				Natural growth in population			
	1940	1970	1986	1989	1940	1970	1986	1989	1940	1970	1986	1989
USSR	31.2	17.4	20.0	17.6	18.0	8.2	9.8	10.0	13.2	9.2	10.2	7.6
RSFSR	33.0	14.6	17.2	15.9	20.6	8.7	10.4	10.7	12.4	5.9	6.8	3.9
Ukraine	27.3	15.2	15.5	13.3	14.3	8.8	11.1	11.6	13.0	6.4	4.4	1.7
Belorussia	26.8	16.2	17.1	15.0	13.1	7.6	9.7	10.1	13.7	8.6	7.4	4.9
Georgia	27.4	19.2	18.7	16.7	8.8	7.3	8.8	8.6	18.6	11.9	9.9	8.1
Armenia	41.2	22.1	24.0	21.6	13.8	5.1	5.7	6.0	27.4	17.0	18.3	15.6
Azerbaidzhan	29.4	29.2	27.6	26.4	14.7	6.7	6.7	6.4	14.7	22.5	20.9	20.0
Moldavia	26.6	19.4	22.7	18.9	16.9	7.4	9.7	9.2	9.7	12.0	13.0	9.7
Lithuania	23.0	17.6	16.5	15.1	13.0	8.9	9.9	10.3	10.0	8.7	6.6	4.8
Estonia	16.1	15.8	15.6	15.1	17.0	11.1	11.6	11.7	-0.9	4.7	4.0	3.7
Latvia	19.3	14.5	15.9	14.5	15.7	11.2	11.9	12.1	3.6	3.3	4.0	2.4
Uzbekistan	33.8	33.6	37.8	33.5	13.2	5.5	7.0	6.3	20.6	28.1	30.8	27.0
Kazakhstan	40.8	23.4	25.5	23.0	21.4	6.0	7.4	7.6	19.4	17.4	18.1	15.4
Kirgizia	33.0	30.5	32.6	30.4	16.3	7.4	7.1	7.2	16.7	23.1	25.5	23.2
Tadzhikistan	30.6	34.8	42.0	38.7	14.1	6.4	6.8	6.5	16.5	28.4	35.2	32.2
Turkmenistan	36.9	35.2	36.9	35.0	19.5	6.6	8.4	7.7	17.4	35.9	28.6	27.3

(Source: *Narodnoe Khoziaistvo v 1989* and *Narodnoe Khoziaistvo za 70 Let*)

children had come to outweigh the 'security for the future' motive for having children (Perevedentsev, 1987). This line of reasoning led to the conclusion that a family of two to three children was to be a likely norm in developed society and this fitted well with demographers' requirements of a regionally or ethnically differentiated demographic policy. The suggestion of a three-child family as the national norm simultaneously intervened in Russian, Slav and Baltic women's reproductive behaviour, asking them to have more children and stay away from work longer, and Central Asian and Transcaucasian women's reproductive behaviour by encouraging them to have fewer children. The family unit became the vehicle for the articulation of this policy. At the ideological level this took the form of concern over high rates of divorce and a re-emphasis of women's true vocation in motherhood.

Family legislation

The concern over the rising rate of divorce was rooted in the belief that low fertility was linked to the rise in divorce and hesitancy among women to remarry. Indeed the ratio of divorces to marriages had been increasing rapidly. In 1960 there were 12.1 marriages and 1.3 divorces per 1000 population, in 1988 this had become just 9.4 marriages but 3.3 divorces. In 1982 the demographer Perevedentsev calculated that 11 per cent of marriages were breaking up within the first year and 25 per cent of all marriages did not last the first five years. This instability in their married lives was seen to be discouraging women from having children and a wide-ranging ideological campaign was conducted to strengthen family values. This included the introduction into schools of a course for ninth- and tenth-grade pupils on 'The Ethics and Psychology of Family Life' (extended to all schools in 1983) which provided students with sex education equipping them for fruitful reproduction rather than pleasure. At the same time a strong press campaign on the dangers of abortion to both physical and mental health was conducted and the virtues of motherhood extolled. The emphasis, once again, was not on 'choice' for women but on natural destiny. A book for newly-married published in 1971, for example, stated:

Pregnancy and childbirth are essential for a woman's organism ... after giving birth a woman ... begins to live life more fully. Women with many children usually look younger for their age, are more energetic and healthier than those who have no children. (Khodakov, 1971)

In legislative terms the strengthening of the family was embodied in the 1981 decree 'On measures to strengthen Government Help to Families with Children' which: instituted for the first time a system of partially paid leave to working mothers for 12 months following birth; established single payments to families on the birth of first, second and third children (a clear indication of the differentiated demographic policy); and increased payments to single mothers (an important recognition of the growing phenomenon of single-parent families). The 1981 decree also made small increases in holidays for women with children and in paid time off to look after sick children.

Of course these measures were experienced by women not as crude ideological manipulations to encourage them to have children they did not want – after all, child benefits were still so meagre that they could hardly be seen to be a great financial incentive – but as minor relief from the heavy double burden placed on them. Moreover, the strengthening of the family was a value shared by most Soviet citizens since the family played an important role in the lives of individuals. Although in the immediate post-revolutionary period there had been broad discussion, and practice, with different social forms of regulating sexuality, by the end of the 1920s the traditional form of the monogamous family as the basic economic (consuming) unit was being promoted as crucial to the stability of the new socialist state. Yet in the post-war period the family in Soviet society has been less an ideological support to the state, bringing up children in the 'spirit of socialism', than a refuge away from the intervention of the state and a key site of

the second economy.[6] Nevertheless the state has
relied on the family as the key unit of reproduction
of the population and socialization of new members
of society, and it is its failure to fulfil this role
adequately that has caused most concern. The bargain
struck between women and the state over women's
reproductive rights and duties was being broken not
only by women, but by the state as well. The advent
of glasnost has revealed the failure of the state to act
out its paternal role in a number of areas. In particular
the state has failed: to protect the health of mothers
and children; to provide adequate child-care; to
guarantee women's control of their own fertility; and
to encourage a redefinition of relations between the
sexes.

**Health of mother
and child**

Despite the money invested in health-care for
pregnant women and infants the rate of infant
mortality in the Soviet Union is extremely high. In
1989 the rate of infant mortality (i.e. the number of
children dying up to one year of age, per 1000 born)
was 22.3. This is 2.5–3 times higher than in the USA,
Great Britain, France, Federal Republic of Germany
and Japan (*SSSR v Tsifrakh v 1989*, 1990). In some
parts of the country the rate is significantly higher
than this – in Central Asia rates vary between 37 and
53. The highest rate is in the Republic of Turkmenia
where one of the major causes of death is dystrophy –
resulting from starvation. This is often caused by
severe protein deficiency in pregnant Turkmenian
women leading to babies being born weak and
severely underweight, often with some kind of
deformity. Maternal mortality is also causing some
concern, especially in rural Russia where there is
poor provision of midwives and low standards of
hygiene in hospitals. The RSFSR has the second
highest rate of maternal mortality (50) after Kirgizia
(53.8) in the USSR.

Another major issue that has been illuminated by the
spotlight of glasnost has been the appalling treatment
of women giving birth to children or having
abortions in state hospitals. Women have little control

over where they have their children (connections and bribes are the only ways women can seek to ensure a place in a reasonable hospital) or over who is present at the birth. Husbands and partners are not allowed to see the child until the woman is released from hospital. Conditions in hospitals are reportedly very poor, with bribes needed to secure clean linen and food. Above all, though, women complain of the abusive way in which they are treated by, mainly female, doctors who are rude, uninformative and often not in attendance at births. Treatment of women having abortions is even worse – anaesthetics are often unavailable and women are left unattended for hours after the operation.

Child-care provision

It is now recognized that the state's formal commitment to the provision of child-care to all families desiring it is an abstract one. Figures show that there are 1 875 000 parents whose applications for pre-school child-care are unfulfilled. There is also serious concern over the standard of care provided. Poor sanitary conditions and overcrowding lead to high rates of sickness among children. Dissatisfaction is also high among child-care staff who complain of extremely low pay, half the national average, and poor working conditions – 70 per cent of nursery-school teachers are also expected to do auxiliary tasks without additional pay. This led nursery-school workers in Moscow to threaten industrial action in May 1990 (Terekhina, 1990, p. 1). For these reasons parents are often highly reluctant to place their children in state day-care institutions and often call upon relatives (especially grandmothers of the children) to take on the role of caring for small children.

Abortion and contraception

One of the most difficult negotiations between women and the state is over the provision of access to birth control. In this respect the Soviet state initially had an extremely progressive position. Abortion was legalized as early as 1920 and in the 1920s there was considerable propaganda about birth control methods. It was in the USSR that the vacuum suction method of abortion was first developed. Free access to abortion alongside the recognition of *de facto* marriage in the post-revolutionary state, however, soon became associated with sexual promiscuity, lack of responsibility and social instability, and a more conservative attitude on women's reproductive rights and duties began to develop. Under Stalin this was embodied in the new family legislation of 1936, which among other things prohibited abortion except where the mother's life was endangered. Although abortion was re-legalized under Krushchev, the Soviet state's policy on birth control remained contradictory: the failure to develop anywhere near adequate provision of contraception has made women dependent on abortion as a method of birth control.

There are currently more abortions than there are live births: 1.39 abortions to one live birth. More than 75 per cent of women of child-bearing age have had at least one abortion; many have had several. Since the early 1980s it has been recognized that repeated abortions may seriously damage a woman's child-bearing capacity, and so aggravate the demographic situation. Nevertheless, recent calls by radical Soviet demographers for the development and production of adequate supplies of effective contraceptives as the only way to increase the birth rate have largely gone unanswered. Although figures on abortion suggest a decrease in their number – from 100.3 per 1000 women of child-bearing age in 1985 to 86.6 in 1988 – the latter figure does not take into account the so-called 'mini-abortions', by vacuum suction method, which are only now being made available to Soviet women. Nor does this figure include the many illegal abortions conducted by 'off-duty' doctors or untrained people. The situation is particularly acute where it concerns under-age girls who dare not approach state doctors, since in order for the doctor to agree to an abortion the girl would have to have an authorizing document, which is given only in the presence of her parents and in conjunction with the bureau for juvenile affairs. In Turkmenistan the situation with back-street abortions became so bad that it was decided to set up an anonymous centre where girls could pay 25–50 roubles, considerably less than the 600 roubles demanded for a back-street abortion, and be treated by professional doctors (Akhmedyarov, 1989, p. 4).

Despite the technological capability for the production of effective contraception, usage remains at an extremely low level for an industrially developed nation. Even in the Russian Republic it is estimated that only one-quarter of the demand for contraception is being met and thus the continued dependence on traditional methods, such as coitus interruptus and condoms, means that birth control methods currently used by Soviet couples are highly ineffective (Popov, 1986).

Unrestructured gender relations

There is also some evidence to suggest that women are abandoning the traditional form of the family because it does not fulfil their aspirations. By 1986 there was one divorce to every three marriages and it is estimated that about 70 per cent are filed for by women. Among young people in general there is a growing irreverence towards marriage. A survey conducted among young people in Azerbaidzhan showed that only 23 per cent of urban and 40 per cent of rural young people thought that marriage was a valuable institution in society (Mansimov and Foteeva, 1982). More than a third of urban young people said that they definitely did not want to have children. Furthermore, only 15 per cent of urban and 18 per cent of rural students expressed disapproval of pre-marital sex. Recent articles show that young people are contemplating and practising different forms of lifestyle including 'trial marriages' and living together as an alternative to marriage. There also appears to be a growing cynicism about marriage. Although for a long time marriage has been seen as a means of moving up the queue for housing, it is now reported that people are applying to get married in order to gain access to special shops for brides and grooms and subsequently not going through with the ceremony. Women are also increasingly choosing to bring up families on their own: a survey conducted in the city of Perm' in 1983 revealed that 41 per cent of children were conceived outside marriage and figures for 1988 show that over 10 per cent of children are born outside marriage.

Under perestroika there has been a growing awareness of the importance of individual choice and this has stretched to discussion of the need for women to be able to define how many children they have and when they have them. There have also been calls for greater availability of different forms of contraception so that women are able to choose a form that suits their individual needs. To this end the association 'Family and Health' was founded in January 1989 under the Ministry of Health's Institute for the Protection of the Health of Mother and Child. This is the first modern family planning centre and offers advice on contraception for a minimal registration fee. In addition there has been increasing criticism of the way in which sex education is taught in schools, and the press has taken it upon itself to initiate a broader discussion. Still, no fundamental redefinition of the bargain with women over their reproductive rights and duties is in evidence. Gorbachev, like other leaders, has emphasized the importance of the family as a 'pillar of socialist society' and has encouraged women to prioritize their role as wife and mother over that of worker. Since men continue to earn much more than women, there is little incentive for men to take up the opportunities of paternity leave that might act as a natural process of democratizing relations between the sexes, while at an ideological level the re-emphasis of stereotypes of masculinity and femininity in contemporary Soviet society actually discourages this and reinforces the mother–child bond at the heart of the nuclear family unit.

Women as decision makers – participation and representation

In this section the question of women's involvement in the defining of the dual role of worker–mother will be explored. It is important to establish whether or not women have participated in the definition of this dual identity. If they have not, it becomes necessary to examine how the political sphere has been constructed through the exclusion of women, and to analyse what this tells us about the nature of power and women's access to it in the Soviet Union.

Women and 'high politics'

Integral to the development of Soviet political culture has been the conscious desire to draw women into politics. Immediately after the October Revolution special commissions for agitation and propaganda among women were organized to encourage women into taking up a more active political role. In 1919 these commissions were reorganized and became known as the 'Women's Department' (*Zhenotdel*). In many respects this project has been successful and, until the recent reforms, women's participation in political institutions in the USSR has been generally higher than in western societies. At the last pre-perestroika elections in 1984, the highest body of power, the Supreme Soviet (or Parliament), had 492 women deputies, i.e. 33 per cent of the total number of deputies. This, the government boasted, compared extremely favourably with the 4.5 per cent of women returned to the US Congress. Moreover, at local levels women were even more active in the soviets (councils) – elections in 1987 to local soviets of people's deputies returned 49 per cent women deputies.

One of the major reasons for this high representation is the ideological premise that women are a 'backward group' in terms of civic consciousness, which led to the promotion of the special commissions for work with women and the introduction of a quota system in representative bodies for certain social groups, including women. In terms of women's access to power, though, it must be remembered that quantity of representation does not necessarily entail quality. The quota system ensured that the women who did sit on council bodies were selected, rather than elected, and that they were good Party workers who could be trusted to toe the Party line. It should also be remembered that although the Supreme Soviet was nominally the highest body of power, in fact its legislative function had been reduced to the ratification of legislation prepared by Party bodies, and its executive function had been curtailed by the domination of the Party, at the local executive committee level, or usurped by the Council of Ministers, at the highest level. If we look to the arenas of real power – to the Party and government circles – women are much less visible. Only one woman has ever been a full member of the Politburo – Elena Furtseva, under Krushchev, and since the early 1920s women have never constituted more than about 5 per cent of the membership of the Central Committee. The problem appears to be that not only do very few women get elected to the intermediary levels of political power – for example only 3 per cent of the *oblast* (regional) level of party committees are women – but that, once elected, women are kept within their own region and channelled into areas such as ideology, and agitation and propaganda, which hold low status within the Party elite. Such positions confine women to a stereotypical 'expressive' function, and because they are low status they do not encourage promotion (Moses, 1978).

Under Gorbachev the 'women's question' has certainly returned to the political agenda. At the twenty-seventh Party congress (February 1986) Gorbachev drew attention to the low level of representation of women in politics and called for the revival of the women's councils (*zhensovety*).[7] The women's councils were intended to provide a mechanism for women's participation in the solving of problems in the social and economic sphere. As democratization gathered pace during 1987 and 1988, however, new ways of solving the 'women's question' had to be found. This was reflected in Gorbachev's 'new approach' to the women's question which went beyond his call at the twenty-seventh congress for the revival of the women's councils as the necessary forum for the separate (and unequal) resolution of specifically women's problems. In his speech to the nineteenth Party conference in June 1988 Gorbachev noted that it was not enough simply to recognize the inability of Soviet women to exercise their constitutional equality with men as a result of the difficulties of everyday life, and to call for the revival of the women's councils. Instead, he argued, paths into the highest levels of politics must be opened to women (Gorbachev, 1989). Shortly afterwards, in September 1988, Alexandra Biriukova was appointed as a candidate member of the Politburo – the first woman to reach such a high level since Furtseva.

The democratization reforms so far, though, have actually reduced the percentage of women at the highest level of government. The slackening of the Party's control over the selection of candidates to the new Congress of People's Deputies meant that the rough quotas based on social background and gender were no longer adhered to. The beneficiaries of this were the intelligentsia, the losers were the working class and women. Female membership of the old Supreme Soviet stood at around 33 per cent, whereas, only 352 (i.e. 15.7 per cent) of the new democratically elected Congress are women. Of these, 75 were elected from the women's councils and so we must expect that, when the reserving of seats for public organizations is abandoned (as it has already been in some republics), women are likely to lose out still further. In addition, the women's councils have failed to develop into any kind of authentic women's movement; they have remained at the level of filling the gaps where other organizations, such as the trade unions or the work collective committees, have failed to work properly. Women's councils have largely remained confined to establishing ordering services and shops at enterprises and work-places, or organizing knitting or child-health circles for women. They are aimed at reducing the double burden on women, not at the redistribution of that burden. According to survey data, the net result of Gorbachev's attempts to find new ways of making women's voices heard has been that women actually feel their input has decreased – almost two-thirds of women felt that women had not begun to play a more active role in public life since the advent of perestroika, although 42 per cent said they would like to participate in some way. When asked what prevented them from doing so, the most frequent response was the 'lack of a thought-out state policy towards women, the lack of trust in them and their undervaluation' (Sillaste, 1990).

Democratization – a new 'equality' for women

In order to understand why democratization has been a negative rather than a positive process in terms of women's participation in the political sphere, we must look at democratization as a gendered concept. Democratization and the strengthening of the rights of Soviet citizens was vital if people were to be encouraged into active participation in perestroika. A new active citizen, who would bear individual responsibility both in the economy and in the political sphere, was to be created through the process of democratization. These citizens had not only rights but duties and it is here that the gendered nature of the new citizenship becomes apparent. Citizens of both sexes were to continue to have equal rights in the formal sense, but their duties were to be very different: women's would be firmly rooted in the moral, spiritual and thus private sphere. Gorbachev and other reformers have made this clear in references to the 'costs of emancipation' (*izderzhki emantsipatsii*), which are defined as the emergence of social problems such as juvenile delinquency, poor labour discipline and immorality. These, it is claimed, are a direct result of women's activity in social production since this activity did not leave women enough time to perform 'their everyday duties at home – housework, the upbringing of children and the creation of a good family atmosphere' (Gorbachev, 1987). What Gorbachev was arguing was that the bringing of women into the labour-force had been well-intentioned but wrong: the negative social phenomena referred to were, in his words, 'a paradoxical result of our sincere and politically justified desire to make women equal with men in everything' (ibid.).

Perestroika, therefore, meant not only a redefinition of citizenship, it also meant a redefinition of equality.

Equality, henceforth, was to be seen not in 'identity' but in 'difference'.

Women's activity and participation

The extent to which women participate in 'high politics', though, cannot fully explain the role women play in decision making nor how women are related to power in society. In order to explore this more comprehensively we have to look to other spheres of women's activity and participation, primarily the sphere of the 'private' or 'domestic'. There is a good deal of evidence to suggest that women are far more active than men in the private sphere and that, through their control of the family budget and regime, they have considerable effective power in this sphere. Indeed some would argue that women have so much power in the private sphere that Soviet society is matriarchal not patriarchal (Tolstaia, 1990). This argument rests on a cultural understanding of the relationship between public and private spheres in society and suggests that in Russian culture it is not 'reason' (male rationality) but the 'soul' (female spirituality) which is prioritized. The spiritual and the moral are, according to this argument, not as undervalued in Russian culture as in western cultures. A second reason why we should look to the private sphere as one of important decision making lies in the development of Soviet rather than Russian culture. The increasingly ritualistic nature of politicking in the Soviet public sphere has led to the devaluation of that sphere. Consequently, the family came to be seen as a space in which people could speak their mind, retaining a 'public persona' for the outside world. The family and kinship network also became vital in economic terms as the state distribution system failed to satisfy people's needs. Especially during the Brezhnev years, people turned to family, relatives and friends in order to gain access to goods and services that could not be obtained in strictly legal ways.

Although this helps us to see better the ways in which women (who are central in the private sphere) have been involved in crucial areas of decision making, it does not help us evaluate how important these areas have been. The culturalist approach allows us to see women as having a separate sphere of power from men, but it does not say anything about the relative nature of that power. Nor can we simply accept as a truism the dominance of women in the new, urban-based private sphere. Although surveys conducted by Soviet sociologists in the 1970s showed that both women and men tended towards seeing women as 'domineering' in family life, there is no evidence to suggest that this dominance can be equated with either effective power or authority. Indeed the 'domineering' nature of women was not attributed to their natural role in the private sphere, but to their bringing home the qualities that they had to show in the work-place, and these qualities were seen (especially by men) to be unfitting to the domestic sphere (Shlapentokh, 1984). The fact that women appear dominant may in fact stem less from any retention of their 'natural' sphere of influence than from the weakening of the traditional male role. The devaluation of the public sphere – the ritualistic and unsatisfying nature of both the political and the economic spheres – has greatly reduced the traditional areas of the development of masculine identity. The widespread abuse of alcohol and the dependency on women that this induces has also led to a generally low regard for men among Soviet women. This weakening of the male 'role' has not led to more egalitarian relations between women and men but to a conservative retrenchment in which women take on many of the roles previously ascribed to men while espousing a desire to be more 'feminine', and men fail to pull their weight in the family while complaining that their wives are 'domineering' and 'unfeminine'.

Women's informal activity

Although democratization has not succeeded in drawing women into the highest levels of decision making, this does not mean that women have been unable to make their voices heard. The unleashing of social forces in the process of the unravelling of perestroika has not by-passed women. Although women have always resisted patriarchal society by, for example, devising their own contraceptive methods, refusing their husbands/partners sex, filing for divorce, having children without marrying the father, passing on their culture, national language or religion to their children, etc, these forms of resistance are often ignored because they do not take place in the public sphere. At this particular historical moment, though, new forms of female activity are evolving in Soviet society.

In some cases, such as that of the action of professional/middle-class women, this activity is familiar to us from the methods adopted by women of similar social backgrounds in western societies. A growing consciousness of their exclusion and subordination has led professional women to set up groups to support women in certain professions and to promote women's access to these prestigious areas of work. Such groups already include: a women's film-makers' union and women's jurists' club, a council of women writers and a Moscow club of women writers, an organizational committee to bring together women in the creative arts, an association of women academics, and a number of organizations and support groups for women in business and management. There have also been attempts to turn the Party-dominated women's councils, which throughout their history have not been taken seriously by mainstream Party bodies, into authentic women's movements. The Women's Council of the Central Aero-hydrodynamics Institute in the town of Zhukovsky near Moscow, for example, has rejected the usual role of the women's council and has set about actively constructing horizontal links between women alongside the vertical structure imposed by the women's council organization. This has resulted in creating women's groups based around common concerns and interests. In many cases the activity of such groups of women is accompanied by overtly feminist ideologies, which range from liberal to socialist feminism and are based on both essentialist and androgenous visions of relations between the sexes.

The movement of professional and intellectual women accounts for only a small, even if the most visible, aspect of growing female resistance to oppression. They have also begun to unite around issues such as the hazardous conditions in which they work and the disproportionate amount of hard, manual labour night-shifts performed by women. Protests have already come from cotton workers in Central Asia poisoned by agricultural chemicals, textile workers with abnormally high levels of heart and respiratory disease, construction workers in the Far East and nursery-school workers in central Russia. In a number of cases this has brought women out on strike and has forced concessions on demands such as more flexible forms of work (part-time, flexi-time and home-based work), better working conditions, and equal access to better paid and more prestigious work.

A key area of growing consciousness and activity is that associated with perceptions of women as women and mothers. Soviet women have protested angrily at the infringement of their rights as mothers. This they attribute to the state's negligence in specific cases, as well as to its generally inhuman attitude to its subjects. Negligence is claimed by women protesting about the infection of dozens of mothers and young children with the HIV virus and about the continuing after-effects of Chernobyl, as well as other environmental problems. The brutality of the state is invoked more broadly by mothers' protests over conditions of army service. Mothers have demanded that their sons be obliged to serve in the Soviet army only within the borders of their own republic, that the widespread incidence of bullying (*dedovshchina*) be stopped, and that the number of soldiers killed while in non-combat service be drastically reduced. The soldiers' mothers quickly organized themselves in the public sphere and, by June 1990, had founded an all-union committee called Mothers' Heart (*Materinskoe Serdtse*) with branches all over the Soviet Union (Shreeves, 1990). In November 1990 Gorbachev issued a presidential decree on the implementation of the mothers' demands. Other women's groups active in the political sphere, such as 'Caratas' in Lithuania and the Moldavian Christian Democratic Women's movement, have put forward platforms based on a sense of 'womanhood' which envisages a primarily spiritual and moral role for women rather than an overtly public one. These movements aim to promote what they see to be women's values and interests in society, retaining an essentialist position on the nature and sphere of activity of women.

In contrast, groups have also formed around the demand for a complete reassessment of women's sexuality – specifically calling for an end to its inherent link with marriage and reproduction. For the first time press space has been given to lesbian women and an Association for the Protection of Sexual Minorities has been formed, publishing a regular, and officially registered, magazine. Such groups overtly reject Gorbachev's vision of an 'equal but different' woman of the future. Another group that reclaims the rhetoric of the 'individual' from the reformers is the Independent Women's Democratic Initiative (NeZhDI).[8] The NeZhDI, formed in July 1990, is one of the off-shoots of an informal group called the League for the Emancipation from Stereotypes which, as its name suggests, rejects traditionalist gender roles in society. Another off-shoot of this league is the Centre for Gender Studies, the first academic institution in the USSR to undertake specifically gender related research. It is the women involved in these organizations who must take much of the credit for the insertion of the 'paternity leave' clause into current legislation.

The ability of all these groups to make women's (dissonant) voices heard is dependent on their capacity to intervene in the policy-making process. Both the soldiers' mothers' committees and the Centre for Gender Studies have so far been highly successful at getting their proposals discussed and accepted at the highest levels. Increasingly, though, like all other 'informal groups', these organizations will find their effectiveness blocked by the instability of the formal political institutions and the greater experience and resources of the older organizations (such as the formalistic Soviet Women's Committee).

The current situation would appear to be one of women's total alienation from the decision-making process. This is manifested in a loss of faith among women in both the old political structures and the new organizations emerging from below. Replies to the 'Women and democratization' survey suggest that this alienation has left women politically schizophrenic, declaring an abstract trust in the 'strong male leader' at the same time as believing that only women themselves can defend their interests (Sillaste, 1991).

Women's personal autonomy

So far the experience of women has been explored in terms of their 'roles' as workers, mothers and citizens. Under perestroika a new question has been opened up – how do women experience being 'women'? By this I mean how do women construct their identity as women, and how is this mediated by the state and, increasingly, the market?

Women's identity before perestroika

One of the problems in analysing how women's identity has been affected by perestroika is the paucity of information on women's perceptions of themselves in the pre-perestroika period. What knowledge we have is confined to official constructions of women's identity that have revolved around images of women as worker–mothers, although at different periods of time one or other role has been emphasized. During periods of heavy industrialization and during World War Two, the role of women as workers was emphasized, although in the latter period this was accompanied by a glorification of the motherland (*mat'-rodina*). In the 1970s fears of the 'demographic crisis' and rising divorce rates led to discussions of female identity being more directly linked to male identity. This emerged in the debate around the 'feminization of men' and the 'masculinization of women'. The argument was that women's non-traditional role in social production was depriving them of their 'femininity'. At the same time women's dominance in the family and their predominance in the caring professions, especially education, meant that boys were unable to develop a strong masculine identity since they had no strong male role model (Attwood, 1990).

The Soviet Union today is undergoing a sexual revolution possibly of equal magnitude to that of the 1920s and this has enormous implications for how women's identity will be shaped in the future. The changing economic and political situation in the Soviet Union has meant that key issues around the role of the state and the market in relation to women have emerged for the first time, bringing liberation for women in some areas and further oppression in others. I want to explore these gains and losses by looking at the way in which the reintroduction of sexuality into Soviet life has affected women's sense of self.

Glasnost and the resexualization of Soviet society

Glasnost has given women the opportunity to establish self-respect as sexual beings. Women have spoken out against the degradation and humiliation they are subjected to when attending abortion clinics and maternity hospitals, and there has been real criticism of the lack of access to contraception. The founding of the association Family and Health marks the creation of the first family planning organization giving consultations and practical help on the prevention of pregnancy. There has also been an end to the taboo on public discourse on sex and sexuality. In this area the youth papers and weeklies have played a major role by serializing and reviewing books on sex and carrying articles on all kinds of issues around sex and sexuality. Discussions have included: at what age one should begin a sexual relationship; the different attitudes to sex between men and women; coping with loneliness and dissatisfaction with relationships; the sexual liberation of the 1920s; and male and female homosexuality.

The liberation that results from this 'sexualization' of society, though, is experienced unequally by men and women since the society being sexualized is an unequal one. As a result men appear as the subjects of sexual relations while women are seen primarily either as victims of men's sexuality or as sexual deviants themselves. This attitude to women's sexuality is apparent in two important issues that have been discussed for the first time under glasnost: prostitution and rape.

Prostitution

The importance of the recognition of the existence of prostitution in the Soviet Union has generally been held to be ideological: such a recognition challenges the classical Marxist assumption that prostitution would end with the socialist revolution. Marx and Engels saw prostitution as inherently linked to the monogamous, nuclear (bourgeois) family on which capitalism depended for the transmittance of property. Nonetheless, Marxism argues, hypocritical bourgeois morality allowed men to abuse oppressed and exploited (working-class) women through the institution of prostitution. Hence, prostitution could not theoretically exist where the bourgeois family did not, and prostitution has not officially existed in Soviet society since the mid 1930s. This also means that prostitution has not been a criminal offence, although prostitutes have been convicted under the parasite laws for living off 'unearned income' or for the conscious spreading of venereal diseases, and have been deprived of their rights over their children under the family law on the grounds that they exert a harmful influence on them.

The recognition of the existence of prostitution in contemporary Soviet society has required the abandonment of the Marxist understanding of the roots of prostitution. Since no alternative socio-economic explanation of prostitution in socialist society has been advanced, the old interpretation has been replaced by an ideological shell much more familiar to westerners: prostitution as the moral dissoluteness or (sexual) deviancy of women. The first, and most prevalent, image of the Soviet prostitute was of a young, hard-hearted woman who targets foreign businessmen at Intourist hotels (hotels for foreigners), motivated by the possibility of marrying her way out of the country or earning foreign currency and the privileges accruing from this. Since then, two other categories of prostitute have been discussed: those who work primarily for roubles; and those who work at stations mainly for alcohol or small sums of money. It is the latter who elicit the most moral distaste, since such women are seen not only as prostitutes but as alcoholics, and thus as having abandoned their motherly responsibilities. In addition, because they tend to be middle-aged (or older), the sexualization of their bodies appears to break even more social taboos. In comparison, the image of the '*interdevochki*' (women working Intourist hotels) is apparently a relatively glamorous one, since their work offers access to hard currency, expensive clothes, perfume and cosmetics and possibly even travel beyond the USSR. One might expect this to offer a positive image of women's sexuality. In fact, since virtually no attention is given to the dangers faced by prostitutes, the material hardship that often drives women (especially single mothers) to prostitution or, most importantly, the culpability of the buyer as opposed to the seller of sex, even the most glamorous Soviet prostitutes continue to appear as perpetrators of sexual deviancy.

Rape

Glasnost has also introduced discussion of women as victims of sexual abuse and this is apparent in the discussion surrounding the rise in the incidence of rape. Statistics released by the Ministry of Internal Affairs showed a 120 per cent increase in the incidence of rape in 1989 over 1988. As we have seen in the spheres of labour and motherhood, the paternal role of the state in the USSR has led to women being highly protected by legislation. The Russian Criminal Code (1960) includes two articles on punishment for coercing women to have sex: one dealing with rape, and group rape: and one dealing with rape within marriage or other exploitation of the dependent position of women. This is highly progressive in that it recognizes the power relations involved in rape, i.e. that women are often coerced into sex by their dependency on husbands, family, employers or landlords. Yet the latter article is rarely used, and is included in only some of the republican criminal codes. Furthermore, studies of rape victims show that a very wide definition of 'mitigating circumstances' in rape is used by judges – almost any case in which the victim and assaulter knew one another before the crime, and in which the victim was not a virgin (Juviler, 1978). This view is shared by those investigating crimes – one Ministry of Internal Affairs (police) official claimed that at least 30 per cent of rapes were 'provoked' by the victim, and he defined such 'provocation' as 'becoming acquainted with their attackers in accidental circumstances, drinking alcohol with them' (Zaichkin, 1989).

Even where women are seen as 'victims' of male abuse, it is the moral virtuousness of the woman which appears to be of more interest to judges than the man's or men's violence towards women. This implication of women in male violence can be seen in the way both rape and other forms of physical and sexual abuse of women are treated. Domestic violence, for example, is most often accredited to male drunkenness and usually includes either open or veiled criticism of the man's wife for not finding time to be loving enough to her husband, thus driving him to the bottle. Probably the greatest concern currently is that voiced over the alarming increase in gang rape. Although the issue has received serious treatment from isolated scholars (Kon, 1989), nonetheless, the most popular images of rape come from its portrayal in a whole series of films, mainly about young people in which rape or attempted rape is portrayed in pivotal scenes. These incidents invariably involve the rape of the girlfriend, daughter or sister of the male 'hero' of the film by a group of men known to the girl. Not only is the victim implicated in the crime by her participation in the group's activities but the rape itself is used as a symbolic event. Neither the psychological consequences for the woman nor the power relations involved in the committing of the crime are explored, and one is left with a sense that what has been portrayed is a visual image of the moral depths to which society has sunk. It is important here that those involved are young people, since youth acts as a symbol of the future of society. Rape thus appears as a dramatic enactment of Marx and Feuerbach's claim that the state of relations between men and women is indicative of the relations within society as a whole: women are reduced to a reflection of the real relations within male society. As a result, the oppression of women remains a question of morality and can be overcome only through a superstructural (or secondary) process of raising levels of culture.

Pornography The debates around prostitution and rape show how change in Soviet society is necessitating new ways of evaluating social phenomena crucial to the way in which women and women's sexuality is constructed socially. One phenomenon that is not only being re-evaluated due to glasnost, but that has been actually created by it, has caused even wider debate in the Soviet Union. This is the phenomenon of pornography. The pornography debate is a crucial one since the advent of pornography for the first time in Soviet society has been blamed on the new openness around sex and has been directly implicated in the rise in the incidence of rape. It is also important because it raises the issue of the role of the state. Although the sale and exhibition of pornography is banned by Soviet law, this law contains no definition of what constitutes pornography and what, for example, constitutes 'erotic art'. The considerable discussion of this matter has focused on the experience of other countries in the regulation of pornography. A resolution by the Soviet Parliament in April 1991 called for the creation of a commission to screen films, journals and other material for pornography and violence and for a classification of films to be established, but did not solve the problem of definition. Another key component in the pornography debate is the issue of the relation of the market to the position of women in society. In this context, the appearance of pornography is linked to a more general theme of the increasing marketization, and thus devaluing, of Soviet culture. This argument is usually employed by the 'high-culture lobby', and is based on the dual argument of the need for freedom of the 'artist' and the classical nature of erotica in art, and the threat posed to true art by the commercialization of Soviet culture under perestroika. Sometimes this argument has a more political slant as, for example, in one author's expression of horror at the way in which the image of Lenin was denigrated in a feature on Russian women in one issue of *Playboy* magazine. The author is horrified by the devaluing of Soviet images, while pornography itself is not seen as a problem, and anyway, the author notes, *Playboy* is not pornography (Gorlov, 1990).

At its current stage, the debate around pornography reveals most of all how, as in the case of prostitution and rape, issues around the oppression of women are channelled into the discourse of morality. In popular consciousness the problem of pornography consists in the unnecessary showing of sex scenes and nakedness in films, on television, in photographs and on stage. Rather than eliciting outrage at the objectification and degradation of the female body, the horror is often at the immorality of what is being portrayed. And, naturally, it is women who are seen to be to blame. One example of this tendency can be seen in letters from viewers of *Little Vera* who expressed their anger at the 'shamelessness' of the sex scene shown in the film. One letter (signed by 'seven married women') declares that the authors obviously do not know who should be on top during the sexual act and who on the bottom because they show Vera – the prostitute – on top (Khmelik, 1990). A second typical reaction from women viewers was that if such films were going to be made then at least they should have chosen someone 'beautiful' to perform the role. This is a typical comment women make on the advent under perestroika of beauty contests – what offends is usually not the objectification of women but that those who win are not really beautiful. The implication of this is that women are divided into 'wives' and 'whores' and the latter are to blame for tempting men away from righteousness. This is made explicit by one women writing to the youth newspaper *Komsomol'skaia Pravda*, following the publication of an article describing approvingly a striptease club in Tallinn. The author accuses the dancer interviewed in the article of breaking up marriages by making men disappointed in their wives and thus turning them off marital sex. An alternative male view, similarly laying the blame for the interest in pornography on women, is that men turn to pornography for tenderness and comfort (expressed in the eyes of the models) that they are denied by their wives who have been turned into man-haters and sadists by the conditions of Soviet reality – lack of cosmetics and domestic equipment (Baskov, 1990).

Glasnost, therefore, is giving women space for the first time to explore their own identity. For young women in particular this will be very important for they will grow up with much more freedom to determine their own sense of self than any generation since the revolution. The ability of women to construct positive gender identities, however, is dependent on a positive and secure notion of female sexuality. Public attitudes towards female sexuality are transmitted via debates such as those on prostitution, pornography and the sexual abuse of women. If these debates remain locked in the discourse of morality, then the freedom brought by the 'sexual revolution' will be experienced only by men.

Conclusion: the ambiguities of change

In material terms, as regards the quality of daily life, women stand to be the greatest beneficiaries of the Gorbachev reforms ... (Walker, 1986)

It is not hard to see what brought Martin Walker to this conclusion. The greater emphasis laid by Gorbachev on the consumer and services side of the economy, the measures introduced to strengthen the family, the ideological resurrection of the individual as opposed to the collective, the stress on 'all-human values' as opposed to the armed competition between

ideologically opposed world views – in short, the
turn towards socialism with a 'human face' – all
seemed to point to the movement of Soviet society
towards a world in which women's views were more
central. The reality of women's experience of current
change in Soviet society, though, has been rather
different. The question of how to solve the perceived
national economic and political problems has once
again dominated the political agenda and sidelined
truly radical alternatives. At the same time, there is a
new openness for the discussion of such alternatives
that retains a radically liberating potential for women.
The experience of Soviet women, therefore, has been
an ambiguous one.

In the economic sphere, for the first time, women
have been able to make choices about how to divide
their working time: to do part-days or weeks in their
paid jobs, and thus have more time to devote to
domestic work and child-care; to opt for flexi-time in
their paid jobs, and so continue with full-time paid
employment but in a more convenient way; or even
to choose temporarily to give up paid employment
altogether. But although, for many women, these
options appear 'enabling', there are also fears that
those who make these choices today will find
themselves without the 'choice' to re-enter the
work-force in the future. If women remove
themselves from the sphere of economic production
at this crucial economic turning point, they may find
themselves permanently confined to a secondary
economic role since the 'choices' are still to be made
only by women. The promise of a more consumer-
oriented economic system, that should have eased the
burden on women by bringing to their lives many of
the convenience products western women take for
granted, has also been realized only very partially.
One major step forward has been the opening in the
Ukraine of a joint venture producing tampons. One
plant, however, cannot supply the entire population
of Soviet women and, like most joint-venture and
co-operative products, prices are very high.

Democratization of the political sphere has also been an ambiguous process for women. Attempts to re-authenticate the public sphere have brought little gain for women. On the basis of a redefinition of what constitutes 'equality', the political sphere is being restructured in a way that excludes women, or rather that relocates them into the private sphere. On the other hand, the internal dynamic of perestroika transformed it from a self-contained Party-led movement for economic reform into a much wider social movement (of revolutionary potential) which was dependent on, but also an inevitable victim of, the unleashing of the forces of individual and collective action. This has led to the emergence of different forms of women's consciousness which has helped women articulate their interests and visions for the future.

The space in which these visions can be articulated has been officially sanctioned by another key component of perestroika – glasnost. Glasnost has allowed the 'women's question' to return to the sphere of debate, and women are finding space to talk about themselves, their experiences and their relations with men and other women. But even this process is far from easy for women. The anger that women vent is often accompanied less by a sense of empowerment through common experience than by a sense of powerlessness to change their situation. Women, then, are facing change with a greater awareness of what unites them, but also of what divides them.

Notes

1   I avoid using the term 'class' here because it is problematic in a Soviet social context. Nevertheless, constituent parts of class identity (level of education, rural/urban background, provincial/central residence, positioning in the labour-market and socio/economic status of parents) do play an important role in the stratification of Soviet society and therefore both unite and divide Soviet women.

2   Statistics cited here are taken from Soviet sources, compiled by the State Committee for Statistics

(Goskomstat). In the Soviet Union, unlike the west, it is
empirical sociology which has been viewed as the most
socially threatening branch of social science, since
'impartial statistics' have the potential to reveal the gap
between ideology and reality. For this reason, collection of
data has been restricted and published only in contexts in
which the data appear to uphold the Party view of the
development of Soviet society. For this reason, statistics
cited should always be viewed with a critical eye.

3   In the period 1975–84, the average monthly money wage
       in trade and the restaurant sector increased by more than
       one-third (34.1 per cent), in public health, physical culture
       and social security by 28.4 per cent, and in the cultural
       sector it increased by 25.3 per cent – in the same period
       the increase in the average monthly wages of workers and
       employees in industry was 26.1 per cent (Gruzdeva and
       Chertikhina, 1987).

4   Sociological studies of the life patterns of workers show
       that while the career patterns of 80 per cent of men
       indicated upward movement, only 45 per cent of women
       moved up in social status, 45 per cent were stationary and
       10 per cent moved downwards (Rimashevskaia, 1988).

5   The 1970 Labour Law provided for maternity leave for
       women of 56 days before and after birth with state benefits
       (70 days for abnormal births) and up to one year's leave
       without pay to look after the child. An amendment of
       1981 allowed partially paid leave of up to one year
       (provided the woman had worked for one year) to look
       after the child, with payment of state benefits for this
       period, plus additional unpaid leave until the child is 18
       months old. In 1987 a further amendment to this article
       allowed women who had taken leave in order to look after
       a child to work part-time or to work from home – women
       retained the right to benefits during the period of partially
       paid leave. In 1990 a further amendment extended the
       period of partially paid leave (with social security payments)
       to look after the child to 18 months. In addition an
       application could be made for leave without pay until the
       child was three years old. Very significantly, this law also
       provided for the partially paid leave and additional leave
       without pay to look after the child to be taken either fully
       or in part by the father of the child, the grandmother, the
       grandfather or other close relatives.

6   The 'second economy' consists of numerous legal, semi-legal and illegal informal means of by-passing the imperfect state-planned supply and distribution system (the 'first economy'). These means can include use of the black-market, bribery, corruption, or simply obtaining goods in short supply and exchanging them with friends and relatives for other goods in short supply to which they have access.

7   The women's councils were established by Krushchev in the 1950s and 1960s and marked the first women's movement since the 1920s. Under Brezhnev, however, they became formal, moribund organizations until Gorbachev's call for their revival in 1986.

8   In Russian the Independent Women's Democratic Initiative is shortened to the acronym NeZhDI which means 'don't wait'.

8 Conclusion

Chris Corrin

In concluding this study of women's experience of
change it is appropriate to consider not only the
similarities and differences between women's
experiences in changing situations and of the various
processes at work in their countries, but also some of
the future trends resulting from political
developments and moves towards marketization.

The year of 1989 certain proved to be a 'turning
point' for most of the countries in central and eastern
Europe. Beginning in January when the Hungarian
reformers forced the communist leadership to accept
a multi-party system, and the first independent
political party was launched in Slovenia in
Yugoslavia, the changes rapidly multiplied in a variety
of ways throughout the year. Round-table talks took
place in Poland from February to April, between the
government and the Solidarity opposition,
culminating in agreement on a period of 'guided
democracy'. By July, Gorbachev was renouncing the
'Brezhnev doctrine' to the Council of Europe, and in
August Tadeusz Mazowiecki of Poland became the
first non-communist prime minister in central and
eastern Europe for at least 40 years.

Perhaps the most visibly dramatic occurrence took
place in August and September when tens of
thousands of East Germans made their exit to the
west via Hungary and Austria. This was viewed by
television watchers all over the region, and elsewhere,
and it was considered that the decision of the

Hungarian authorities *not* to close their borders gave a thrust to the revolutionary potential in the region. That the Soviet Union did not intervene at this point was a pivotal signal to the old regime in East Germany.

By September the Hungarian constitution was agreed by the Communist Party and opposition representatives and in October the Party had reformed itself as the Hungarian Socialist Party. In East Germany in October and November there were major demonstrations in various cities against communist rule, and in October Honecker resigned as East German head of state, replaced by Egon Krenz. By November the Berlin Wall was tumbling down, with over 50 crossing points established by the end of the month. In Prague, in November, an anti-government demonstration was violently disbanded by police and more demonstrations took place around the country, with the Czech opposition groups forming Civic Forum on 19 November. Egon Krenz lasted less than two months in office, resigning on 6 December. Another resignation followed when Czechoslovakia's Party leader, Milos Jakes, resigned and a non-communist government took power, headed by Vaclav Havel, former dissident and writer. The balance sheet at the end of 1989 showed that the communist leaders were well and truly challenged by opposition groups and that in Hungary and Czechoslovakia new non-communist governments were being organized.

By March 1990, elections in East Germany had resulted in a victory for the right-wing coalition, the Alliance for Germany (48 per cent), over the Social Democrats who had been expected to do quite well. In the multi-party elections in Hungary the Democratic Forum won the biggest share of the vote (42 per cent) and went on to head a three-party coalition against the opposition coalition headed by the Free Democrats (who received the second largest vote). By May the communists had been voted out in multi-party elections in two Yugoslav republics, Croatia and Slovenia, and right-wing parties came to

power. In the June multi-party elections in
Czechoslovakia the Civic Forum and its sister
organization in Slovakia, Public Against Violence,
were swept into power. At the same time the
Warsaw Treaty Organization (Warsaw Pact) made an
agreement to transform itself into a political body.
From July, when German monetary union took
place, to September, when the signing of the 'Four
plus Two' talks (four allied powers plus the two
Germanies) took place in Moscow, German
unification was prepared. The two Germanies were
officially unified on 3 October 1991. This unification
of a divided country was taken by many as a signal for
the unification of the whole of Europe – no longer
east and west but a 'new Europe'. In terms of the
new political structures the Appendix (pages 256–63)
shows some of the most fundamental moves away
from the rigid Party systems.

Yet, it is fair to say that no definitive picture emerges
from the outlines of these changes given in the
Appendix. In the most general terms, all the countries
have rejected the rigid systems of Party control over
state and societal structures and relations, yet in
Poland and Hungary where distinct changes have
been continuing for at least a decade there are
apparent differences in aims and political mechanisms
for achieving change. Perhaps the frequent use of the
word 'former' signifies much in terms of the former
GDR, the former Yugoslavia and the former Soviet
Union. With the disintegration of republican systems
we are witnessing enormous changes. The impact
upon women of such changes will be various and in
some situations fundamental. Women in Croatia
during late 1991 were facing the terrible experience
of losing sons and husbands to the war while trying to
continue with 'normal' life amid shelling and
destruction. Many people in certain of the former
Soviet republics and in Romania and the former
Yugoslavia during the winter of 1991–92
experienced cold from fuel shortages, and hunger
from either food shortages or inefficient distribution
systems. Many women and men are now

experiencing their first period of unemployment and the associated hardships that accompany it.

In political terms there is much talk about how 'democratic' each country is. In Poland the great solidarity of Solidarnösc and the unifying factor of the Roman Catholic Church gave expression to homogeneity in Polish life and allowed for more participation for the majority of working people, yet for women there is apparent oppression in this linking of Church and state, especially in terms of women's rights to control their fertility. The remarkably fragmented results of the October 1991 elections in Poland meant that forming a coalition was very difficult and clearly showed classic symptoms of 'voter alienation', which given the large number of parties could lead to political impotence in dealing with the bad economic situation.

In Hungary, while there were very democratic (if complicated) electoral arrangements, the leading party in the ruling coalition (Hungarian Democratic Forum) has proven itself to be a party of talk rather than action, and there remains confusion within Hungary as to the way forward politically and economically. While the Church has signatures on petitions against abortion rights, the Parliament is 'waiting to see' what the mood will be.

In Czechoslovakia the Civic Forum was deeply divided before it quietly dissolved in April 1991. The genial 'unifier', Havel, is under pressure within the more divided party situation. The incident of eggs being thrown at him in Bratislava in October 1991 was symptomatic of the heightened nationalist tensions between the peoples of Slovakia and the Czech lands.

For people in the former GDR certain aspects of life have become shocking, especially in terms of price rises and unemployment. It is hard to imagine the effects of becoming unemployed in the abstract, and certainly there were no practical examples of people living without work in a period of rising inflation. A fairly low average wage under the communists, say

1200 marks (£400) a month secured a stable and relatively comfortable standard of living. Now that subsidies have been lifted from rents, energy, food and consumer goods even those in work are suffering. In some towns though, such as Liepzig, unemployment had reached 50 per cent by April 1991. The poor showing of Kohl's Christian Democrats in his own region is a measure of the disappointment felt by West Germans in terms of tax rises and added economic burdens.

In the former Yugoslavia the declaration of hostilities on 6 May, coupled with the subsequent failure to elect a head of state, led to a constitutional crisis. It is difficult to foresee a short-term resolution to this ongoing conflict, and in the meantime women's lives are equally caught up in the 'cross-fire'.

In the Soviet Union, Gorbachev's offer to resign in April 1991 turned out to bolster support for his continuation, yet Yeltsin's subsequent election as President of the Russian Republic proved timely in terms of securing Gorbachev's release during the August coup. On 31 December 1991 the Soviet Union ceased to exist, and within the new Commonwealth of Independent States serious questions are now being asked regarding the future collaboration in the region, particularly in military terms. Growing nationalist aspirations will have their impact as the 1990s unfold.

As the body of this study shows, there are some points that need to be emphasized regarding the situation for women in this time of transition. The push and pull factors leading towards a greater role for market mechanisms in each of these countries have some similar roots yet will often result in different consequences.

I will centre these concluding remarks initially on our three analyses: of women's involvement in production and reproduction; of women's participation and representation in decision making; and of women's personal autonomy.

Women as producers and reproducers – workers and mothers

It is apparent that in the arenas of production and reproduction women's lives will be vitally affected. In terms of work, women will lose some of their opportunities in paid production. Childbearing and child-caring in this changing climate are actively being promoted as women's prime concerns and direct responsibility. From Gorbachev's 'women's true mission' speech to the legislation privatizing state nurseries and placing limits on women's rights to abortion, it is apparent that women's choices are again being limited in terms of working outside the home, with state support for families. Women are attempting to resist new legislation in many areas, especially that limiting rights to abortion which is now being incorporated into several parliaments. Table 8.1 indicates the level of women's work-force participation.

Table 8.1

Women's labour-force participation 1970–1988

Female Employment as a percentage of the total labour-force

Country	1970	1980	1985	1988
Bulgaria	42.5	48.7	49.9	–
Czechoslovakia	45.0	46.2	47.2	47.3
Hungary	41.9	44.8	45.7	46.0
GDR	48.6	50.5	50.2	49.9
Poland	39.4	43.5	44.7	45.5
Romania	30.2	37.2	39.4	40.0
USSR	50.8	51.2	50.8	50.8

(Source: Kroupova, 1990, quoted in *Swasti Mitter*, Vienna Report)

The high level of labour-force participation by women has been an important factor in the 'double burden' arguments concerning legislative definitions of women as workers and mothers. This has set up, to some extent, a false dichotomy. It need not be the case that women have to choose between such limited options. Flexibility is the key to twinning possibilities concerning paid work and child-care. Such flexibility has not been present within the countries under consideration, either from the perspectives of training and retraining for women of all ages, job-sharing or flexibly timed working hours, or from the perspectives of men sharing care within the home. Similar problems are present within the economies of western Europe, in terms of the devaluing of women's worth and the under-emphasizing of the possibilities of more creative ways of organizing paid work and unpaid domestic work.

In terms of the full employment policies it was often the case that there was over-employment in certain spheres so that several people 'shared' a job that required little effort and paid very little. Such over-employment and the general top-down approach within enterprises meant that working people felt demoralized and had little respect for the style of management. In some countries, like Hungary, it was possible to have second and even third jobs within the second economy. This in turn, though, placed strain on people's personal lives. It is apparent that many women in these countries have been forced to work to supplement the family budget. Within the present situation there are many women throughout the former Soviet Union and central and eastern Europe who would be happy to be able to spend time at home with their growing children. Many women have worked long hours in poor conditions for low pay, and for many years. There is a difference between women choosing domestic work, in the knowledge that their families will be provided for, and having basically no choice. In former times there was no choice about working; it was a duty to work. Yet the economic scene is such that many women will have little choice about returning to the home, and will in fact be forced to become unpaid domestic workers, possibly having to deal with a constantly shrinking budget. Women in the lower income groups, single parents, and those who are unskilled and made redundant from large factories will not have many choices. Within the changing environment, with a continually shrinking job market and the closure of crèches and kindergartens, the fact that women are still seen as primarily responsible for child-care and domestic work means there may be no choice concerning unemployment. In fact, in many countries, hidden unemployment has existed for some time.

Recent figures on unemployment show varying trends. At the beginning of 1990 in Poland there were 46000 people unemployed, yet by the end of December 1990 this figure had increased to 1 126 100 – 8.3 per cent of the total work-force. Women made up 51 per cent of this figure, which is high given that women workers are 45 per cent of the total work-force. That the majority of women unemployed are in the 31–40 age group causes concern, as this is a time of increased expenditure on children and in the family generally. Vesna Pesic notes that the large-scale lay-offs that began at the end of 1990 in Croatia and Slovenia showed 216000 registered unemployed at the end of January 1991 – 38 per cent higher than in the same month in 1990 (Pesic, 1991). Although women in Hungary seem to have been slightly less affected than men so far, it is now recognized that there are a large number of women employed in the heavy industries (largely as ancillary staff – cleaners, clerical workers) and as these industries are closed or privatized women will face unemployment in roughly equal numbers with men. In Czechoslovakia generally, to date, the figures on unemployment remain almost universally low in comparison with the other countries under consideration, except the former Soviet Union.

Women's unemployment differs across these countries according to comparable data on qualifications and skills. In some countries, notably the former Yugoslavia and GDR, it appears that a large proportion of the unemployed women have a high level of education, including university degrees. In

Hungary, Poland and Czechoslovakia the situation seems somewhat different in that the majority of highly educated women can find employment, except those in certain academic circles as academia is being drastically reorganized. The boards of some banks and commercial concerns in Hungary are composed of up to 50 per cent women. While most of the higher education institutions are being reorganized in central and eastern Europe the tenure of those employed remains uncertain. In Czechoslovakia and Hungary it is likely that those women without skills training or those in semi-skilled occupations will suffer most from unemployment, certainly in the shorter term. Hungary and Czechoslovakia have the most highly developed market economies and are following similar paths in terms of closing down and privatizing heavy industrial concerns and diversifying into other commercial and technological sectors including banking and information technology. In these countries then, women with certain educational qualifications will be able to take up some posts in these sectors, whereas the opportunities for less qualified women will decrease.

In terms of training and retraining of women, very few schemes exist in these countries at present. The various ministries of labour seem to assume that it is men who will be trained or retrained in the necessary skills, or that women's particular employment needs can be subsumed under general labour-market requirements. The fact that women-headed households make up an increasing number of family groups and that in some countries, especially Poland and Hungary, this number is increasing, seems not to be taken account of.

Economic conditions

In the former Yugoslavia, Poland and the former GDR the picture seems less clear and altogether less optimistic. Poland is in the worst situation economically, in terms of its IMF debt and the forced cut-backs of the 'short shock' treatment that have been biting into Polish society. With the budget running at 10 000 billion zloty (£525 million) deficit in mid 1991, the Government attempted to get monetary restrictions eased by the IMF in order to be able to counter the recession. In June 1991 Solidarity was demanding that the effects of recent rises of more than 100 per cent for domestic energy be compensated. Since the October 1991 election the situation can be seen to have deteriorated in that the centre-right forces in coalition are in opposition to Walesa's economic reform plans.

In the former GDR, while the economic situation is less obviously desperate in terms of external borrowing, the psychological effects of the West German 'take-over' have been dramatic, with blatant infringements of the unification treaty in terms of the 'down-grading' of certain GDR qualifications and other practices which destroy people's prospects. As noted, unemployment in some cities such as Leipzig is reaching the 50 per cent mark. Suicide rates have risen alarmingly.

In the former Yugoslavia, while the massive inflation has been curbed, the extremely precarious political situation is one in which the economy can barely function. With the declared independence of Slovenia and Croatia, and their economic plans to split from the other republics, it remains unclear how the various economies can develop. Certainly further aid from the European Community will be linked with political stability, and the current impasse between the right-wing governments in the 'break-away' republics and the communist hardliners in Serbia and Montenegro seems unlikely to be resolved quickly. Women's employment in Yugoslavia was always uneven across republics but now unemployment is increasing, especially for certain groups of women. In the current confused political climate women's needs are even less regarded yet their difficulties increase.

In the former Soviet Union, on the other hand, the picture is contradictory yet optimistic. Precise information on the economic front is not so easy to obtain, though it is apparent that the national income has fallen markedly. The perceived need for western investment within the economy ties the republics to moving further in the direction of market-oriented reforms. The restructuring of outdated industrial organizations will bring with it unemployment, which will of course vary across republics and will affect men and women differently. The initial figures signalling unemployment are not yet broken down according to gender.

There are some existing networks that could be made use of with regard to women gaining new skills or retraining for other employment. The forums of the trade unions could be activated on women's training initiatives. One model might be the Women's Association Mission in Moscow. There are also Associations of Entrepreneurs in Czechoslovakia and Hungary which might be approached to initiate cross-national networking. Certainly various courses in assertiveness training would be useful to women. At present, because of lack of funding for such courses, it is only women who can afford to pay for them who can take part. Trade-union projects could be particularly important for women in terms of co-ordinating retraining for those wishing to pursue alternative forms of work.

There is a certain level of government co-operation between Hungary, Poland and Czechoslovakia in the fields of labour policy and labour-power planning yet these mechanisms have not yet been extended to develop women workers' skills specifically. In Hungary the governmental organizations have been quite effective to date in promoting self-employment among women but, of course, the great majority of women cannot become self-employed. Social support systems such as child-care facilities and flexible working, plus mechanisms for effective wage bargaining need to be encouraged by governmental organizations and worked towards by people in their work-places and trade unions.

Domestic work   In terms of work within the home between women and men, progress seems to have been slow. As in western Europe, there are some modern, democratic family groupings present in all of these countries, often at the professional, middle-class levels. In many families at all levels men take part in caring for children but, as women are aware, the domestic division of labour is not primarily about 'who does what'. The fundamental changes needed for women to become equal partners with men in society concern primarily attitudinal changes, that is changes in people's value orientations – their priorities concerning what is 'valued' and in which ways. What is required is a re-evaluation of work in all of its forms, so that domestic work and caring do not remain undervalued and relegated as secondary and less important. Here the cash nexus weighs heavily. If all things are valued in monetary terms then of course work that is unpaid and that does not create obvious wealth in the recognized, public 'productive' sense is bound to be downgraded and viewed as relatively unimportant. Yet in terms of the quality of life and indeed the regeneration of the human race, and of course work-forces, domestic work is vital to all other forms of production.

The main aim of some of the women's groups that are active in highlighting the importance of domestic work, across Europe and internationally, is threefold. First they wish to create a recognition that domestic work can be enjoyable, certainly in terms of spending time with children, and that men are missing out by not being more involved in this. At the same time, as cleaning in various forms seems less enjoyable, it should be shared democratically. Second, parenthood, not just motherhood, needs to be recognized as a social contribution and as something to be chosen. Third, notions of 'sex roles' need to be broken down so that it becomes acceptable for women to be out working as bank managers or train drivers and for men to be able to work in the home.

Choices are being made about who is employed within the countries under consideration in this transitional period, but the entrepreneurs or state officials making many of these choices are definitely not considering women as equally good and important employees. A public debate on the old ideas of 'sex roles' is vital to protect women's interests. If all women can do is to argue against such traditional ideas within their own domestic situations, in their own lives, then they not only suffer personally, but their opportunities to gain strength collectively are denied.

Women as decision makers – participation and representation

During 1989 women were highly visible on the streets in demonstrations, organizing meetings, electioneering and voting. When the new governments were being formed, however, and people were taking their places in the new power structures, women seemed to disappear from view. The reasons for this differ across countries, but two primary factors are the still-current belief that politics is a 'man's world' and that women have other priorities. The former has many causal links with the 'dirty' politics of the old regimes and the view that the political world is a ruthless one. An underlying, yet very important aspect of this, is another commonly articulated belief that people will not vote for women. In Hungary the leader of the Hungarian Socialist Party (the reformed Communist Party) was criticized for her dress sense rather than her policies.

In terms of women's priorities, given that they are generally paid workers as well as having the primary responsibility for home-work and domestic care, they certainly have a lot less time to participate in evening meetings. This need not be the case, but the prevailing attitudes are such that women are much more acceptable as behind-the-scenes organizers in trade-union or party offices, while the men carry out the, often less onerous, public duties.

There are important theoretical issues here in terms of differences between *emancipation* – equality on men's terms and within a male-oriented and dominated framework – and *liberation* – which includes a concern with the expansion of social space to the benefit of women, men and children, so that this is an extended notion of equality that can liberate people from limited expectations about what people can and cannot do.

Within feminist groups worldwide participation in formal politics is a hotly debated issue, yet there is a general recognition that without the presence of women in decision-making bodies, women's interests cannot be truly represented. Some feminists argue that women have to undermine the prevailing patriarchal attitudes in which men's values are accorded priority, and that women can thereby create a 'women-friendly' culture. The case of Icelandic women is often cited. There women made their breakthrough political *after* such a culture had begun to be built up. With many men away for up to six months at a time, Icelandic women had prepared the ground by building up their confidence and support and were then able to act boldly in unison, and became a definite force to be reckoned with. Women in central and eastern Europe and the former Soviet Union are unlikely to get such opportunities, any more than women in most other countries. It is going to be a slow process to undermine the dominant male cultures apparent throughout most countries of Europe.

Women's activity towards change

The liberation of women in any society involves a dual process – entry into the national economy and relative withdrawal from the domestic economy. Experience demonstrates that the burdens of domestic work are not automatically lessened by nationalization of the means of production. It also confirms that structural changes must be accompanied by some form of cultural revolution aimed at the elimination of gendered power imbalances and the opening up of domestic opportunities and responsibilities – caring for children can be a pleasure denied to men. Notions of masculinity and femininity need to be extended and explored.

A numerical drop in the numbers of women in the higher levels of the governmental structures has been apparent since the Communist Parties lost power. As noted, much of this participation was numerical and

token, rather than actual and active. The numbers of
women now involved at this high level are at least
equal with certain western democracies such as
France and Britain, yet obviously fall far short of such
higher participation in Sweden and Iceland. That
women are active in party offices, writing social
policy documents, working in the trade unions and
labour offices, is apparent, and such women will be
pivotal in the coming years in making women's
demands heard. So too will those women who do
not actively intervene in 'high politics' but who are
making decisions on an everyday level in their
homes, at their children's schools and in their local
housing communities. How women are to gain the
confidence in their abilities to change their
surroundings is the key question for the 1990s.

**Women's rights
over their bodies
– abortion and
sexuality**

It is apparent that the availability of abortion is
becoming restricted in many countries in central and
eastern Europe. It is well to point out that women in
these countries have never argued for abortion as a
form of birth control, but that in situations where
other forms of contraception were not readily
available women needed the choice of having
abortions in order not to be forced to bear children
they could not care for or support, for whatever
reasons. That abortion was used as a means of birth
control in some countries, such as the Soviet Union
where some women had as many as 12 abortions, is
not to say that women wanted this. The effects of
abortion on women are traumatic, especially when
the clinics in which they are carried out are set up like
assembly lines with women watching others having
their abortions, sometimes without anaesthetic.

Women in central and eastern Europe today are
arguing that rather than return to the horrors of
'back-street', illegal abortions, they want a safer, legal
option to be available, if need be.

**Women's
personal
autonomy**

Women's autonomy can be gained in a variety of
ways, not least by learning about ways to achieve it.
One foundation in Hungary, Ariadne Gaia
Foundation, runs a variety of personal development

courses including training courses in educational areas which aim to raise awareness, including assertiveness and leadership courses, and courses concerned with healing and spirituality. Such foundations, given adequate funding, could provide a useful link between governmental organizations and individual needs. To be able to do this their services would need to be recognized and supported as being beneficial in terms of social regeneration and effective skill training.

It can be seen that women's active participation is attempting to effect change, linked with women's autonomy. The large variety of 'women's groups' that have been forming over the last year or two, be they any of the 37 varieties available in Czechoslovakia or at the level of the Gender Studies Centre in Moscow are evidence of this. There has been a growth in international conferences to which a variety of women from the former Soviet Union and central and eastern Europe countries have had opportunities to travel – a shift from the past when it was the self-appointed, official women's representatives who generally attended such gatherings. One important decision taken at the Women's Conference on Security and Cooperation in Europe (CSCE) in Berlin in November 1990 was to form a network of women from central and eastern Europe. The text of the declaration is set out below.

Women from East-Central and East European countries present at the first Women's CSCE came to the conclusion that it is of vital importance to create a network of East-Central and East European women in order to coordinate activities of women's organizations in their countries and share information about the actual situation of women on the broad international level. Such a network is necessary especially as the newly emerging democracies have proved to be conservative and authoritarian regarding women. They perpetuate and promote male dominance in these societies. The best examples to prove this statement can be found in the tendencies to raise the percentage of unemployed women beyond that of men and to curb or even ban the right of abortion.

It is necessary to develop close relations with women from all other parts of Europe and the world because we share the same problems, even if the manifestations are different – in East Europe increasing nationalism and ethnic conflicts, and in the West racism and xenophobia have similar roots in the patriarchy and have the same disastrous impact on all women.

East-Central and East European participants of the Women's CSCE are convinced that the worsening situation of women in their countries, which is due to the transition period, could be stopped and the most difficult problems overcome only if women organize themselves and struggle against the still very dominant patriarchal culture and structures in their societies.

With the spreading of the women's movement from below, women from East-Central and Eastern Europe have a general chance to change the societies they are living in and influence all levels of power structures.

This historic document says a good deal for the resolve of those women present to attempt to initiate women's activism towards progressive change within their societies.

Drawing together the interwoven threads of this book is both an easy and a difficult task. It is easy in the sense that common themes and experiences have come through each country under consideration. Yet it is also very difficult in that what we have tried to present is a study that shows the differences between and within countries in the context of varying experiences of the 'Soviet style' of political organization and its social consequences. Since the major upheavals of 1989 the previous commonality in these countries' politics has been transformed, so that they are moving away from the Soviet-style economistic way of organizing their affairs towards more open and pluralistic methods of decision making. This is happening at a different pace in each country, and the October 1991 elections in Poland certainly showed that timing is an important variable in changing political structures. Polish people 'voted with their feet' – the average turnout was 43.2 per cent and the numbers elected from different parties meant that it was extremely difficult to form a strong government.

The complications surrounding the 'double burden' remain very much a factor in women's lives in the former Soviet Union and in central, eastern and southern Europe. For women in western and northern European countries, juggling child-care and jobs remains a difficulty. With the wider marketization in the countries we have looked at one general consensus among analysts of women's lives is that the various experiences women face across Europe are now becoming more comparable. Common features are emerging in terms of choices women may make as to their full-time participation in the work-force, the organization of child-care (in that state care will continue to become reduced over the transitional period) and in terms of their organization as women, for themselves.

It remains the case, and this is the difficult part for most people as it makes all considerations more 'complicated', that in every country in the world certain women and their communities are always considered as 'different', be they Romany women, Jewish women, black women, migrant women, disabled women, lesbian women, or very old and poor women – the list is long. While the authors of this book agreed on many common aspects of our project, we are aware that a short collective book of this size barely scratches the surface of the variety and enormous complexity in women's lives. Our aim was to inform readers in an accessible way about some aspects of women's lives in a part of the world that has experienced a great deal of change. Now massive changes are taking place again and we wanted to point up the similarities and differences within these countries at a time when women are caught in what could be seen as 'the worst of both worlds'. Nurseries and crèches are being privatized or priced out of many women's reach while women's rights to good contraceptive advice and abortion are being challenged. Women and men are experiencing unemployment differently across these countries of Europe, especially in that women are seen to have a 'natural' alternative to a career – becoming full-time mothers. Not all women want this option, yet it is obvious that having been denied the right to stay home with children many have quite romantic notions of 'how nice it would be ...'. Yet most women know that it is not romantic to be poor and to be unable to buy life's necessities. For some women, especially in the former GDR and in Poland, their dream of spending more time with their children now that they no longer have paid work has turned into the nightmare of having to go from place to place to try to buy food at reasonable prices. In the former Soviet republics in early 1992 the queues were long for small food stocks that had tripled in price in a matter of days.

Some women in Russia, Romania and various other areas in different countries try to find things to sell – small piles of mint leaves on a piece of newspaper, handfuls of wrinkled apples and a multitude of handiworks are evidence that many women are now poor yet want and need to be able to provide the bare minimum for their families. It is often women from the so-called minority groups – such as Romanies or ethnic minorities within larger national groups – who suffer most as they are generally poorer, less protected by social policy measures, and have less access to resources such as health care, education and, of course, jobs.

'Reform' is not gender neutral and it varies in each country according to national conditions, historical developments and current resources and levels of prosperity. One major factor that is pivotal to this work is that the advancement of women's interests is most definitely not seen as an official priority by the newly-appointed governments in central and eastern Europe in present times. It must be added that even in those countries of the world where the advancement of women's interests is officially prioritized, the reality is often disappointing. Some would argue that having women's interests written into the old 'state socialist' rhetoric did women more harm than good. From the case studies we have considered, it is obvious that many women's lives were very hard and there remained areas of prejudice and injustice against women in these societies. Yet it is also the case that most women in these countries, other than women in oppressed ethnic groups, are by and large well-educated and view working outside their homes as something they expect to be able to have choice in. Regardless of choices that may be made regarding full-time parenthood, many women will remain active within the labour-market and will have expectations instilled from the former period that will give them a drive to fulfil their own desires. This confidence and ability among women will not disappear in the coming years, and it may well become strengthened in the new, more open and democratic conditions.

The question 'whither Europe?' remains a challenge for the peoples of central and eastern Europe and the former Soviet Union. Some groups of people, including leading political forces in Slovakia, the former Yugoslavia, Romania and the former Soviet republics, are looking towards organizing their societies along ethnic/religious lines that will lead to great upheaval. The fragile political climate of the Balkan peninsula will heighten tensions during the early 1990s, and despite a more participatory social and political situation in some countries the reality of nationalism, racism and war radically affects people's lives. In such a situation different groups of women often become fundamentally important as a source of anti-nationalism and peace activism. On issues of reproductive rights, violence against women and generally changing women's situations for the better, women across Europe – east, west, south and north – continue to share communication and activism, which could well become one of the most positive aspects for change as this century ends.

Appendix
Fundamental political changes

Name of country:	**The Hungarian Republic – Hungary**
Background uprisings:	1956 revolution (now recognized as a revolution).
Timing of revolutionary changes:	Recognition post-1956 of Soviet influence in the area. Began economic experimentation from mid 1960s (1968 NEM). Various oppositional groupings publishing samizdat materials. By mid 1980s Communist Party was reforming to certain extent. By 1989 the transition was smooth in that communist rule caved in as locus of power had shifted.
Main revolutionary movements/parties:	Association of Free Democrats arose from opposition groupings. Young Democrats FIDESZ very active from 1988.
	Hungarian Democratic Forum largest party; not radical.
Name of transformed CP:	Hungarian Socialist Party part of opposition in Parliament.
Has leading role of CP been officially denied?	Yes. Decision taken at Party congress in 1989. Constitution changed in October 1989.
Date of elections:	24 March to 8 April 1990.
Name of former president:	János Kádár (1957–88).

Name of current president:	Arpád Göncz.
Make up of new government:	Centre-right coalition of Hungarian Democratic Forum (largest party), plus Christian Democrats and Smallholders.
	Opposition includes Association of Free Democrats (second largest party), Young Democrats and the Hungarian Socialist Party (former communists).
Current pressing issues:	Enthusiasm for EC entry. Eager for western investment. Inflation at 30 per cent in first quarter of 1991. Aims to close or privatize 75 per cent of heavy industrial concerns in next five years. Tensions could arise between the communist-controlled unions in mining and steel industries over the number of anticipated unemployed.
	Obvious divisions between rich and poor is causing concern. Budapest and other areas are experiencing bad pollution. EC financing some environmental projects.
	1991 war in Yugoslavia affecting life in Hungary – thousands of refugees, fears for ethnic Hungarians in Serbia and infringements of Hungarian airspace.
Name of country:	**Poland**
Background uprisings:	1956 uprising.
	1976 opposition.
	1980/91 development of Solidarnösc.
Timing of revolutionary changes:	State/society confrontation since 1970s. Martial law declared 1981.
	Government reforms rejected by referendum 1987. By first round of more open elections in 1989 Solidarity gain over communists.

Character of changes:	Long-term confrontations between workers and government. Strikes and demonstrations. 1981 martial law was turning point in state–society relations. August 1989 Solidarnösc offered to form new coalition with the communists and Mazowiecki was appointed first non-communist prime minister in central and eastern Europe.
	October 1991, free elections failed to secure a clear coalition.
Main revolutionary movements/parties:	Solidarnösc was the major opposition grouping containing differing groups and factions.
Name of transformed CP:	Social Democracy of the Kingdom of Poland.
Has leading role of CP been officially denied?	Yes. The Sejm eliminated the leading role of the Communist Party in government on 29 December 1989.
Date of elections:	First round of free elections June 1989. New government formed in August 1989.
	27 October 1991.
Name of old president:	General Jaruzelski.
Name of current president:	Lech Walesa.
Make up of new government:	Uneven combination with centre-left holding majority of seats but centre-right coalition.
Current pressing issues:	Unemployment and negative balance of foreign debts. Short-shock treatment has led to much poverty and less foreign investment than Hungary or Czechoslovakia.
	£350 million loan from IMF.
	Tension between government and workers' protests.

Name of country:	**Czech and Slovak Federative Republic (CSFR) – Czechoslovakia**
Background uprisings:	Late de-Stalinization.
	1968 uprising Prague Spring – all opposition heavily suppressed during the 1970s and 1980s.
	Charter 77 formed a focus for other political groups in Europe.
	After the brutal suppression of the Prague Spring the secret police were very active. Many people felt implicated and political opposition was limited.
Timing of revolutionary changes:	The 'Velvet Revolution' of late November 1989 was very short – less than three weeks.
	The very large, peaceful demonstration soon coalesced around Vaclav Havel and Civic Forum, with the Slovakian sister organization Public Against Violence.
Main revolutionary movements/parties:	Civic Forum and Public Against Violence. Some tension with former communists. Public Against Violence strongly supported in Slovakia.
Name of transformed CP:	Remains unchanged.
Has leading role of CP been officially denied:	Yes. Constitution changed November 1989.
Date of elections:	Elections were held in June 1990, six months after the new government was formed.
Name of old president:	Gustav Husak.
Name of current president:	Vaclav Havel.
Make up of new government:	Broad social democratic coalition. Clearer party lines emerging since Civic Forum was dissolved in April 1991.

Current pressing issues:	Federal tensions between Czech lands and Slovakia.
	Enthusiasm for trading links with other central and eastern European countries.

Name of country:	**German Democratic Republic** now five länder in united Germany.
Background uprisings:	1953 uprising.
	1961 Berlin Wall built.
Timing of revolutionary changes:	Summer 1989 citizens travel through Hungary.
	October 1989 70 000 demonstrate in Leipzig: Krenz replaces Honecker; November government and politburo resign.
	Berlin Wall reopened.
Character of changes:	Peaceful vigils, especially in Leipzig – 'We the people'.
Main revolutionary movements/parties:	New Forum, Social Democratic Party, Christian Democrats Union, Green Party, United Left.
Name of transformed CP:	Party of Democratic Socialism (PDS).
Has leading role of CP been officially denied?	Yes – by a parliamentary vote, Volkskammer 1 December 1989.
Date of elections:	18 March 1990.
Name of old president:	Erich Honecker.
Name of current president:	Kohl – all-German Chancellor.
Make up of new government:	Christian Democratic majority.
Current pressing issues:	Unemployment.
	Rise of nationalism.
	Protests in five länder of former GDR about poverty and unemployment.

Resentment in West Germany about increased taxes required for refloating the eastern economy.

Kohl less popular in local polls.

Name of country: **Yugoslavia**

Background uprisings: Broke with Soviet Union in 1948.

Uprising in Kosovo in 1981.

Timing of revolutionary changes: Adopted policies of decentralization and self-management. Tito imposed unity until he died in 1980.

1987 Milosevic became leader of Serbian Party with nationalist rhetoric over Kosovo.

By 1989 inflation reached 2500 per cent. Croat PM Markovic stabilized the dinar by April 1991.

War declared in May 1991 with constitutional crisis when Serbs refused to recognize the Croatian premier in the rotation of all-Yugoslav leadership.

Main movements/parties: The Serbian communists backed by the Montenegrins wanted all-Yugoslav federation – some see this as 'greater Serbia'. The Slovenes and Croats favoured independence.

Name of transformed CP: Name unchanged (League of Communists of Yugoslavia, LYC).

February 1990 the Slovene League of Communists was renamed the Party of Democratic Renewal.

Has leading role of CP been officially denied? Yes. January 1990.

Congress of the LYC agrees to abolish constitutionally guaranteed leading role. Congress indefinitely adjourned after Slovene walkout.

Date of elections:	April–May 1990 multi-party elections in two republics: Slovenia and Croatia. Right-wing parties elected over communists.
Name of last federal prime minister:	Ante Markovic.
Name of current president:	15 May 1991 failure to elect a president, rejection of normal rotation, meant constitutional crisis.
Make up of new government:	Republics of Croatia and Slovenia announced their independence 26 June 1991.
Current pressing issues:	Recognition of independence of Croatia and Slovenia by European Community. UN peacekeeping force in place.
	Holding the ceasefire; negotiating territorial and political settlements. Re-establishing independent economies.
Name of country:	**Russia and the former Soviet republics**
Background uprisings:	Occasional popular disturbances since the 1960s and large-scale demonstrations against communist rule since about 1988. About 1000 lives lost in inter-ethnic conflicts since the same date.
Timing of revolutionary changes:	Political change, though launched by the Party leadership, came increasingly to reflect pressure 'from below'. The first-ever largely competitive elections in March 1989 were followed by republican and local elections in 1990 in which nationalist and other movements gained power in six of the 15 republics, and in Moscow and Leningrad.

Main revolutionary movements/parties:	The principal political force opposing the Communist Party on a national basis is 'Democratic Russia', a loose coalition of liberals and radicals whose candidate Boris Yeltsin was elected Russian President in June 1991. About 500 parties are active at the republican level.
Name of transformed CP:	Following the August coup, the activity of the Party was suspended in a number of republics. No new communist grouping has yet been forged.
Has leading role of CP been officially denied:	Yes. In March 1990 the Third Congress of People's Deputies voted to reword Article 6 of the 1977 constitution so as to end the monopoly of power previously enjoyed by the CPSU.
Date of elections:	Elections were held in 1989 and 1990 under a revised electoral law adopted in December 1988.
Name of old president:	Andrei Gromyko (1985–88).
Name of last president:	Mikhail Gorbachev.
Make up of new government:	Following the failed coup of August 1991 a temporary governmental structure was put in place. It included a two-tier union (political and economic) of those republics wishing to join, and a bi-cameral Parliament. Each former republic is forming its own governmental structure.
Current pressing issues:	The collapse of the economy, with national income falling 14 per cent in the first quarter of 1991; market oriented reforms under discussion and western assistance is seen as essential to its success. Also the military and national questions.

Bibliography

Hungary

Adamik, Mária, 'Hungary: A loss of Rights?', *Feminist Review*, no. 39, winter 1991, pp. 166–70.

Béres, Zsuzsa, 'Women's Liberation: Words of Ill Repute', *Budapest Week*, vol. 1, no. 2, March 1991, p. 11.

Biró, David, 'A "teremtés koronái" es a "gyengébb nem"' (The 'masterpiece of creation' and the 'weaker sex'), *Valósag*, no. 9, 1982.

Böhm, Antal and László, Pál, 'Between Town and Village' in A. Böhm and P. Kolosi (eds.) *Structure and Stratification in Hungary*, Institute for Social Sciences, Budapest, 1982.

Corrin, Chris, *Magyar Women's Lives*, Macmillan Education, 1992.

Corrin, Chris, 'The Situation of Women in Hungarian Society' in Júlia Szalai and Bob Deacon (eds.), *Social Policy in the New Eastern Europe*, Gower, 1990(a).

Corrin, Chris, 'Women's Experience of Change in Hungary', in Phizaklea, Rai and Pilkington (eds.), *Women in the Face of Change*, Routledge, 1992.

Eberhardt, Eva (with Szalai, Júlia), *Women of Hungary*, supplement to *Women of Europe*, European Community, January 1991.

Ferge, Zsuzsa, *A Society in the Making: Hungarian Social and Societal Policy 1945–1975*, Penguin, 1979.

Hanak, Katalin, 'Fantasticality - Reality - Fantasy' in *Jel Kép* (Symbol), special edition, Mass Communications Research Centre, 1984.

Hann, C. M., *Changing Cultures – Tázlár: A Village in Hungary*, Cambridge University Press, 1980.

Hegedüs, András, Heller, Agnes, Márkus, Mária, and Vajda, Mihaly, *The Humanisation of Socialism: Writings of the Budapest School*, Allison and Busby, London, 1976.

Heinrich, Hans-Georg, *Hungary: Politics, Economy and Society*, Pinter, London, 1986.

Kamarás, Oroszi and Bárány, *Longitudinal Marriage Survey*, Population Statistics Department, Hungarian Statistical Office, Budapest, 1984.

Koncz, István, *Nepszabadsag*, 10 December 1977.

Konrad, Gyorgy and Szelenyi, Ivan, *The Intellectuals on the Road to Class Power*, Harvester Press, Brighton, 1979.

Koves, Rózsa, article on International Women's Day issues, *Népszava* (People's Voice), 8 March 1978.

Kulcsár, Rósza, 'The Development of the Socio-economic Conditions of Women in Hungary', conference paper for 'Changes in the Status of Women in Eastern Europe', George Washington University, December 1981.

Kulcsár, Rósza, 'Marriage and Social Mobility', *New Hungarian Quarterly*, no. 72, winter 1978, pp. 141–46.

Ladó, Mária, 'Women in the Transition to a Market Economy: The Case of Hungary', United Nations Conference on the Impact of Economic Reform on the Status of Women in Eastern Europe and the USSR, Vienna, 8-12 April 1991.

Márkus, Máriá, 'Change in the Function of Socialization and Models of the Family', *International Review of Sociology*, no. 3, 1975.

Márkus, Máriá, 'Factors influencing the Fertility of Women: The Case of Hungary', *International Journal of Sociology of the Family*, no. 2, 1973.

Mátyus, Aliz, *Holnapon Innen, Tegnapon Tul* (This Side of Tomorrow, the Other Side of Yesterday), Szépirodalmi Könyvkiadó, Budapest, 1980.

Sándorné, Dr. Horváth, Erika, *A Gyestöl a Gyedig*, (From the Child Care Allowance to the Child Care Benefit), Kossuth Könyvkiado, 1986.

Sas, Judit, 'Way of Life and Family Aspirations', in Szánto, *Ways of Life*, Corvina Books, Budapest, 1977.

Szabody, E. (ed.), *Nök – Gazdaság – Tarsadalom: Tanulymanyok A Nok Helyzeterol* (Women – Economy – Society: Essays on the Situation of Women), Kossuth Könyvkiado, Budapest, 1976.

Szalai, Júlia, 'Some Aspects of the Changing Situation of Women in Hungary in the Process of Transition', in A. Tóth and L. Gábor (eds.), *Beyond the Great Transformation,* Budapest, 1991.

Tamás, Pál, 'Hova Lett a Magyar Feminizmus?' (Where has Hungarian Feminism gone?), *Elet és Irodalom* (Life and Literature), 1 May 1987, p. 5.

Tóth, A. and Gábor, L., 'Hungary Under Reform', *Sociological Studies*, Budapest, 1989.

Vajna, T., 'Problems and Trends in the Development of the Hungarian New Economic Mechanism: A Balance Sheet of the 1970s', in A. Nove et al, *East European Economies in the 1970s*, Butterworth, 1982.

Valkai, Zsuzsa, *Miért Isznak a Nök?* (Why do women drink?), Magvetö Kiadó, Budapest, 1986.

Poland   Dobraczynska, Matgorzala, 'Dilemmas of Polish Women – Let's Work', paper given at CSCE Women's Conference, Berlin, November 1990.

Kuratowska, Zofia, 'The Present Situation of Women in Poland', paper prepared for the United Nations Seminar on 'The Status of Women in Eastern Europe and the USSR', Vienna, April 1991.

Petrusewicz, Marta, 'Women and Opposition in Poland: Some Considerations on the Political Participation of Women', in Yolande Cohen (ed.),

Women and Counter Power, Black Rose Books, Montreal, 1989.

Report on Legal Discrimination of Women in Poland, Governmental Plenipotentiary for Women's Affairs, Warsaw 1990.

Siemienska, Renata, 'Women and Solidarity in Poland in the early 1980s', in Yolande Cohen (ed.), *Women and Counter Power,* Black Rose Books, Montreal, 1989.

Titkow, Anna, 'Let's Pull Down the Bastilles Before they are Built', in Robin Morgan, *Sisterhood is Global,* Penguin, 1984.

Women in Poland, Main Office of Statistics, Warsaw, November 1990.

CSFR   Cermakova, M., Hradecka, I. and Navarova, H. (eds.), *K. Postaveni Zen v Ceskoslovenske Spolecnosti,* Sociologicky Ustav Interni Edice, Prague, 1991.

Hanzlova, D., *Vliv VRSR na Postaveni Zeny ve Spolecnosti,* Prague, 1977.

Hauserova, Eva, mimeograph, 1991.

Heitlinger, Alena, *Women and State Socialism: Sex Inequality in the Soviet Union and Czechoslovakia,* Macmillan, London, 1979.

Hradecka, I., unpublished research results at Skoda Factory, 1989.

Kroupova, A., *Women: Employment and Earning in Central and East European Countries,* Prague, 1990.

Navarova, H., in *Mladez a Male Socialni Skupiny,* Prague, 1989.

Okruhlicova, Anna, 'The Influence of Social and Economic Changes in the Czech and Slovak Federal Republic on the Position of Women', paper presented to United Nations seminar on The Status of Women in Eastern Europe and the USSR, Vienna, April 1991.

Solcova, M. J. *Postaveni Zeny v Socialisticke Sbolecnosti,* Prague, 1984.

Unpublished internal material (UIM), 'Rovnopravnost Zen a jeji Socialie Skonomicke Podminky v CSFR', Sociological Institute, Prague, November 1990.

Valterova, A., editorial in *Zena 91*, April 1991.

Venerova, Ludmila, 'Brief survey of the Situation of Czechoslovakian Women at the Beginning of the Transitional Period from Centrally-planned to Market Economy', paper presented at United Nations seminar on The Status of Women in Eastern Europe and the USSR, Vienna, 1991.

GDR   Beyer, Marina, 'The Situation of East German Women in Post-Unification Germany', *Women's Studies International Forum*, vol. 15, no. 1 (special issue, 'A Continent in Transition: Issues for Women in Europe in the 1990s').

Dölling, I., 'Between Hope and Helplessness: Women in the GDR after the "Turning Point"', in *Shifting Territories: Feminisms in Europe*, special issue of *Feminist Review*, no. 39, 1991.

Einhorn, B., 'Socialist Emancipation: The Women's Movement in the German Democratic Republic', in S. Kruks, R. Rapp and M. Young (eds.), *Promissory Notes: Women in the Transition to Socialism*, Monthly Review Press, New York, 1989.

Einhorn, B., 'Where Have All the Women Gone? Women and the Women's Movement in East Central Europe', in *Shifting Territories: Feminisms and Europe*, special issue of *Feminist Review*, no. 39, 1991.

Fischer, E. and Lux, P., Ohne uns ist kein Staat zu machen: DDR-Frauen nach der Wende, Verlag Kiepenheuer & Witsch, Cologne.

Heinen, J., 'The Impact of Social Policy on the Behaviour of Women Workers in Poland and East Germany', in *Critical Social Policy*, issue 29, vol. 10, no. 2, 1990.

Herminghouse, P., 'Legal Equality and Women's Reality in the German Democratic Republic', in E.

H. Altbach et al (eds.), *German Feminism: Readings in Politics and Literature*, State University of New York Press, 1984.

Kolinsky, E., *Women in West Germany: Life, Work and Politics*, Berg, Oxford, New York, Munich, 1989.

Martin, Brigitte, 'Im Friedrichshain' (In the Freidrichshain Hospital') in B. Martin, *Der rote Ballon* (The Red Balloon), Buchverlag Der Morgen, Berlin, 1978.

Meier, U., 'Equality without Limits? Women's Work in the Socialist Society of the German Democratic Republic', in *International Sociology*, vol. 4, no. 1, pp. 37–49.

Nickel, Hildegard-Maria, 'Frauen in der DDR' (Women in the GDR), in *Aus Politik und Zeitgeschechte, Beilage zur Wochenzeitung Das Parlament*, B, 16–17, 13 April 1990.

Rosenberg, D., 'The Emancipation of Women in Fact and Fiction: Changing Roles in GDR Society and Literature', in S. L. Wolchik and A. G. Meyer (eds.), *Women, State and Party in Eastern Europe*, Duke University Press, 1985.

Rueschemayer, M., 'Socialist Transformation and Gender Inequality: Women in the GDR and Hungary', in D. Childs, T. A. Baylis and M. Rueschemeyer (eds.), *East Germany in Comparative Perspective*, Routledge, London, 1989.

Schwarz, G. and Zenner, C. (Eds.), *Wir wollen mehr als ein 'Vaterland'*, Rowohlt Verlag, Hamburg, 1990.

Shafer, S. M., 'The German Democratic Republic', in G. P. Kellv (ed.), *International Handbook of Women's Education*, Greenwood Press, Westport, Conn., 1989.

Shaffer, H. G., *Women in the Two Germanies: A Comparative Study of a Socialist and a Non-Socialist Society*, Pergamon Press, Oxford, New York, Toronto, 1981.

Stachowa, A., 'Und der steinerne Elefant' (And the Stone Elephant), in *Stachowa, Stunde zwischen Hund und Katz*, Mitteldeutscher Verlag, Halle-Leipzig, 1976.

Unsere Fibel, (Our Reader, a first reading text), Volk und Wissen, Berlin, 1978.

Winkler, G. (ed.), *Frauenreport 90*, Verlag Die Wirtschaft, Berlin, 1990.

Winkler, G. (ed.), *Sozialreport 90: Daten und Fakten zur sozialen Lage in der DDR*, Verlag Die Wirtschaft, Berlin, 1990.

Witzlack, G. et al, *Bald bin ich ein Schulkind* (Soon I'll Be a Schoolchild, a text to prepare children for school), Volk und Wissen, Berlin, 1977.

Wolf, C., *Cassandra*, Virago Press, London, 1984.

Wolf, C., *A Model Childhood*, Virago Press, London, 1982.

Wolf, C., *The Quest for Christa T.*, Virago Press, London, 1982.

Wolter, Christine, *Ich Habe Wieder Geheiratet* (I've remarried), 1978.

Wolter, Christine, *Wie ich meine Unschuld verlor* (How I Lost my Innocence), Aufban-Verlag, Berlin, 1976.

Yugoslavia

Donzelot, J., *The Policing of Families*, Hutchinson, London, 1979.

Licht, S., 'Abortion Policies in Yugoslavia', unpublished paper, 1991.

Pesic, Vesna, 'The Impact of Reforms on the Status of Women in Yugoslavia', paper presented at United Nations seminar on The Status of Women in Eastern Europe and the Soviet Union, Vienna, 1991.

Riley, D., 'Am I That Name?', *Feminism and the Category of 'Women' in History*, Macmillan, London, 1988.

Saraceno, C., 'Porodicno vreme i zenski diskontinuitet', *Marksizam u svetu* (Marxism in the world), 1981, pp. 8–9.

Svetlik, Ivan, 'From a One-dimensional to a Multi-dimensional Welfare System', in B. Deacon and J. Szalai, *Social Policy in the New Eastern Europe*, Avebury, 1990, pp. 164–78.

Russia and the former Soviet republics

Akhmediarov, V., 'Abort do shestnadtsati', *Komsomol'skaia Pravda*, 29 July 1989.

Attwood, L., *The New Soviet Man and Woman: Sex Socialization in the USSR*, Macmillan, Basingstoke, 1990.

Baskov, 'Golaia zhenshchina', *Gorizont*, no. 4, 1990, pp. 19–24.

Bodrova, V., 'Rynok, uvy, ne dzhentel'men', *Pravitel'syvennii Vestnik*, no. 40, September 1991, p. 8.

Bridger, S., *Women in the Soviet Countryside*, Cambridge University Press, Cambridge, 1987.

Browning, G., *Women and Politics in the USSR*, Wheatsheaf, Brighton, 1987.

Buckley, M., *Women and Ideology in the Soviet Union*, Harvester, 1989.

Golodnenko, V. and Strakhova, D., 'Rabotaiushchie zhenshchiny – ne vtoroi sort', *EKO*, no. 8, 1990, pp. 56–62.

Gorbachev, M., 'O khode realizatsii reshenii XXVII s"ezda KPSS i zadachakh po ugubleniiu perestroiki' (speech at the nineteenth Party conference, 28 June 1988), *Izbrannie Rechi i Stat'i*, vol. 6, Politizdat, Moscow, 1989, pp. 323–97.

Gorbachev, M., *Perestroika*, Collins, London, 1987.

Gorlov, V., 'Striptiz', *Komsomol'skaia Pravda*, 11 January 1990, p. 3.

Gruzdeva, E. and Chertikhina, E., 'The Occupational Status and Wages of Women in the USSR', *Soviet Sociology*, vol. 26, no. 3, 1987.

Helgeson, A., 'Demographic Policy', in A. Brown and M. Kaser (eds.), *Soviet Policy for the 1980s*, 1982, pp. 118–45.

Holland, B. (ed.), *Soviet Sisterhood*, Fourth Estate, London, 1985.

Juviler, P., 'Women and Sex in Soviet Law', in Atkinson, Dallin and Lapidus (eds.), *Women and Russia*, Harvester, 1978, pp. 243–66.

Khmelik, M., *Little Vera*, Bloomsbury Publishing Ltd, London, 1990.

Khodakov, N., *Molodim Suprugam*, Meditsina, Leningrad, 1971.

Kon, I., 'Proshcheniia net', *Nedeliia*, no. 46 (13–19 November), 1989, pp. 10–11.

Lapidus, G., *Women in Soviet Society, Society, Equality, Development and Social Change*, California University Press, Berkeley, 1978.

Lenin, V. I., *On the Emancipation of Women*, Progress, Moscow, 1965.

Mamonova, T., *Women and Russia*, Basil Blackwell, Oxford, 1984.

Mansimov, Ch. and Foteeva, E., 'Osobennosti predstavlenii molodezhi Azerbaidzhanskoi SSSR o semeinoi zhizni', *Sotsiologicheskiie Issledovaniia*, no. 3 (July–September), 1982, pp. 128–31.

Moses, J., 'Women in Political Roles', in Atkinson, Dallin and Lapidus (eds.), *Women in Russia*, Harvester, 1977, pp. 333–54,

Perevedentsev, V., 'Vid s vershiny', *Ogonek*, no. 10 (March), 1987, pp. 4–7.

Piiasheva, L., 'Podumaite, chto vazhnee? ...', Dubna, 22 May 1991, p. 6.

Popov, A., 'Regulirovanie rozhdenii v sovremennikh Sem'iakh', in M. Bednovo (ed.), *Sem'ia, Zdorov'e, Obshchestvo*, Mysl', Moscow, 1986, pp. 181–206.

Rimashevskaia, N., 'Current Problems of the Status of Women', *Soviet Sociology*, vol. 27, no. 1, 1988, pp. 58–71.

Sakwa, R., *Soviet Politics – An Introduction*, Routledge, 1989.

Shlapentokh, V., *Love, Marriage and Friendship in the Soviet Union*, Praeger, New York, 1984.

Shreeves, R., 'Sexual Revolution or Sexploitation?', *Radio Liberty Report on the USSR*, vol. 2, no. 31, 1990, pp. 4–8.

Sillaste, G., 'Zhenshchina v labirinte mnogopartiinosti', *Partiinaia Zhizn*, no. 14, 1991, pp. 34–42.

Sillaste, G., 'Zhenshchiny i politika', *Izvestiia*, 6 August 1990, p. 2.

SSSR v Tsifrakh v 1989, Goskomstat, Moscow, 1990.

Telen', L., 'Kakaia zhe ona, zhenskaia dolia?', *Sotsialisticheskaia Industriia*, 22 January 1988.

Terekhina, V., 'Bastuet detsad', *Komsomol'skaia Pravda*, 3 April 1990.

Tolstaia, T., 'Notes from the Underground', *New York Review of Books*, vol. 37, no. 9 (31 May 1990), pp. 3–7.

Voznesenskaia, J., *The Women's Decameron*, Quartet Books, London, 1986.

Walker, M., *The Waking Giant*, Michael Joseph Ltd, London, 1986.

Waters, E., 'Restructuring the "Woman Question"', *Feminist Review*, no. 33 (autumn), 1989, pp. 3–19.

Zaichkin, A., in *Nedeliia*, no. 46, (13–19 November), 1989, p. 11.

Zakharov, N., Posadskaia, A. and Rimashevskaia, N., 'Kak my reshaem zhenskii vopros', *Kommunist*, no. 4, 1989, pp. 56–65 (translated and summarized in *Current Digest of the Soviet Press*, vol. 41, no. 19, p. 22).

Zhenshchiny v SSSR, Goskomstat, Moscow, 1988.

General

Ash, Timothy Garton, *The Polish Revolution: Solidarity*, Cornet, 1985.

Ash, Timothy Garton, *We The People*, Granta/Penguin, 1990.

Ball, Alan, R. and Millard, Frances, *Pressure Politics in Industrial Societies: A Comparative Introduction*, Macmillan, 1986.

Cohen, Yolande (ed.), *Women and Counter Power*, Black Rose Books, Montreal, 1989.

Corrin, Chris, 'Women's Liberation in Socialist Patriarchy', *Slovo: A Journal of Contemporary Soviet and East European Affairs*, vol. 3, no. 2, November 1990(b).

Deacon, R. and Szalai, J., *Social Policy in the New Eastern Europe*, Avebury, 1990.

Dennis, M., *German Democratic Republic: Politics, Economics and Society*, Pinter, London, 1988.

Drakulic, Slavenka, *How We Survived Communism and Even Laughed*, Hutchinson, 1992.

Edwards, G. E., *GDR Society and Social Institutions: Facts and Figures*, Macmillan, London, 1985.

Einhorn, B., 'Sisters Across the Curtain: Women Speak Out in East and West Europe', in *END Journal of European Nuclear Disarmament*, no. 8, Feb–Mar 1984.

Engels, F., *Origin of the Family, Private Property and the State*, Pathfinder Press, New York, 1972.

Ergas, Yasmine, 'Convergencies and Tension between Collective Identity and Social Citizenship Rights: Italian Women in the Seventies', in *Women in Culture and Politics: A Century of Change*, Firedlander, Cook, Kessler-Harris and Smith-Rosenburg (eds.), Indiana University Press, 1986.

Evans, J. et al (eds.), *Feminism and Political Theory*, Sage, London, 1986.

Evans, Mary, *The Woman Question: Readings on the Subordination of Women*, Fontana Paperbacks, 1982.

Fehér, Ferenc and Heller, Agnes, *Eastern Left, Western Left: Totalitarianism, Freedom and Democracy*, Polity Press, 1987.

Fehér, Ferenc, Heller, Agnes, and György, Márkus, *Dictatorship over Needs: An analysis of Soviet Societies*, Blackwell, Oxford, 1983.

Francome, C., *Abortion Freedom: A Worldwide Movement*, George Allen & Unwin, London, 1984.

Fritz, Jan M., 'Female Labour Force Participation in Eastern Europe: An Analytical Framework', *Humanity and Society*, vol. 8, no. 2, 1984, pp. 151–62.

Fry, M., *Patronage and Principle*, Aberdeen University Press, 1987.

Glenny, Misha, *The Rebirth of History*, Penguin, Harmondsworth, 1990.

Grosser, Alfred, *Germany in our Time*, Penguin, 1970.

Hankiss, E., *East European Alternatives*, Oxford University Press, Oxford, 1990.

Heinen, Jacqueline, 'Inequalities at Work: The Gender Division of Labour in the Soviet Union and Eastern Europe', *Studies in Political Economy*, autumn 1989, pp. 39–61.

Jallade, J. P. (ed.), *The Crisis of Distribution in European Welfare States*, Trentham Books, Stoke-on-Trent, 1988.

Kaldor, Mary, *Europe from Below*, Verso, 1991.

Kaldor, Mary, *The Imaginary War: Understanding the East West Conflict*, Blackwell, 1990.

Keane, John, *Civil Society and the State*, Verso, 1988.

Keane, John, *The Rediscovery of Civil Society*, Verso, 1988.

Kolonkiewicz, George and Lewis, Paul, *Poland: Politics, Economics and Society*, Pinter, 1988.

Konrad, Gyorgy, *Antipolitics*, Quartet, 1984.

Kroupova, Alena, 'Women, Employment and Earnings in Central and Eastern European Countries', paper presented for Tripartite Symposium on Equality of Opportunity and Treatment for Men and Women in Employment in Industrialized Countries, Prague, May 1990.

Kruks, S., Rapp, R. and Young, M. B., 'Promissory Notes: Women in the Transition to Socialism', Monthly Review Press, New York, 1989.

Lovenduski, J., *Women and European Politics: Contemporary Feminism and Public Policy*, Wheatsheaf Books, 1986.

Lovenduski, J. and Hills, J., *The Politics of the Second Electorate*, Routledge and Kegan Paul, London, 1981.

Lovenduski, J. and Outshoorn, J. (eds.), *The New Politics of Abortion*, Sage, London, 1986.

Lovenduski, Joni and Woodall, Jean, *Politics and Society in Eastern Europe*, Macmillan Education, 1987.

Mellor, Roy, *Eastern Europe: A Geography of the Comecon Countries*, Macmillan, 1975.

Molyneux, M., 'The "Woman Question" in the Age of Perestroika', in *New Left Review*, no. 183, 1990, pp. 23–50.

Molyneux, M., 'Women's Emancipation under Socialism: A Model for the Third World?', in *World Development*, no. 9/10, 1981.

Morgan, Robin, Sisterhood is Global, Penguin, 1984.

Morgen, S. and Bookman, A. (eds.), *Women and the Politics of Empowerment*, Philadelphia Temple University Press, 1988.

Rakovski, Marc, *Towards an East European Marxism*, Allison and Busby, London, 1978.

Randall, Vicky, *Women and Politics*, Macmillan Education, 1991.

Rich, Adrienne, *Of Woman Born: Motherhood as Experience and Institution*, Virago, London, 1972.

Rowbotham, Sheila, *Women's Consciousness, Man's World*, Penguin Books, Harmondsworth, 1973.

Schapiro, J. and Potichnyi, P. J. (eds.), *Change and Adaption in Soviet and East European Politics*, Praeger, New York, 1976.

Scott, H., *Does Socialism Liberate Women?*, Beacon Press, Boston, 1974.

Scott, H., 'Eastern European Women in Theory and Practice', in *Women's Studies International Quarterly*, no. 1, 1978.

Scott, H., *Sweden's Right to be Human: Sex Role Equality, the Goal and the Reality*, Allison and Busby, London, 1976.

Scott, H., *Women and Socialism*, Allison and Busby, London, 1976.

Sharpe, Sue, *Double Identity: the Lives of Working Mothers*, Penguin, Harmondsworth, 1984.

Silnitsky, Frantisek and Larisa, Reyman Karl, *Communism and Eastern Europe*, Macmillan, 1987.

Siltanen, J. and Stanworth, M. (eds.), *Women and the Public Sphere,* Hutchinson, London, 1984.

Szelény, Iván, *Urban Inequalities under State Socialism*, Oxford University Press, 1983.

Szelény, Ivan and Konrad, Gyorgy, *The Intellectuals on the Road to Class Power*, Macmillan, 1979.

The Minority Rights Group, 'Minorities in the Balkans', report no. 82, London, 1989.

Tomaszewski, Jerzy, *The Socialist Regimes of East Central Europe: Their Establishment and Consolidation 1944–67*, Routledge, 1989.

White, Gardner, Schopflin and Saich, *Communist and Post Communist Political systems: An Introduction*, Macmillan, 1990.

White, Stephen, *Handbook of Reconstruction in Eastern Europe and the Soviet Union*, Longman Current Affairs, 1991.

Wolchik, Sharon L., *Czechoslovakia: Politics, Economics and Society*, Pinter, London, 1991.

Wolchik, Sharon L. and Meyer, Alfred G. (eds.), *Women, State and Party in Eastern Europe*, Duke University Press, 1985.

Index

Figures in italics indicate tables.

Also available from Scarlet Press

The European Women's Almanac
Paula Snyder

The European Women's Almanac is an essential reference guide to the status of women in the Europe of the 1990s. Packed with facts and information, **The Almanac** has everything you want to know about how women in 26 countries – including the European Community, eastern Europe and Scandinavia – live, love, spend and earn. Paula Snyder uncovers some extraordinary facts.

- Did you know that the Austrian Institute for Economic Research estimates that the value of housework done by women is AS400 billion each year?
- On 14 June 1991 an estimated 500 000 Swiss women left their jobs and homes and took strike action in support of equality. Four men were reported as having set up an emergency open-air ironing service in the centre of Bern.
- In 1982 lesbian activist Uschi Sillge addressed East Germany's first public conference on lesbianism and homosexuality to be held since the Second World War.
- In Sweden men lost the right to hit their wives in 1864.
- In October 1975 Icelandic women staged a one-day strike. As a result, equal rights legislation was passed within a year.

This indispensable book provides for the first time a comparative overview of rights and provisions for women in Europe in the areas of work, family issues, politics, the law, sexuality, education and health. Arranged country by country, the information is punctuated by personal testimonies from women living in the nations covered, together with easy-to-read tables, comparative charts and maps.

ISBN 1 85727 005 3 pb / 1 85727 015 0 hb